THE GERMAN PÍCARO AND MODERNITY
Vol. 2

Series Editor:

Imke Meyer

New Directions in German Studies

Volumes in the series:

Improvisation as Art: Conceptual Challenges, Historical Perspectives
by Edgar Landgraf

Citation and Precedent: Conjunctions and Disjunctions of German Law and Literature
by Thomas O. Beebee (forthcoming)

Vienna's Dreams of Europe: Culture and Identity beyond the Nation-State
by Katherine Arens (forthcoming)

From Kafka to Sebald: Modernism and Narrative Form
edited by Sabine Wilke (forthcoming)

Thomas Mann in English: A Study in Literary Translation
By David Horton (forthcoming)

The German Pícaro and Modernity

Between Underdog and Shape-Shifter

Bernhard F. Malkmus

continuum

Continuum International Publishing Group
80 Maiden Lane, New York, NY 10038
The Tower Building, 11 York Road, London SE1 7NX

www.continuumbooks.com

Cover image: Paul Klee, Ohne Titel [Gefangen, Diesseits—Jenseits/Figur],
um 140; Öl, ausgesparte Zeichnung mit Kleisterfarbe auf kleistergrundierter
Jute auf Jute, 55.20 x 50.10 cm x 2 cm; © 2011 Artists Rights Society (ARS),
New York/VG Bild-Kunst, Bonn; image courtesy of Foundation Beyeler,
Riehen/Basel; Foto: Peter Schibli, Basel

Library of Congress Cataloging-in-Publication Data

A catalog record for this book is available from the Library of Congress.

ISBN-13: 978-1-4411-4615-1

Typeset by Fakenham Prepress Solutions, Fakenham, Norfolk NR21 8NN
Printed and bound in the United States

'—ich bin plötzlich mitten in diesem Traume erwacht, aber nur zum Bewusstsein, dass ich eben träume und dass ich weiterträumen *muss*, um nicht zu Grunde zu gehen: wie der Nachtwandler weiterträumen *muss*, um nicht hinabzustürzen.'

'—I suddenly awoke in the middle of this dream, but only to the consciousness that I am dreaming and that I *must* go on dreaming lest I perish—as the sleepwalker has to go on dreaming in order to avoid falling down.'

Friedrich Nietzsche[1]

---

1 *Die fröhliche Wissenschaft*, 417; *Gay Science*, 63 (§54).

Contents

Acknowledgements

One of the lessons I learnt from picaresque writing is that authorship is a mere confidence trick. This book is a case in point: it has not, as erroneously stated on the front cover, been conceived and executed by one author, but rather forms a collaborative effort. It was inspired and written by many people. Sifting through its pages, I can hear the voices of Norbert Nadler and Gerhart von Graevenitz; I am again listening with gratitude and joy to the rich and thought-provoking discussions with David Midgley and Judith Ryan; I can see individual ideas and phrases evoke memories of critical interventions by Peter Arnds, Matthias Bauer, Nicholas Boyle, Vicente Cantarino, Ian Cooper, Manuel Dries, Richard Gordon, Michael Minden, Victoria Moul, Julian Preece, Ernest Schonfield, Peter Stenberg, Rochelle Tobias and John Zilcosky. The unwavering support offered by my colleagues at the Department of Germanic Languages and Literatures at The Ohio State University provided a rich ostinato for orchestrating the final manuscript. All these voices have given the wayfaring pícaro a temporary home. Special thanks go to Mark Nicholls, librarian at St John's College, Cambridge, and his assistant Peter Hutton for their good humour and expert advice; they took pleasure in dusting both their astonishing manuscript collection and my bookish broodings. Many of the ideas that give this project structure and coherence were concocted on the second floor of their sacred precincts. This list, far from complete, shows that the only claim to authorship the author of this study can legitimately make pertains to its errors and inconsistencies.

I am most grateful for the generous support I received from the following institutions: *Studienstiftung des deutschen Volkes* for initial research at Harvard University, St John's College, Cambridge, for the Benefactors' Scholarship, and the Arts & Humanities Research Council (UK) for a tuition grant.

This book is dedicated to my parents, who tried their utmost to prevent me from becoming a pícaro, and my sister, who always wanted me to be more of one. It would not have been finished without the *élan vital* and loving companionship of Marie and Nikolai.

Introduction: Boxing (In) Life Stories

We are surrounded by tricksters, rogues, pícaros and confidence men who 'know one trick more than the devil', as the Spanish proverb goes.[1] Even if we are not in the middle of a credit crunch or an economic recession (when comparisons between the financial elites and literary characters of mixed reputation abound), we frequently conjure up the image of the hard-nosed or scheming rogue and the tight-fisted or secretive trickster to describe our political and economic establishment. What is more, for many centuries writers have furnished our imagination with the ramblings, success stories and failures of a hero who lives on the fringes of society and makes ends meet by mastering many skills at the same time—namely, the quick adaptation to a vast range of social and cultural practices, the art of mimicking social decorum, and, last but not least, an unfailing sense for the right moment to poke fun at others. In all likelihood, this literary hero resonates with his readers and captivates their imagination because he is not all that different from them.[2]

The trickster figure populates folk and fairy tales across many cultures, often as an embodiment of fertility and omnipotence, and forms one of the universal mythological imaginaries of humankind.[3] The confidence man, by contrast, is a specific historical product of the rise of capitalism, emerging from the streets of New York during the 1840s and brought to literary prominence by Herman Melville in his social satire *Confidence-Man. A Masquerade* (1857). The classic

---

1 '¡Sabe un punto más que el Diablo!'

2 Henceforth reference to the 'pícaro' will consistently be made in the third person singular masculine. This is due only to the fact that all the novels discussed in the main body of this study feature a male protagonist and is not meant to extend any generalizations with regard to gender.

3 See, for example, Erdoes and Ortiz, *American Indian Trickster Tales*. For an anthropological discussion of the trickster figure in Native American mythology see Radin's influential study *The Trickster*. Honold, 'Travestie und Transgression', 211–16, comments on Radin with regard to the German picaresque.

pícaro, who enters the scene as a literary character during the sixteenth century in Spain, is heir to some of the mythical qualities of the trickster and, at the same time, foreshadows the complexities of individuality in modern capitalism, as embodied by the confidence man.

As Yirmiyahu Yovel has suggested, the origin of the pícaro can be described as a birth 'from the death of shame'.[4] He regards the classic pícaro as a reflection of the particular situation of Spanish Jews, who, in 1492, were forced either to leave Spain or convert to Christianity. Those who stayed, the so-called *conversos* (or 'New Christians'), found themselves in a psycho-social double-bind. The better they integrated into Spanish Catholic society, the higher was the degree of suspicion and social envy they faced in a culture increasingly obsessed with ethnic homogeneity. It is the sense of 'shame' resulting from this situation, Yovel argues, that is at stake in picaresque tales, many of which were written by authors with a *converso* background: 'a conflict arises in the text between the private and the social dimensions of shame. Cautiously but unmistakably, protected by the device of irony and allusion, the individual is emerging *as individual*—in opposition to the objectified, self-suppressing state in which he existed when accepting the verdict of external stigma.'[5] The process of freeing oneself, by narrating the self as an articulation of 'private shame', from a social stigma and from the related sense of 'social shame' is the mark of the Spanish picaresque tale.

In the twentieth century the pícaro made a comeback. As in Yovel's reading of the Spanish model, the main issue in this literary revival is the conflict arising 'between the private and social dimensions of shame', yet shame in this case is not any longer determined by one specific historical predicament such as the one faced by many *conversos*, 'the verdict of an external stigma'. It rather encompasses a wide range of contradictory reactions to the social, political and economic situation of what we have come to call modernity. I use the term modernity here as a historical category applicable to the majority of so-called Western societies. It delineates the change from a stratum-based to a meritocratic society, principally during the last third of the eighteenth century, and is marked by the gradually unfolding effects of the Enlightenment, the French Revolution and the various phases of industrialization, as well as the related rise of capitalism. We may also add these defining aspects, identified by Reinhart Koselleck: the acceleration of time; the development of an 'open future' marked by inventions, innovations and discoveries; and the (retrospective and

---

4   Yovel, *The Other Within*, 273.
5   Yovel, 'Birth of the Picaro', 1322. (Emphases are always in the original, unless otherwise stated.)

self-descriptive) organization of time into epochs. Koselleck stresses that with 'the opening of the world, the most different but coexisting cultural levels were brought into view spatially and, by way of synchronic comparison, were diachronically classified'.[6] It was only during the late eighteenth century that the idea gained cogency that various historiographies of the same historical event can coexist and, indeed, be equally true.[7] One of the corollaries of this insight was a kind of uncertainty principle, namely the idea that representation cannot be separated from the point of view of the observer. In sum, modernity defines a world 'that seeks its meaning in the *future*' and places unprecedented emphasis on the various forms of imagining, conceptualizing and representing that future as a logical product of our observer-inflected understanding of the past and present.[8] It shapes a society which 'unlike any preceding culture lives in the future rather than in the past'.[9]

Like no other literary character, the picaresque hero dramatizes the challenges resulting from the accelerated rate of change and mobility in modernity—from its 'Mercurian' (rather than 'Apollonian') nature, to use Yuri Slezkine's terms.[10] And no other literary character comes as close to forming an imaginative correlative for this idea of the 'Mercurian' nature of Jewish traditions in Europe and for what Slezkine calls the 'Jewish' nature of European modernity in general: 'Virtually all of those who associated Jews with modernity judged them according to the traditional Apollonian-Mercurian oppositions of natural versus artificial, settled versus nomadic, body versus mind. Especially body versus mind: what was sterile rationality to Sombart was intellectual ability to Jacobs, but both agreed on the centrality of the two concepts and the permanence of their attachments.'[11] This opposition is part of the socio-political situation the modern pícaro has to negotiate. However controversial we deem attempts that compare the complexities of *converso* life in Spain during the sixteenth century to the equally complex situation of post-emancipation Jewry in Germany, it cannot be denied that there is, in both cases, a striking prominence of Jewish writers who used the picaresque.[12] In doing so, they made invaluable contributions to a reflection on early modern Spanish society, as

---

6   Koselleck, 'Beginning of Modernity', 166.

7   Foucault, 'Of Other Spaces', 26.

8   Moretti, *The Way of the World*, 5.

9   Giddens and Pierson, *Conversations*, 94.

10   Cf. Slezkine, *Jewish Century*, 40–1.

11   Ibid., 56. Slezkine refers to the controversy between Werner Sombart (*Die Juden und das Wirtschaftsleben*, 1911) and Joseph Jacobs (*Jewish Contributions to Civilization*, 1919).

12   Cf. Yerushalmi, *Assimilation and Racial Anti-Semitism*.

well as on early twentieth-century German-Jewish assimilation and the Holocaust.

It may come as a surprise that the literary creations of a bureaucrat from Prague and a recluse from Switzerland open the interaction between the rather sanguine and extraverted heroes of this study, but it will not be entirely unexpected that this study focuses on the German-speaking world. Some of the most memorable picaresque characters of the twentieth century penned their lies and fabled their biographies in German, and they did so at a time when Central Europe both became a particularly overheated catalyst for modernizing processes and witnessed their barbaric implosion in the autocratic militarism of the late Wilhelmine period and the racist ideology of National Socialism.

'To begin at the beginning'—this is how Dylan Thomas famously opens his radio play *Under Milk Wood*, as if 'the beginning' was always easy to determine and intuition would never let a poet down on this most crucial question, where to begin? Oskar Matzerath, Günter Grass's picaresque narrator in *Die Blechtrommel*, whimsically declares that he lacks the instinct Thomas takes for granted: 'wie fange ich an?' ['how shall I begin?'], he asks himself—an ambiguous question that pertains both to the origins of the narrator and the beginning of the narrative (and therefore is widely debated by picaresque narrators).[13] Most biographical, autobiographical or, as Matthias Bauer calls the picaresque, 'pseudo-autobiographical' narratives offer the moment of birth, the hatching of the egg, as it were, as the natural point of departure.[14] The classic pícaro tells his story *ab ovo*, a convention denigrated by Horace for its sterility. The Roman poet preferred being thrown into the middle of things by the epic narrator and had no patience for the desire to construct an artificial beginning merely for the vanity of a racy plot (which, in the case of the *Iliad*, would have been the egg, hence *ovo*, of Leda, fertilized by Zeus as a swan).[15] Laurence Sterne, similarly dismissive of the poetic urge to 'begin at the beginning', pokes fun at this convention by taking it at face value: *The Life and Opinions of Tristram Shandy* literally begins with Tristram's conception. Oskar pushes the mock *ab ovo* beginning back one generation: *Die Blechtrommel* starts with the conception of his mother.

---

13 Grass, *Blechtrommel*, 8; *Tin Drum*, 5.

14 Bauer, *Schelmenroman*, 8–9. For a first flavour of the complexities of life-writing see Eakin, *How Our Lives Become Stories*; Gusdorf, 'Conditions and Limits of Autobiography'; Hart, 'Notes for an Anatomy of Modern Autobiography'; Olney, *Metaphors of Self*.

15 Horace, *Ars Poetica*, vv. 146–52.

Bertolt Brecht's fragmentary picaresque story "Der Lebenslauf des Boxers Samson-Körner", written in 1926, captures the spirit of competition, chaos, con trickery, fluid identities and social fatalism that has been described as the trademark of the Weimar Republic.[16] Like Sterne's and Grass's unique novels, it begins in a remarkable way, too: with a double birth. Paul Samson-Körner (who is modelled on the light heavyweight boxer and actor of the same name, whom Brecht admired) adopts a fake identity as the offspring of Swedish settlers in Utah in order to avoid being arrested as a prisoner of war in the United States during World War One. His narrative, jotted down by 'Brecht' in the role of the interviewing journalist, unfolds as follows:

> Wenn man etwas über sein eigenes Leben aufschreiben soll, ist es wirklich schwierig, alles unter einen Hut zu bringen. [...]
>
> Ich will es daher gleich bemerken, dass ich in Beaver im Staate Utah, U.S.A, geboren bin, im Mormonendistrikt, fast am Großen Salzsee. Ich kann auch andeuten, warum ich dort geboren bin: es ist, weil Beaver im Staate Utah, U.S.A., an keiner Eisenbahnlinie liegt. Sie können dort zwölf Frauen ehelichen, aber Sie können, wenn Sie nach meinem Geburtshaus schauen wollen, nicht anders als zu Fuß hinkommen. [...]
>
> Andererseits bin ich in Zwickau in Sachsen geboren, weil ich dort das Licht der Welt erblickte. In Zwickau hielt ich mich ungefähr dreizehn Jahre auf, und zwar vorwiegend im Hotel 'Deutscher Kaiser'. Dieses Hotel gehörte einem Onkel von mir. Ich lernte dort spielend Tür aufmachen, Koffer tragen und Stiefel wichsen. Das war mir gelegentlich sehr nützlich, als mir in England, ein kleines Jahr später, das Wasser ziemlich an den Hals ging [...]. (216)[17]

> When they ask you to write something about your own life it isn't all that easy to get it together. [...]
>
> So let me say right away that I was born in Beaver, State of Utah, U.S.A., in the Mormon area close to the Great Salt Lake. I can also suggest why I was born there: it was because Beaver, State of Utah, U.S.A., is not on the railroad. It is a place where you can marry twelve wives, but if you want to look at the house where I was born you can't get there except on foot. [...]
>
> To look at the other side: I was born in Zwickau, Saxony, because that's where I first saw daylight. I remained in Zwickau

---

16 Cf. Sloterdijk, *Kritik der zynischen Vernunft*, 849–59.

17 The main primary sources under scrutiny in each chapter are referenced directly in the text. References to the original will be followed by references to the English translation, e.g. 216/207.

> for roughly thirteen years, most of which I spent in the Hotel Deutscher Kaiser. The hotel was named after the Emperor of Germany and belonged to one of my uncles. There I learned a game known as opening doors, carrying bags and cleaning shoes. This came in very handy a bare year later in England, when the wolf was somewhat at the door [...]. (207)

Brecht playfully transforms the literary topos of origin into a double birth. In so doing, he not only parodies conventions of life-writing, but also introduces a picaresque narrative logic: projection (into the future) precedes origin (rooted in the past), roleplay precedes social identity. The order in which these two versions of the birth are told places the picaresque confidence trick before the physical birth. Not surprisingly, Samson-Körner's fragmentary story as a boxer does not tell us much about boxing but focuses on the stages in his life story that lead up to his boxing career—what he calls 'eine Reihe Unternehmungen von unserer Seite, für die man uns *nur versehentlich nicht ins Loch* steckte' ['initiatives of ours which we might easily have been jugged for if only they had thought of it'] (220/211). This is the characteristic picaresque adventure story: a tale that moves between two social realms seemingly opposed to one another, the established social and the criminal world, and that blurs the boundary between them. Other features Brecht's story has in common with the picaresque tradition (apart from the complicated family history and the play with origins) are the themes of exile, initiation and various master–servant relationships.

Above all, the narrative structure itself allows us to read Brecht's fragment as a showcase for some of the main features of modern picaresque fiction. First, the 'Lebenslauf' (which translates to 'walk of life', 'life story' and 'curriculum vitae') is embedded in an interview, which Samson-Körner uses in order to justify the twists and turns of his life. Yet, the reader has to decipher the subtexts of the answers without knowing the questions. This particular frame, the pícaro's attempt to defend himself when faced with questions or accusations that are unknown to the reader, is a common feature of the classic picaresque form. Second, the related frame of social mimicry poses additional questions with regard to how the text stages the negotiation between society and individual. Why do we listen to somebody who claims that he was born in Utah as well as in Saxony? In what ways does the boxer and confidence man Samson-Körner (with his telling double name) highlight issues of trust in a social context?[18] Related to

---

18 The name Samson-Körner refers to two figures representing freedom: the biblical figure of Samson who serves in God's plan to deliver the Israelites from the Philistines (Judges 13–16); and the poet Carl Theodor Körner, who gained

these issues of credibility and mimicry is also the question of why the modern picaresque is predominantly the site for male gender negotiations and constructions—as opposed to classic picaresque fiction, in which pícaras had a substantial share, albeit exclusively imagined by male authors.[19] From its very beginnings, picaresque fiction has been used as a tool for exploring the ambiguities of social roles, including gender roles. This proved to be particularly important with regard to picaresque heroines such as Francisco López de Úbeda's Justina, Hans Jakob von Grimmelshausen's Mother Courage and Daniel Defoe's Moll Flanders. Why the modern revival of that tradition pursues that same goal, but limits the exploration to the ambiguities of male roles and gender constructions, will remain one of the unanswered questions of this investigation. In the course of the discussion I will offer a tentative argument that revolves around the observation that Nietzsche's concept of the artistic self as *Übermensch* has a profound impact on the way in which the modern picaresque renders the key issues of credibility and mimicry (which are also at stake in Brecht's piece). It is this particular subtext and its insertion into the ever more prominent autobiographical subtext of self-fashioning in the picaresque tradition, I argue, that was more conducive to being appropriated by male authors, who by the early twentieth century were less and less able or inclined to write about female protagonists, especially in narrative modes with a pronounced life-writing component. The strong Nietzschean undercurrents and overtones of the revival of the picaresque may have prevented it from being used more productively by female authors until the revival of the pícara in various literatures during the past 30 years. Why this Nietzschean subtext may have provided a particularly inviting imaginary template for male gender reflections and negotiations is one of the equally powerful and problematic dimensions of the modern picaresque and will be addressed in readings of specific novels.

---

fame for his liberation songs during Napoleon's occupation of the German lands.

19   A survey on the pícara as literary heroine can be found in Gillespie, 'Pikara und Schelmin'. The Spanish pícara is discussed in Hanrahan, *La mujer en la novela picaresca española*, II, chapter 7, and Dunn, *Spanish Picaresque Novel*, chapter 7. While the picaresque heroine plays a significant role in most picaresque traditions, her appearance is notably less frequent in the twentieth century (Doris in Irmgard Keun's *Das kunstseidene Mädchen*, Tino in Else Lasker-Schüler's *Die Nächte Tino von Bagdads* and Beatriz in Irmtraud Morgner's *Trobadora Beatriz* may serve as borderline examples). See also Rodríguez-Luis, 'Pícaras' and Daghistany, 'The Picara Nature'. English-language literature of the last 30 years has, however, witnessed a new prominence of the pícara, see Strobel, *Pikara als Grenzgängerin*, chapter 5.

In very general terms, the pícaro is a figure who, confronted with conflicting role expectations, has to stage himself rhetorically within a given social framework. In his classic definition of the Spanish pícaro, Claudio Guillén adumbrates this situation: the pícaro *'can, in short, neither join nor actually reject his fellow men.* He becomes what I would like to call a "half-outsider"'.[20] He relates this position to the medieval anthropology of the dual man (*homo duplex*), which is based on the assumption that there is a direct correspondence between the visible actions of a human being as he appears in society (*homo exterior*) and his invisible motivations (*homo interior*). The picaresque tale, as it emerged in sixteenth-century Spain, used this template and reversed it by emphasizing rifts and ruptures rather than congruence between these two poles: that is, the split between inner and outer man, between reflection and action, between the narrator of a projected self and various narrated social roles—or, as in Samson-Körner's case, between a diegetic persona who is able to play the servant ('spielend Tür aufmachen, Koffer tragen und Stiefel wichsen') and an extradiegetic one who wants to give a comprehensive account of everything by hindsight ('alles unter einen Hut bringen'). It is this rupture, the breaking up of the unity of the dual man, which is spelt out in the picaresque, Guillén maintains: its language of dissimulation facilitates a characteristic 'double perspective of self-concealment and self-revelation'.[21] While picaresque writing, both in Spain and across Europe, has undergone dramatic changes since its inception, this double perspective has played a major role in its modern revival.

The guiding hypothesis of this study is that the revival of the picaresque reflects the human condition in modernity, which is marked by the emergence of the individual through the exchange between two social roles: the active shape-shifter, who is marked by flexible social role-play and a satirical use of language, and the passive underdog, who is often related to the social logic of scapegoating. While the enfranchisement of the bourgeois and the participation of an increasing part of the population in a wider share of more readily available products leads to an unprecedented empowerment of individuals and to an acceleration of social mobility (from the country into the cities, from dependency to self-organization), the same development also leads to an increased interference of bureaucratic administration, creating or corroborating structures of alienation, exploitation and exclusion that threaten to undermine newly earned liberties.[22]

---

20   Guillén, *Literature as System*, 80.
21   Ibid., 82.
22   With regard to the terminology of the self, I follow the modern philosophical usage, which defines 'subject' as *general* self-consciousness, 'person' as *particular*

The picaresque hero, like no other (re)creation of modern literary imagination, epitomizes this very predicament between empowerment and disenfranchisement. Both of these concepts are defined by their failure to be fully one thing or another in this context: the seeming autonomy of the adaptive shape-shifter is jeopardized by the results of his actions and is often portrayed as leading to narcissistic self-absorption; the seeming innocence of the underdog is compromised by his complicity with various suppressing social and political apparatuses. As an underdog, he presents himself as a victim of society, marginalized by the cruelty of a perverted moral cosmos or by the growing inclusion of man's bodily existence in mechanisms and calculations of state power.

Michel Foucault notes with regard to this latter development: 'For millennia man remained what he was for Aristotle: a living animal with the additional capacity for political existence; modern man is an animal whose politics calls his existence as a living being into question.'[23] This increasing tendency to engineer social and physical life, according to Foucault, endows the individual with unprecedented liberties and, at the same time, subjects the human body to power structures that potentially call into doubt most basic rights.[24] Giorgio Agamben takes this one step further and points out that in modernity man's physical existence as such—he calls it 'bare life'[25]—begins to converge with the political realm, 'as if politics were the place in which life had to transform itself into good life and in which what had to be politicized

---

self-consciousness, and 'individual' as *separate* self-consciousness, see Frank, 'Subjekt, Person, Individuum', 9. In the context of the picaresque, 'individual' will be used consistently as the most appropriate term. The term 'subject' is generally avoided, in order to prevent unnecessary interferences with a terminology deeply rooted in idealism and *Subjektphilosophie*. The modern picaresque dramatizes an agency that cannot be squared with the tenets of idealism but rather challenges its dialectical foundations. It is only within this particular context of intellectual history that I use the term 'individual *as* subject'; otherwise I will restrict myself to the more neutral term 'individual', in order to highlight that picaresque identities are formed in the interaction with the environment through projected forms of self and society.

Needless to say, the point here is that, in the context of the picaresque, 'in-dividuality' in its etymological sense is in fact a kind of persona, but as such an indispensable one; on this issue see Hamacher in 'Disgregation of the Will', 121–2 and 136–8. (On the semantics of 'I' see also Tugendhat, *Selbstbewußtsein und Selbstbestimmung*, 73–5.)

23 Foucault, *History of Sexuality*, I, 188.
24 Cf. ibid., 140.
25 'Bare life' (*la nuda vita*) is a reference to Benjamin's phrase 'bloßes Leben' in 'Zur Kritik der Gewalt', 201 ('mere life' in the English translation, cf. 'Critique of Violence', 250).

were always already bare life'.[26] He argues that this convergence becomes ever more prevalent in modern nation states, whose constitutional law is based on perpetually turning *'bare* life' (the Aristotelian *zoe*) into *political* life (*bios*) and, in the process, reinstating its sovereign power. The modern citizen here emerges as marked both by subjection to sovereign power and by individual liberties.[27] As the second half of this investigation shows, much of modern picaresque writing dealing with the experience of World War Two is pitched against this backdrop. From the perspective of the picaresque stranger, outcast and ethnic or social hybrid, citizenship is a form of social mimicry—an aspect best illustrated by Grass's Oskar Matzerath, who is at once Polish, German and Kashubian and defies the categories of Nazi biopolitics.

As a shape-shifter, the modern pícaro avoids trouble and makes sure he keeps on changing his appearances in order to succeed in his environment, but he also changes the shape of society in the process. The modern picaresque demonstrates the dialectics of opportunity that exists between the human potential to create something innovative and the constant danger of becoming dependent on this potential as the sole foundation of identity. This dialectics is based on the increased importance of flexibility in modernity, which allows humans to mould their individuality in relation to certain role models. Ralf Dahrendorf highlights this duality, calling society 'an irritating fact [...] which we cannot escape with impunity', irritating in the sense that humans have no chance to escape the conflicting role models imposed by society.[28] He conceives of the human being as a role-player who adopts individuality as a communicative confidence trick among fellow humans. Irrespective of whether a role is ascribed or acquired, it inevitably involves a process of both internalizing external role patterns and, ultimately, depersonalizing individuality.[29]

In the same vein, Anthony Giddens remarks: 'Roles may be played at as well as played.'[30] The picaresque is a variation on this basic theme of playing with and at roles. Little Lázaro, for example, the most well-known (and arguably first) pícaro in the Spanish tradition, does both. He plays the role of a respectable member of society in order to clear his reputation (and that of his wife) from accusations about their moral conduct (see Chapter One below)—a communicative frame modelled

---

26 Agamben, *Homo Sacer*, 7.
27 Cf. ibid., 49–62.
28 'Homo Sociologicus', 194. (All translations from non-English secondary sources are by the author, unless otherwise stated.)
29 Ibid., 348.
30 Giddens, *Social Theory*, 119.

on contemporary legal practice (possibly also the Inquisition) and the tradition of the Catholic confession. At the same time, he plays *at* this frame or format in his construction of an implied reader, vis-à-vis whom he boasts his rhetorical and literary virtuosity. In so doing, he satirically denigrates society and fashions himself as an educated social commentator.

Brecht's Samson-Körner also plays roles and plays *at* these roles, both by inventing alternative roles for himself and by referring to his role as a narrator, for example at the very beginning of his story: 'Wenn man etwas über sein eigenes Leben aufschreiben soll, ist es wirklich schwierig, alles unter einen Hut zu bringen.' ['When they ask you to write something about your own life it isn't all that easy to get it together.'] He successfully manages the coherence of the impression he makes on two levels, which is typical of the modern picaresque.[31] First, he plays roles: his narrative allows the readers to witness how he manipulates the impression he makes on his environment, how he uses social mimicry to advance himself. Second, he plays *at* his role playing: by satirically mocking society, he turns the reader into an accomplice at the expense of society. The interaction between the narrator and the reader is in itself an extension of picaresque trickery. The reader never quite knows what to make of that complicity.

The picaresque narrator, in the attempt to convince others of the heavily edited version of his life, fabricates a particular implied reader persona, 'a textual structure anticipating the presence of a recipient without necessarily defining him: this concept prestructures the role to be assumed by each recipient'.[32] While the pícaro appeals to the implied reader by sharing the external perspective of the satirist (and an implicit moral consensus), he simultaneously subjects her to his diegetic perspective: he turns her into the victim of his autobiographical confidence trick. The (implied) reader shares a laugh about the unreliable world with a blatantly unreliable narrator. Much of the playful joy created by the picaresque narrative is related to the reader's ability or inability to decode the satirical persona as yet another picaresque persona, to decipher the extradiegetic reference of the satirist (and the implied reader persona it offers) as yet another confidence trick.

The picaresque hero adopts an ambivalent perspective on society: he envisages himself as part of a specific social lifeworld and, at the same time, shares a satirical bird's-eye view on society with the (implied)

---

31 Erving Goffman, for example, describes communication as a form of impression management that focuses on maintaining the coherence of its framing codes, see *Presentation of Self*, 222. See also Schlenker and Pontari, 'Impression Management and Self-Presentation', 201–10.

32 Iser, *Act of Reading*, 34.

reader, which marks him as an outsider to that very lifeworld. This double perspective can be linked to the position of a 'half outsider' between internal and external perspectives, between social adaptation and individualism. The picaresque 'dialectics of the social self'[33] is best captured at the beginning of Günter Grass's *Blechtrommel*. From an asylum, Oskar Matzerath looks back on the 30 years of his life as an observer who claims to understand his environment as a system of connections (albeit an absurd one); at the same time, he reinvents these 30 years as a specific lifeworld embedded in history. The picaresque situation is defined by this paradox, combining diegetic and extradiegetic references: it evokes both involvement and detachment in the same act of self-narration. It is this referential paradox which teases us into listening to somebody like the boxer Samson-Körner, who claims he was born in Beaver/Utah as well as in Zwickau/Saxony. The double reference paradoxically endows him with a surplus of credibility by mapping two opposite strategies of engendering credibility on top of each other, even if he makes obviously incompatible statements: mimetic identification and satirical detachment. Thus, he manages to achieve what F. W. Chandler describes as a fundamental feature of all picaresque writing: 'we do not so much look at the rogue as borrow his eyes with which to look at the world'.[34]

These and related aspects of the picaresque narrative template provide the incentive for twentieth-century writers to turn to this unique narrator persona, who is both participant and observer, active shape-shifter and passive underdog. My overarching argument is that modern picaresque fiction is marked by the impossibility of separating these two poles and is concerned with combining self-assertion and ostracism in one character. It thus dramatizes the ambiguous character of human agency in modernity, celebrating its exuberance and creative potential and, at the same time, highlighting the precarious nature of its epistemological, social and economic presuppositions.

I have limited myself to five representative novels, focusing on the two phases of highest productivity of the picaresque form: the early twentieth century and the time after World War Two. Brecht's "Samson-Körner" demonstrates that the Weimar period, too, was rife with a con man mindset and produced a wide range of interesting picaresque writings. Yet most of these writings explore various picaresque features within a largely non-picaresque narrative structure; Alfred Döblin's *Berlin Alexanderplatz*, which I will briefly discuss in the conclusion, may serve as a prominent example. Therefore I have opted for the

---

33   Guillén, *Anatomies of Roguery*, 390.
34   Chandler, *Romances of Roguery*, 60.

following combination of novels: two early examples that are never or only rarely discussed in this context (Robert Walser's *Jakob von Gunten* and Franz Kafka's *Der Verschollene*); the two undisputed masterpieces of the modern German picaresque (Thomas Mann's *Bekenntnisse des Hochstaplers Felix Krull* and Günter Grass's *Die Blechtrommel*); and one example that should belong to that canon, but has not yet received the critical appreciation it deserves (Edgar Hilsenrath's *Der Nazi und der Friseur*). Apart from being representative of the 'return of the pícaros', the choice of primary texts is also motivated by the structural and thematic features I regard as particularly relevant for the reinvention of the pícaro.[35]

Kafka and Walser display some of the most striking features of the modern picaresque tradition and anticipate some of its limits, which is the main reason for the prominence they receive in the overarching design of my argument. Karl Roßmann in Kafka's *Der Verschollene* is a pícaro who is neither able to narrate his own story nor to take his fate into his own hands. Rather, he keeps running into the same problems, a vicious cycle of guilt and emotional dependencies. While many of the modern German-language pícaros do take control of their lives by manipulating them in their autobiographical stories, they keep on referring back to this underlying circular structure of guilt. Walser's *Jakob von Gunten* pushes the boundaries of the picaresque tradition to its limits and creates what I describe as a self-parody of the picaresque: the narcissistic pícaro invents himself in the narrative act through diminishing himself, severing ties with family, society, culture and tradition. While Kafka establishes the circular structure of guilt at the core of his picaresque itinerary, Walser adds a second latent centre around which subsequent novels revolve: a narcissistic solitude underneath the ludic exuberance of self-fashioning that always retains the power of self-parody.

Felix Krull's confidence tricks with fellow human beings, by contrast, take on a different colour and have to be seen in the context of his rhetorical understatement: as a confidence man (*Hochstapler*) he devours the world in its imagined totality, as a *Tiefstapler* he presents that very world as corruptible and shares a good laugh about it with the reader. While playful, resourceful and entertaining, Felix is also a victim of himself and of what he establishes as 'his self' through his confidence tricks. Most modern pícaros combine two personae in one character: the ludic shape-shifter and the marginalized underdog, the *Hochstapler* and the victim. Oskar Matzerath in *Die Blechtrommel*, for example, is overdetermined by conformism (the 'Trommler' for the Nazis), subversion (the drummer against the Nazis) and ostracism

---

35 Schumann, 'Wiederkehr der Schelme', 474.

alike (he is constantly in danger of being subjected to the Nazi euthanasia programme). Hilsenrath's *Der Nazi und der Friseur* pushes this
dual nature of the modern pícaro to its extremes in the parallel biographies of the SS officer Max Schulz and his Jewish childhood friend Itzig
Finkelstein, whom he claims to have killed in a concentration camp.
Max adopts Itzig's identity after the war, in order to start a new life as
a 'Jewish' barber in Tel Aviv, so he maintains. Yet, the reader is left in a
haze as to who survived the war: Max the ruthless perpetrator or Itzig
the survivor-guilt ridden victim. The skilfully composed novel allows
both readings.

There is no shortage of alternative examples, varying in nature, scope
and quality.[36] For instance, Walter Serner's *Letzte Lockerung. Handbrevier
für Hochstapler und solche die es werden wollen* (1927) provides a reflection
on confidence trickery. Alfred Döblin's *Berlin Alexanderplatz* (1929)
and *Babylonische Wandrung oder Hochmut kommt vor dem Fall* (1934),
as well as Thomas Mann's *Joseph* tetralogy (1933–43) are also rooted
in the picaresque tradition. The two Germanies after World War Two
both developed productive traditions of picaresque writing. Examples
like Martin Beheim-Schwarzbach's *Die diebischen Freuden des Herrn von
Bisswange-Haschezeck* (1952), Albert Vigoleis Thelen's *Die Insel des zweiten
Gesichts. Aus den angewandten Erinnerungen des Vigoleis* (1953), and Paul
Pörtner's *Tobias Immergrün* (1962), to name but a few, are evidence that
this type of narration resonated with the West German readership. Novels
such as Erwin Strittmatter's *Der Wundertäter* (1957), Manfred Bieler's
Bonifaz oder der Matrose in der Flasche (1963), or Irmtraud Morgner's *Leben
und Abenteuer der Trobadora Beatriz nach Zeugnissen ihrer Spielfrau Laura*
(1974) testify to the fecundity of the genre in East Germany.[37]

In her study *Wendekrisen*, Miriam Gebauer investigates the importance of the picaresque format for the reflection of German reunification
and its aftermath. She focuses on novels by Thomas Brussig, Jens
Sparschuh and Fritz Rudolf Fries. Whether or not we agree with her
selection and terminology, she makes abundantly clear that pícaros
(and now and again pícaras) still populate contemporary German
imagination after reunification.[38] They also feature as harbingers of
Popliteratur aesthetics, for example in novels by the Swiss writer
Christoph Simon (*Franz oder warum Antilopen nebeneinander laufen*, 2001,

---

36   Surveys can be found in Jacobs, *Der deutsche Schelmenroman*; Schöll,
    'Wiederaufleben einer literarischen Tradition'; Seifert, 'Die pikareske Tradition';
    van der Will, *Pikaro heute*.
37   On the ideological paradox of the picaresque 'extreme individualism' within a
    socialist setting see Marckwort, *Schelmenroman der Gegenwart*, 3–6.
38   On Gebauer's debatable definition of the modern picaresque see *Wendekrisen*,
    50–5.

and *Planet Obrist.. Ein Schelmenroman*, 2005) or by the Russian-German writer Wladimir Kaminer (*Militärmusik*, 2003).

All these pícaros navigate a territory that still bears the mark of modernity, and they are heir to the two main strands of modern picaresque writing—playful self-exploration (which is very pronounced in the decade before World War One) and self-assertion in spite of social ostracism (which is dominant after World War Two). They are involved, yet disengaged; they are detached from their fellow human beings, yet dependent on the ties they establish with them; they are marginalized, yet at the same time they use their marginalized status to push their agenda. As 'half outsiders' they can neither integrate into society nor opt out of it. This distinctive position demands a twofold analysis: one that takes into account both the narrative technique of the modern picaresque novel (as well as the reader response it elicits) and the social implications it reflects. In conducting such analysis, I also hope to provide, among other things, a re-reading of German modernism by exploring its underrepresented picaresque textual practices and both their (socio-political and imaginative) potential and limitations. This study thus contributes to a project David Bathrik, Andreas Huyssen and others started over 20 years ago, namely peeling away 'layers of scholarly reification of the classics of the twentieth century'.[39]

For a clearer understanding of the picaresque form we now have to turn to the Spanish tradition. All the German-speaking authors discussed in this book were, in one way or another, aware of the Spanish roots of the picaresque tradition: they either read some of its most illustrious examples in translation, relished Cervantes' parodic take on it (in some of his *Novelas Ejemplares* and in several passages of *Don Quixote*), or gained indirect access to it through German baroque translations, imitations and reflections of the Spanish heritage.[40] Yet, there is not necessarily a direct connection between each modern picaresque novel and the Lázaros and Guzmáns we will encounter in the following chapter. It is important that we do not base our understanding of productive creative encounters and literary cross-fertilization across the centuries exclusively or predominantly on the size of an author's library. None of the authors I am discussing in detail set out to write a novel based on the Spanish model.[41] Yet, all of

---

39   Bathrick and Huyssen, *Modernity and the Text*, 3.

40   For the readers' convenience I comply with the common English (and ancient Spanish) spelling of Don Quixote, although the modern spelling is Don Quijote.

41   Of all German writers, Fritz Rudolf Fries has the most developed awareness of the Spanish tradition, see *Der Weg nach Oobliadooh* (1966) and *Don Quixote flieht die Frauen oder die apokryphen Abenteuer des Ritters von der traurigen Gestalt* (1995).

them arrived at narrative solutions for addressing specific problems germane to human self-understanding in the particular context of Central-European modernity that have vital features in common with the Spanish precursors.

This digression to sixteenth-century Spain will then also provide us with an opportunity to discuss some of the literary traditions that form the context for the demise of the picaresque during the nineteenth century, namely the *Bildungsroman*, and its re-emergence during the twentieth century. Goethe famously called his model *Bildungsroman* hero Wilhelm Meister 'ein armer Hund', 'a poor sod'—someone who never manages to overcome his mediocrity.[42] The pícaro, both classic and modern, typically starts off much worse than Wilhelm, as an orphan and without the support of a middle-class education and environment, but then succeeds in advancing himself further, neither remaining 'arm' nor turning into a 'Hund'. He starts off as a veritable underdog who may well run with the pack for most of his life, but never goes to the dogs.

---

42   Gräf, *Goethe über seine Dichtungen*, II, 954.

1. The Spanish Picaresque Tradition and Its European Repercussions

Hermano mío, mal sientes de la verdad, que ni ha de ser ni conviene ser: tú lo haces que sea y que convenga. *Libre albedrío* te dieron con que te gobernases. La estrella no te fuerza ni todo el cielo junto con cuantas tiene te puede forzar; tú *te* fuerzas a dejar lo bueno y te esfuerzas en lo malo, siguiendo tus deshonestidades, de donde resultan tus calamidades.

My brother, you are wrong about the kind of truth you think shouldn't be true and which does not suit you. you do whatever you think you have to do and whatever is fine for you. You have been given *free will* with which you are supposed to manage your life. Your fate [*estrella*] cannot compel you to do anything, nor do the skies with all their stars [*estrellas*]. It is you who is forcing *yourself* to leave behind what is good, and it is you who brings upon himself what is bad—by following your misguided inclinations, which cause all your problems. (I, 464, emphases added, trans. B.M.)

This passage can be found towards the end of the first part of one of the seminal Spanish picaresque novels, Mateo Alemán's *Guzmán de Alfarache* (1599/1604). Here the pícaro Guzmán defends himself against his ignorant and pusillanimous environment and the concept of predestination that disregards the power of human decisions.[1] His

---

1 The etymology of *pícaro* remains a bone of contention. Monteser, *Picaresque Element*, 14, offers the following possible origins: 1. *picado*—'pitted with smallpox'; 2. *Picardy*—the province where Spaniards saw ragged, dirty characters in the time of Carlos V; 3. *pico*—'sharp'; 4. *picante*—'sharp or biting'; 5. *picar*—'to pinch'. The first use of the term *el pícaro* is recorded in Diego Hurtado de Mendoza's burlesque piece *Carta del Bachiller de Arcadia al Capitan Salazar* (1548). The first use in English, according to the *OED*, occurs in the Jacobean tragicomedy *The Spanish Gipsy* (1623).

emphatic focus on free will and responsibility for one's own actions articulates a profound concern with individual self-assertion, an aspect often overlooked in discussions of the novel (which does, admittedly, tend to spill more ink about 'misguided inclinations' than about 'free will'). It is, however, precisely this feature of 'libre albedrío' and its complex repercussions that allowed the pícaro to emerge again as a major player in the social and literary imagination of the twentieth century.

While the picaresque is conventionally associated with ostracism and social injustice, it is also an unprecedented imaginative effort to reflect on a new sense of individual mobility and freedom which was about to develop in the course of the modern age. 'Your fate cannot compel you to do anything'—what Guzmán formulates in this passage is a powerful plea for human responsibility and self-empowerment and against the fatalism of astrology ('la estrella'). As a degraded individual in a degrading environment, which is marked by a seemingly endless chain of deception (*engaño*) and disillusion (*desengaño*), he nourishes the seeds of self-assertion and independence within him.[2] At the same time, he tells his story as a series of adventure episodes of a marginalized low character who moves through many social strata in sixteenth-century Spain and its empire and, more often than not, follows his 'misguided inclinations'.[3] In other words, we are never quite sure what to make of his lofty aims, since they are expressed in an ambiguous communicative context, namely as part of a picaresque autobiography that is notorious for the unreliability of its narrator, whose exhibition of penitence could be either pretended or genuine. Guzmán's confessional self-flogging could simply be a sham, designed to further his numerous petty endeavours, it could, however, also reveal a genuinely humanist voice. In many picaresque tales both voices coexist and it is often difficult to tell them apart.[4]

---

2   Ramon Llull's influential notion of free will may have played a role in shaping the concept of adventure, both for the medieval epic and for its picaresque parody, see Nerlich, *Abenteuer*, 252.

3   In all likelihood, this is a reference to the *stimulus carnis* (the desire of the flesh) mentioned in St Paul's letter to the Corinthians (12.7) and the Church Fathers. It has to be seen in the context of Counter-Reformation theology after the Tridentine Council. For context see Darst, *Counter-Reformational Closure*.

4   Research on the Spanish picaresque has been divided between scholars who favour a strict narratological approach and those who focus on socio-economic conditions. For a summary of the debate see Wicks, 'The Picaresque in Literary Scholarship', 23–5. Bataillon, *Le roman picaresque*; van Hoogstraten, *Estructura mítica de la picaresca* and Bauer, *Schelmenroman*, along with Guillén's structuralism and Rico's focus on a unified viewpoint, represent the narratological approach, while thematic aspects are emphasized in Maravall, *La literatura picaresca*, Barrio Olano, *La novela picaresca*, Tierno Galvan, *Sobre la*

Contexts: The Golden Age and the Renaissance

The time of Guzmán's life story, the so-called Golden Age in sixteenth-century Spain (*El Siglo Oro*), was marked by socio-economic predicaments often occluded from our general perception of the Age of Discoveries and Iberian world hegemony. There had been problems smouldering at the core of Spanish society long before the defeat of the Armada fleet in 1588 relentlessly exposed them. Overseas colonies transformed Spanish society and economy and paved the way for mercantilism. The huge influx of new products and gold turned the traditional market upside down and undermined the stratum-based structure of society. This gave rise to a new class of merchant upstarts, who posed a major challenge to the aristocracy and whose speculative entrepreneurship left behind a whole class of destitute losers. Particularly affected by these social transformations was the impoverished *hidalgo* from the lower ranks of the nobility. Traditionally, the *hidalgos* were bound by their class code and therefore not allowed to pursue any kind of professional work. Economic changes, however, forced them to sell most of their estates and possessions and finally take up random or even humiliating jobs.[5] Most famously, Cervantes' Don Quixote epitomizes this figure in the parodic form of an anti-hero who seeks redemption in the surrogate world of medieval chivalry. The classic *pícaro* is equally a victim of economic change—a poor orphan and outsider, the victim of large-scale impoverishment of the rural population due to the collapse of the Spanish agricultural market under the strain of competition from colonial products.[6] The picaresque hero tries to make ends meet in this hostile environment and, by traversing the entire social spectrum, exposes the conflict between traditional hereditary claims and parvenu ambitions.[7]

Apart from this socio-economic upheaval, Spain was also changed by the continuing effects of a mono-ethnic ideology. The unification of Spain under Fernando II de Aragon and Isabela I de Castilla (1492) led to the expulsion of most Jews and Muslims who were not prepared to convert to Catholicism. This was only the culmination of a long history of uneasy cohabitation between Jews and Christians on the Iberian Peninsula. Anti-Semitism, increasingly motivated by racial rather than religious stereotypes, escalated in riots throughout the fifteenth

---

novela picaresca. Wicks calls his approach, to which I owe a fair deal, 'modal': he explores fictional modes according to the relation they establish with the realities of their (assumed) readers, and thus offers a first synthesis of the two approaches, see 'The Nature of the Picaresque Narrative', 240–2.

5   Cf. Ruiz, *Spanish Society*, 74–5.
6   Cf. Herrero, 'Renaissance Poverty', esp. 200–3.
7   Cf. Maravall, 'La aspiración social'.

century, a period during which converts, or *conversos*, to Christianity of Jewish (and, to a lesser degree, Muslim) origin became increasingly successful both in politics and in the church nomenclature.[8] While the Inquisition never attained any specific jurisdiction over Jewish communities, it did, however, become a crucial element in turning anti-*converso* sentiment into anti-Semitism by endorsing the doctrine of purity of blood (*limpieza de sangre*), which 'was to provide the rationale for the isolation, and eventually the destruction of the *conversos*'.[9]

With regard to the converts who abandoned Judaism, an important theological distinction was made by Jewish leaders: while the voluntary converts (if that is an applicable term, given the all-pervasive social and religious pressures during and after the so-called Reconquest) were considered Gentiles and addressed as *meshumad* (or as *marranos*, originally a derogatory term), the forced converts, called *anûs*, unofficially retained their status as Jews. As Norman Roth points out, however, many converts were 'neither forced nor sincere, but rather motivated simply by a desire to improve their social standing and avoid the increasing difficulties associated with being Jewish'.[10] Although socially and economically quite successful, they often found themselves doubly marginalized, both by the Jewish communities as apostates and by Christians as 'secret' Jews.[11] As Jews they had long been perceived as living outside the body politic; as *conversos*, *marranos* or 'new Christians', however, they were increasingly seen as a contamination of the body politic—an ideological perception that was to shape Central European anti-Semitism during the nineteenth and twentieth centuries, too.[12]

Benzion Netanyahu, in his influential study *The Marranos of Spain*, challenged the academic consensus by arguing that the aim of the Inquisition 'was not to eradicate a Jewish heresy from the midst of the Marrano group [which is his term for all *conversos*], but to eradicate the Marrano group from the midst of the Spanish people'.[13]

---

8   The situation of Jewish communities throughout the fifteenth century and the conversion issue in Spain after the pogroms of Castile (1391) have received much scholarly attention. Interpretations vary considerably, cf. Beinart, *Expulsion*; Netanyahu, *Marranos of Spain*; Roth, *Conversos*.

9   Roth, *Conversos*, 115.

10   Ibid., 73.

11   *Conversos* of Muslim origin (*moriscos*) found themselves in a similar situation and were finally expelled in 1609 (Harvey, *Muslims in Spain*, 3–44).

12   Cf. Yerushalmi, *Assimilation and Racial Anti-Semitism*; Stallaert, *La España inquisitorial y la Alemania nazi*.

13   Netanyahu, *Marranos of Spain*, 4. On the debate surrounding Netanyahu's account of Spanish Judaism see his own engagement with critiques in *Marranos of Spain*, 275–93. For context and a critique see Yovel, *The Other Within*, 398–400.

His account of the Inquisition's role in these changes has been contested, but it is evident from his research that the fifteenth century witnessed a shift from social envy to a fully-fledged racial doctrine that led to social paranoia and culminated in the expulsion of both Jews and Muslims from Spain in 1492. The remaining *conversos* found themselves under incessant pressure to avoid (public) confrontation with their ostracized original cultural identity. Coming to grips with these internal conflicts and various layers of (crypto-)identity was to become the trademark of picaresque fiction. The picaresque novel has frequently been read, most prominently by Américo Castro, as a reflection of the *converso* experience of having to adapt to an environment of increasing social hostility.[14]

Many of the predecessors and early practitioners of the picaresque were *conversos* of Jewish origin, for example Fernando de Rojas (*La Celestina*, 1499), Francisco Delicado (*La Lozana andaluza*, 1528) and the aforementioned Mateo Alemán, although it would be misleading to assume a uniform *converso* mentality among them.[15] Even if we do not agree with Castro's exclusive focus on this socio-cultural aspect, we still have to acknowledge the *converso* background as a vital source for the imaginary power of the picaresque tradition and its existential urgency in dealing with the issue of social trust. This allows us to appreciate thematic connections between the social imaginary of the picaresque, on the one hand, and the cultural situation of the *conversos*, on the other; Yovel lists, for example, 'the narrator's lowly extraction and suspected "impure" blood; his being doomed to social exclusion [...]; the ubiquity of a covert real world opposing the Spanish normative world; and the unrelenting rebuke of hidalgo values and applause for personal achievement'.[16]

The second major context for understanding the pícaro as a cultural index is the restructuring of the order of knowledge in Renaissance Europe. Stephen Greenblatt's explorations of Renaissance England characterize the early modern episteme as vacillating between an unprecedented assertion of the executive power of will, on the

---

14 Cf. Castro, *Aspectos del vivir hispánico*, 90–114; *Hacia Cervantes*, 262–301; *La realidad histórica*, 28 and 72–5. See also Márquez Villanueva, *España judeoconversa*, 43–74 and 75–94. Parker argues against the *converso* theory in *Literature and the Delinquent*, 13–14 and 31–2.

15 The authorship of *Lazarillo de Tormes* is shrouded in mystery, but a *converso* connection is possible. Navarro Durán, in *Alfonso de Valdés*, argues that the *converso* humanist Alfonso de Valdés is the author of *Lazarillo*, but her argument was conclusively confuted by Pérez Venzalá, see 'El Lazarillo sigue siendo anónimo'. In 1620, Juan de Luna, an Erasmite *converso*, published a sequel of *Lazarillo* with a strong *converso* subtext.

16 Yovel, *The Other Within*, 265.

one hand, and its administration and engineering, on the other—between social mobility and an increasing degree of surveillance and governance: '[I]n the sixteenth century there appears to be an increased self-consciousness about the fashioning of human identity as a manipulable, artful process.'[17] Though Castro cautions us against applying 'historical principles derived from other parts of Europe' to the Iberian Peninsula, we can safely assume that Greenblatt's observation has some validity in the Spanish context, too.[18] After all, a censored version of *Lazarillo de Tormes* (which appeared on the *Index Librorum Prohibitorum* in 1559), was reissued in the early seventeenth century as part of a collection of courtly manuals reflecting the change of etiquette at the court of Philip III. *Lazarillo*'s role as foundation myth of the picaresque stems from this mutilated version, rather than from the original satire, which was both addressing a wider audience and launching a more specific criticism against the church and the clergy.[19]

From Baldassare Castiglione's *Il Cortegiano* (1528) to Baltasar Gracián's *Oráculo manual y arte de prudencia* (1647), generations across cultural boundaries were obsessed with court manuals and their instructions for the art of dissimulation as a means of creating the impression of authenticity. The successful courtier has to maintain a façade of impartiality and decorum, and simultaneously convey the impression of elegant leisure (*otium*) as a way of successfully conducting business (*negotium*). The crafting of identity was based on the adherence to rules which were, paradoxically, designed to impart the impression of self-conduct without rules. The prime self-fashioners in Golden Age Spain were high aristocrat courtiers and those upstarts who managed to make use of the rapid changes and climb the social ladder quickly in times of fundamental social and economic change. Their social status depended on the balance between visible codes of behaviour and their deliberate occasional transgression—a status that was carried over into the so-called age of disillusionment during the early seventeenth century, when the 'optimism of the Renaissance had given way to a disenchantment with contemporary life, and the prevalent attitude was one which sought to expose abuses and dispel illusions'.[20]

Texts: Inventing and Defending the Self

The picaresque novel or tale projects this social logic, the schizoid combination of complicity and transgression in one character, onto

---

17 Greenblatt, *Renaissance Self-fashioning*, 2.
18 Castro, *Idea of History*, 16.
19 On the contextualization of *Lazarillo* within the contemporary literature of manners see Sieber, 'Literary Continuity', 147–9.
20 Whitbourn, 'Moral Ambiguity', 7.

the dimension of low life.[21] It inflects the Renaissance spirit of self-fashioning in various, partly contradictory, ways and was imbricated with the widespread craze about theatre and histrionics that formed such an important part of the Golden Age.[22] Arguably, its new tone and structure appealed predominantly to a discontented middle-class readership, which paradoxically revelled in both the idea of social mobility and the moral predicament of the parvenu.[23]

The Spanish picaresque tradition displays a number of characteristic features, which I shall illustrate by using the example of *La Vida de Lazarillo de Tormes y de sus Fortunas y Adversidades* (1554).[24] The first edition of the widely circulated picaresque novel *La Pícara Justina* (1605) by Francisco López de Úbeda features a frontispiece that shows two boats floating on what is called 'rio del olvido' (river of forgetting). The larger boat has several of the well-known Spanish pícaros and pícaras on board, among them Guzmán de Alfarache; they look rather disoriented, somewhat bedraggled and clearly lack a navigator. The smaller boat, by contrast, shows Lazarillo (Little Lázaro), who looks relatively content and displays a clear sense of direction by operating what seems to be a rudder.[25] While set apart on his own little boat, Lazarillo is portrayed as the fictitious character who gives the entire tradition some direction in the struggle of the human mind against the river of forgetting. (The allegorical frontispiece is the best proof that there was a sense of tradition.)

Lazarillo tells his own story *ab ovo*, rejecting Horace's dictum in the prologue. It is the story of one of the poorest of the destitute, an orphan who suffers from the widespread indigence of early modern Spain and, in order to make ends meet, hooks up with various masters.

---

21 The term novel is problematic with regard to the sixteenth century, see Dunn, *Spanish Picaresque Fiction*, 29–30. Guillén defends the term emphatically, stressing the conflict between the individual and society as trademark of the novel, see *Literature as System*, 78.

22 Cf. Gumbrecht, Eine *Geschichte der spanischen Literatur*, I, 350–88.

23 Cf. Guillén, *Literature as System*, 151.

24 While I agree with Parker and others that *Guzmán de Alfarache* should be regarded as the most influential pattern of the classic picaresque, I do not concur with his far-reaching denial of any structural cohesion of the picaresque tradition. His focus on the figure of the delinquent and related thematic issues has even led him to the rather unorthodox belief that *Lazarillo de Tormes* should be excluded from the canon of 'pícaros-as-delinquents', see *Literature and the Delinquent*, 4. While this approach may have provoked new insights, its fundamental thrust has not gained much purchase among scholars. A summary of the counter-arguments can be found in Whitbourn, 'Moral Ambiguity', 9–10, and Dunn, *Spanish Picaresque Novel*, 136–7.

25 See the reprint of this frontispiece as the front plate of Valbuena Prat's collection *La novela picaresca española*.

These dubious mentors come from all three estates of late medieval society: the warriors (*bellatores*) are represented by an entirely impoverished *hidalgo*, the workers and peasants (*aratores*) by a blind beggar and a tambourine painter, the clergy (*oratores*) by a Mercedarian friar, a fraudulent pardoner, a cathedral chaplain and a polygamous archpriest; a constable and an attorney also make their appearance as masters—a reflection of the rising class of civil servants after the Spanish unification. Lazarillo learns indispensable lessons about a society governed by the principle of omnipresent warfare (*bellum omnium contra omnes*), and, 'unlike the Christian hero of romance, [...] boasts that success in the quest of everyday objects is the result of his diligence and enterprise'.[26] His journey is also a panoramic literary rendition of society, from the world of beggars to the realm of clergy and finally low aristocracy.[27] Within the clergy, he moves from an indulgence trader to a friar and chaplain and, finally, to the aforementioned archpriest, with whom he strikes an unconventional deal: by marrying his new master's concubine, Lazarillo secures his material welfare and social protection (and covers up the archpriest's lechery).

In order to adjust to the various demands his masters make on him and face up to the challenges their lessons pose to him, Lazarillo turns into a shape-shifter. Efficient role-play for him, as opposed to the aristocratic Renaissance self-fashioner, is not a luxury but a survival strategy. As a satirical narrator persona the pícaro levels criticism against hypocrisy, as a narrated persona he embraces and implicitly justifies an amoral social ethos. Lazarillo furthers the perpetuation of the picaresque world, which is the very object of his satire; his tentative and unsustainable integration into society is based on mutual distrust.[28] A good example to illustrate this duality is the scene in which the blind beggar, Lazarillo's first master, discovers that he is being tricked:

> Todo lo que podía sisar y hurtar traía en medias blancas, y cuando le mandaban rezar y le daban blancas, como él carecía de vista,

---

26   Resina, 'Life of the Novel in Spain', 295.

27   His name alludes to the Spanish *lacería* (misery, poverty) and refers to the two Lazarus figures in the Gospels: the man from Bethany raised from the dead by Christ (John 11.1–44); the beggar who reclines in the bosom of Abraham while the rich man, who refused him alms, suffers in hell (Luke 16.19–31). In Spain, Lazarus is the patron saint of lepers.

28   This double thrust of satirizing and perpetuating the social world is anticipated in the literary traditions that contributed to the emergence of the picaresque: ancient satyr plays, the Menippean satire, the medieval *satyra divina* and *Ständesatire*. These traditions anticipate the paradoxical interrelation between a position *extra legem* and containment, culminating in pieces such as *Liber Vagatorum* (1510), *Till Eulenspiegel* (1512) and Teofilo Folengo's *Baldus* (1517).

no había el que se la daba amagado con ella, cuando yo la tenía lanzada en la boca y la media aparejada, que por presto que él echaba la mano, y iba de mi cambio aniquilada en la mitad del justo precio. Quejábaseme el mal ciego, porque al tiento luego conocía y sentía que no era blanca entera, y decía:

'¿Qué diablo es esto, que después que conmigo estás no me dan sino medias blancas, y de antes una blanca y un maravedí hartas veces me pagaban? En ti debe estar esta desdicha.' (29–30)

Everything which I could pinch or steal I changed into half-pennies. When they got him to make one of his prayers, and gave him pennies, I would take advantage of his not being able to see, and as soon as the penny was held out I would snatch it and pop it in my mouth, and then I would give my master a half-penny instead, which I had ready for the purpose, so that no matter how quickly he grabbed for the penny, thanks to my exchange he never got more than half. The blind villain could tell by the feel that he was not getting whole pennies, and he complained.

'What the devil is going on here?' he said. 'Ever since you've been with me they've been giving me nothing but half-pennies. They never used to give me anything smaller than a whole penny, and often it was bigger coins than that. I swear it's your fault that I'm out of luck.' (15–16, trans. Merwin)

Lazarillo speaks with two voices, one satirically exhibiting the beggar's meanness and, implicitly, the social system that produces such a character (as, for example, in the curse), the other voice slipping into the role of a victim who is even worse off than the crippled beggar (and has to change the alms he has stolen into half *blancas* to continue his survival trickery). His ultimate confidence trick, as this passage demonstrates, is to criticize the very attitudes he emulates. He ridicules the blind beggar for his greed and stinginess and, at the same time, proves to be his best disciple. What are the roots of this seemingly contradictory narrative? The answer lies in the particular way in which the pícaro uses his satirical autobiography as an *apologia*, a self-legitimizing epistle written in response to an unknown public inquiry or a benefactor's request. This addressee and the underlying motivation or obligation is, however, never spelt out or explained.[29] The picaresque narrative as a confessional epistle deliberately mutes potential or actual qualms and accusations by this incognito inquirer.

In the case of *Lazarillo de Tormes*, the protagonist first unmasks the social interaction of three of his masters as dissimulation, in order to

---

29 Cf. Rico, *Point of View*, 2–5.

deflect attention from his own social mimicry. This culminates in the seventh and final chapter, where Lazarillo tries to create the impression that he did not know about the *ménage-à-trois* he is entangled in as the husband of the archpriest's concubine.[30] In fact, his social emancipation is extremely fragile since he is entrenched in unsustainable legal and financial arrangements and always runs the risk of being unmasked. This chapter offers more insights into the *apologia* core of Lazarillo's story, responding to an indictment levelled against him, possibly by ecclesiastical authorities (or even the Inquisition) embodied by 'Vuestra Merced' ('Your Worship')—an 'anonymous *destinataire* or recipient of Lázaro's text, who is also its originating authority'.[31] The prologue to the story has already introduced this 'hidden authority' to the narrative, but the satirical persona throughout the story creates a permanent tension with that hidden reference point, keeping the implied reader poised between following the *apologia* pattern (which draws one into the story) and latching on to the satirical perspective (which keeps one detached from the story). The narrative is thus doubly encrypted for two different implied addressees.

On the one hand, the narrator-protagonist superimposes some kind of teleology on his life story, which makes his position as a low civil servant—he is a town crier or bailiff (*pregonero*)—appear well-deserved, honourable and legitimate:

> En el cual el día de hoy vivo y resido a servicio de Dios y de Vuestra Merced. Y es que tengo cargo de pregonar los vinos que en esta ciudad se venden, y en almonedas, y cosas perdidas, acompañar los que padecen persecuciones por justicia y declarar a voces sus delictos: pregonero, hablando en buen romance. (129)

> In which post I have continued to this day, in the service of God and your Excellency. My function is to cry up the wines which are to be sold in this city, and to announce auctions and lost articles, and to go along beside those who are being prosecuted for the sake of justice, and call out what crimes they committed: in good plain terms, I'm a town crier. (114, trans. Merwin)

On the other hand, he has to defend his wife against accusations of adultery and himself against social envy in view of his amorality and criminal record. The ambiguity lies in Lazarillo's double bind, which makes him both predator and prey. He has to strike a delicate

---

30   The chapters in *Lazarillo* are called *tratados*, literally treatises, a reference to the conventional form of humanist moral philosophy.

31   Dunn, *Spanish Picaresque Fiction*, 32. See also Scholes, *Nature of Narrative*, 143.

balance. If he downplays his hardship, he cannot expect mercy with regard to his criminal past. If he exaggerates his struggle, however, he will undermine the credibility of his repeated claim that he has managed to change his life. Lazarillo's case is both omnipresent and strangely absent in the story, it is both woven into the narrative and suppressed: Lazarillo has to both respond to the accusations and at the same time divert from them. This double bind prevents the classic picaresque tale from being, strictly speaking, episodic in the sense of a potentially endless series of adventures; it is rather linear in rhetorical terms and concerned with structural analogies and argumentative stringency.[32]

The narrated initiation of the picaresque hero into the world, the moment when the blind beggar teaches him that, in order to make ends meet, he has to comply with a world that wants to be deceived, is also an initiation of the reader into the confidence game of the narration. The readers themselves are always exposed to the picaresque strategies of faking and feigning, since they are never given other perspectives on the story than the narrator's take. They have to read it against the grain and thus become complicit with his satirical mockery of society. Both in his apologetic confession and in his satirical social critique, the pícaro is a craftsman of manipulative rhetoric.

For the sake of his argument, Lazarillo exploits (and exaggerates) his humble origins and the insurmountable difficulties of his life, as well as the corruption of society. While his *apologia* implies a conventional condemnation of criminal social behaviour, it aims at eliciting praise for his own adoption of morally corrupt principles. The reader's interpretation vacillates between accepting the picaresque narrator as a victim and doubting his contrivances as a trickster. This endows him with an ambiguous identity poised between victim (turned decent citizen) and deceiver, an ambiguity which was to become decisive for the re-emergence of the picaresque in the twentieth century. The socio-political background of this double bind is the Spanish *hombre bueno*, the social climber, as opposed to the impoverished *hidalgo*: he has to legitimize his position, which he did not inherit, by perpetually

---

32 Nerlich uses this feature of the Spanish tradition to argue against its influence on what he calls the modern 'Schelmenroman', which he defines as any novel with one or several rogues. ('Plädoyer für Lázaro', 9–12) While he is right in pointing out that there is no 'tradition' transmitting the 'formal solidity' of the classic picaresque tale, he ignores the fact that there is a core of modern picaresque texts that use both figural and structural elements comparable to those that played a decisive role around 1600. My readings aim at highlighting the rhetorical coherence of the modern picaresque, while acknowledging the fact that the (narcissistic) episodic structure is taken to new levels.

proving his moral values and virtues.[33] Nevertheless, it is Lazarillo's main aim to 'arrimarse a los buenos, por ser uno dellos'. (15) David Rowland's translation from 1586 inadvertently seems to reduplicate, in its convoluted syntax, some of the trials and tribulations associated with that goal: 'to inhabit among such as were virtuous and honest, to be of that number.' (57) *Los buenos*, the emerging mercantile class, are the unattainable role model for the Spanish pícaro, and throughout the history of picaresque fiction there is an elective affinity between the circulation of money, the rise of capitalism and picaresque itineraries— especially when the pícaro hits the road again in more recent fiction.[34]

Contrasting historicity and personal plausibility, the picaresque form also incorporates elements of private introspection based on the model of confessional literature since Augustine.[35] The narrative frame highlights what I regard as the seminal element of the picaresque structure, a double narrative voice: the story is simultaneously told by the aged pícaro (the reflecting voice), and the naïve young pícaro (the experiencing voice). It combines and contrasts the education and self-awareness of the mature narrator with the limited perspective of the deprived narrated persona, who develops his own narrative tone and viewpoint: 'In an analogous and complementary manner, Lázaro the author records both what was perceived by Lázaro the protagonist and, in addition, the very act of perception.'[36] Hans Ulrich Gumbrecht contextualizes this specific narrative structure of the picaresque within an oscillation which he regards as characteristic of the Spanish Golden Age—the oscillation between the religious idea of cosmological time and a new Renaissance-inflected historical worldview: '[…] while the protagonist exploits the spaces of Subjective action and Subjective world-interpretation, the narrator clearly adapts his discourse to the religious cosmology that was newly institutionalized in the Spanish Empire […]'.[37]

This pseudo-autobiographical format of the picaresque allows both self-parody and self-assertion within the framework of 'Subjective action' and 'religious cosmology'. It stresses the divergence between fact and fiction, so that it could 'pass for truth and be identified as a fable', and simultaneously operates with an emphatic notion of verisimilitude.[38] This has the paradoxical effect that the readers both

---

33 Ruiz, *Spanish Society*, 65–81.
34 Cf. Malkmus, 'Economies of Circulation'.
35 See Jauss's controversial article 'Ursprung und Bedeutung der Ich-Form' on *Lazarillo* as a travesty of the Christian life confession.
36 Rico, *Point of View*, 18.
37 Gumbrecht, 'Cosmological Time', 314. Cf. also Gumbrecht, Eine *Geschichte der spanischen Literatur*, I, 284.
38 Rico, 'Lazarillo de Tormes', 150.

sympathize with and have confidence in an obviously unreliable narrator, mainly because they are blinded by the narrator's erudition and social experience. The credibility of the picaresque emphasis on an encyclopedic approach to verisimilitude counterbalances the unreliable pseudo-autobiographical split of the narration.[39] The complexity of the reader persona constructed through this picaresque *apologia* calls for a reader response analysis, which will enable us to appreciate better the specific advantages of the picaresque narrative template as a reflection and refraction of particular social imaginaries, not only related to specific historical crises such as the economic dilemma of sixteenth-century Spain, but also of the modern human condition in general.[40]

The pícaro's obscure birth contributes decisively to his position as a social outsider. Prematurely in charge of his own life and initiated into the struggle for survival, he recklessly works his way through the echelons of feudal society by virtue of his versatility in playing the shape-shifter. Socially underprivileged, he cannot develop what is conventionally defined as social integrity and would allow him full participation in society. Therefore he chooses to secure his share in society by tricking its representatives and, at the same time, adopts their mask of social integrity. The ensuing circular movement of the pícaro's excommunication from society, followed by his acceptance into society through his skills as simulator and, finally, the de-masking of these practices of simulation, are constitutive elements of the picaresque—elements that open the narrative form up to philosophical reflections on human nature in general.

The Fatherless Child and his Heritage: European Itineraries

Drawing comparisons between related literary modes across centuries is always fraught with concerns about the fallacy of anachronism. Peter N. Dunn rightly cautions us against superimposing contemporary critical (and ideological) categories on certain narrative forms, which have to be understood in the context of their literary and epistemic premises. This is particularly true of modern concepts of religious freedom and individual independence. Yet, Dunn's assumption that the early reader of a Spanish picaresque tale 'would not have decoded the text existentially and taken the protagonist seriously as a human

---

39 Bauer, *Schelmenroman*, 9.

40 Cf. Reed, *The Reader in the Picaresque Novel*. Bauer, *Schelmenroman*, 36, has a more comprehensive approach in mind when he analyses the picaresque as a fictitious autobiography that aims at showing 'situations of conflict between humans refracted in a way [...] which forces the reader to engage in a reading that complements the reading offered by the narrator'. Friedman offers a contestable reading, arguing that the satirical narrator persona is identical with the author censoring the narrated persona, see *Antiheroine's Voice*, xiii.

being' falls into the opposite extreme.[41] He bases his perception of possible reader responses to a new aesthetic development, such as the picaresque, exclusively on recorded reader responses to previously established, related aesthetic practices. Accordingly, he roots the original picaresque firmly within traditions of comic story-telling and the contemporary social skill of telling jokes without offence 'in judging the appropriate moment for the story and the appropriate story for the moment' (*facetudo*).[42] Without doubt, this will have shaped the reception of the new picaresque art of story-telling, but we should not cease probing further here.

As mentioned above, the inclusion of *Lazarillo* in manuals for courtiers, for example, suggests a certain affinity to Renaissance self-fashioning and related changes in the concept of individuality. The *converso* topic and its connection with Counter-Reformation theology and rhetoric in Guzmán, to name another example, cannot be dismissed as a negligible subtext without any bearing on the narrative structure.[43] And even if it were so and the readers of the Spanish picaresque did not, as Dunn suggests, appreciate its innovative narrative structure as a harbinger of certain epistemic changes, this would not entail that it does not exist as a social imaginary or could not have provided a creative stimulus for authors of later generations or different cultures. Whether or not they were exposed to the original picaresque tradition, many twentieth-century authors used, among a multitude of other literary forms, a narrative template comparable to the Spanish one and thus testify to its imaginative power of engagement with the world, as Thomas Pavel remarks: 'Beginning in the midsixteenth century, a new kind of picaresque story gradually freed itself from laughter and viewed human imperfection with the deliberate seriousness that had previously been reserved for the description of human perfection.'[44]

This productive exchange begins with Cervantes, whose dislike of the picaresque is also a profound reflection of its power: in the hands of the pícaro, social mimicry as individual self-advancement turns easily

------

41   Dunn, *Spanish Picaresque Fiction*, 39.

42   Ibid., 32; see also Rico, *Point of View*, 4–5.

43   *Guzmán* was written by a *converso* author in the spirit of the Counter-Reformation; the refusal of the doctrine of predestination and the Christocentric reformulation of the doctrine of the Trinity at the Council of Trent (1545–63) provided the spiritual breeding ground for new concepts of saintliness, emphasizing the role of the individual believer as sinner and, as a consequence, the notion of literature as a truthful moral account rather than an idealistic transfiguration (such as in the pastoral and the romance), see Parker, *Literature and the Delinquent*, 21–5 and 39; and Resina, 'Life of the Novel in Spain', 298–300.

44   Pavel, 'The Novel in Search of Itself', 9.

into a parody of mimetic forms of representation, a topic elaborated in his satire on the picaresque confession and *apologia* structure in 'Coloquio de los perros' and his ironic treatment of the *mundus inversus* topic in 'Rinconete y Cortadillo' (both pieces from *Novelas Ejemplares*). Cervantes' *El ingenioso hidalgo Don Quixote de la Mancha* (1604/15) is a network of genre cross-referencing, which makes it difficult to determine the extent to which it makes use of the picaresque. In the figure of Ginés de Pasamonte, a convicted criminal, the pícaro figure is obviously parodied as a literary fashion. Cervantes, however, also uses picaresque elements to portray the impoverished *hidalgo* class and to buttress his parody of the late medieval heroic epic. Don Quixote's excessive emulation of the perished stratum of migrating knights is an attempt to simulate literature in order to escape reality. This desperate play of simulation is underpinned by references to the picaresque tradition. Like a picaresque imposter, for example, Quixote adopts the title 'Don', which a *hidalgo* in the seventeenth century was not entitled to carry. The picaresque in *Don Quixote* governs one of its main philosophical implications: Cervantes renders self-knowledge as a process of differentiation rather than one of identification. His parody and self-reflexive use of the picaresque is a good example for a response to new creative developments that moves outside the box and thereby exploits its potential. By ridiculing the readers' fascination with the picaresque imaginary, Cervantes also highlights that there is something different about this mode of writing about the human: it looks like an epistle, confession and *apologia* in one, yet at the same time constitutes something new altogether, namely a reflection on the individual as emerging through social dialogue (as a form of impression management) and susceptible to (self-)deceit.

The attitude toward the pícaro in Spain changed tremendously throughout its relatively brief period of flourishing (with the prime examples being *Lazarillo*, *Guzmán*, *Pícara Justina*), which quite possibly demonstrates the curtailed hopes of an emerging merchant and middle class. Alemán's *Guzmán*, published around 1600, is a vehicle for a multi-layered exploration of religious sentiment and social morals, launching criticism against some of the glaring injustices in Spanish society, sometimes explicitly, sometimes in disguise. Francisco de Quevedo's *Historia de la vida del buscón llamado Don Pablos*, published in 1626, a quarter of a century later, by contrast, openly turns against its protagonist. The author persona implicitly mocks the double persona of narrating and narrated pícaro, Don Pablos (and with him quite possibly the *converso* population in Spanish society), as a rascal who does not only work against his own God-given moral instincts but also against a God-given (semi-feudal) social order: 'After its initial sympathetic portrayal in *Lazarillo*, the image of the pícaro declines until he becomes a scapegoat in the hands of Quevedo. *El buscón* embodies the ideology of a ruling class still militantly occupied with the repression of upward mobility.'[45]

While the moral and religious focus was maintained when various European cultures began to adopt this Spanish tradition, the picaresque continued to provide insights into different social strata, economic injustice, and the changing opportunities for and obstacles to social mobility. It is the *desengaño* story of a half-orphan with rather dubious origins, who also happened to be, as numerous translations and adaptations in England, France, Germany and elsewhere show, the father of many children across Europe.

In England, picaresque writing was seen more broadly as a set of themes and motifs that blended easily with roguish adventure tales and, later on, with Henry Fielding's notion of the novel as a 'comic Epic-Poem in Prose'.[46] In France, *la novela picaresca* was perceived in the literary context of the *roman comique*, a large umbrella term encompassing a wide variety of comedies of manner in prose.[47] The *Schelm* of the German baroque and his female counterpart (often called 'Landstörtzerin') originally tended to stick relatively closely to the conventions set by Aegidius Albertinus' translation of Alemán's *Guzmán*, most notably in the works of Hans Jakob Christoffel von Grimmelshausen, before the English and French influences became more pronounced during the late seventeenth century.[48] Grimmelshausen's *Der abentheuerliche Simplicissimus Teutsch* (1668) relates the long journey of Simplicius Simplicissimus from a kind of presocial state of naivety to self-knowledge. The majority of his stories, however, are about the trials and tribulations of life in Central Europe during the Thirty Years' War and his various experiences as victim and perpetrator.

---

45 Pellón and Rodríguez-Luis, 'Introduction', 18.

46 Fielding, *Joseph Andrews*, 4. The English tradition does not fully exploit many of the major features of the genre and focuses on roguery, episodic structure and the realistic vein of the comedy of manners; see Blackburn, *The Myth of the Picaro*, 19 and 104–11. Prominent examples are: Nashe, *The Unfortunate Traveller* (1594); Head and Kirkman, *The English Rogue* (1665–71); Defoe, *Moll Flanders* (1722); Fielding, *The Life of Jonathan Wild the Great* (1743) and Tobias Smollett's *The Adventures of Roderick Random* (1748).

47 Prominent examples are: *La Vie Genereuse des Mercelots, Guenz, et Bosmiens* (anon., 1596); Charles Sorel, *La Vraye Histoire Comique de Francion* (1622); Alain-René Lesage's *Gil Blas de Santillana* (1705–35).

48 On Albertinus see Rötzer, 'Schelmenroman und seine Nachfolge', 131–4; on the German reception of *Guzmán* see Hoffmeister, 'Das spanische Modell'; on the German reception of *Lazarillo* see Röcke, 'Zur Poetik von Schwankdichtung und Schelmenroman', 15–19. Two other baroque writers with picaresque leanings were Hieronymus Dürer (influenced by Albertinus' translations) and Johann Beer (influenced by Grimmelshausen).

Now recognized as one of the classics of early modern European literature, the influence of *Simplicissimus* should, however, not be overestimated; its impact on contemporary writers as well as on the modern picaresque in general is limited. It is true that Mann acknowledged *Simplicissimus* as one of his sources and a 'model', when Oskar Seidlin reminded him of it and pointed out analogous structures between Grimmelshausen's didactic strain and Mann's philosophical irony.[49] And we could add the obvious parallels between the Beau Aleman episodes in *Simplicissimus* (II, 3) and Felix Krull's stint in Paris or the two central leitmotifs (the world wants to be deceived and is marked by the paradoxical constancy of inconstancy, both of which allow the pícaro to develop his manipulative skills). It is also true that Grass praised Grimmelshausen for his art of rendering, in the form of pseudo-autobiographical novels, the scarring and scorching conflicts of the seventeenth century, which, for him, constitute the single most decisive caesura in modern German history. In chapter four of book II, Simplicissimus is dressed in borrowed clothes and forced to play the drummer during an inspection led by the Swedish military, which allows him to refine his strategy of combining conformism and independence. Grass adopts the intermeshing of these two elements in the character of Oskar the drummer—the *Mitläufer* and the rebel. And it is also true that, as Ulrich Wicks highlights, '[p]hysically, psychologically, and narratively, Simplicissimus is almost solipsistically trapped, in his cave, in his thought, in his story'[50]—as are Felix Krull in his prison (and retirement home) and Oskar Matzerath in his asylum. Yet, all these obvious episodic, structural, thematic and narrative parallels or even structural homologies cannot be translated into a conclusive concept of literary genealogy; rather, they demonstrate quite powerfully that the early modern narrative model of the picaresque provides a flexible format for reflecting the kind of social crisis that turns victims into victimizers, irrespective of whether that format is, in fact, emulated or rather reinvented.

While the Spanish pícaro can never really escape the logic of the world of petty crime, through which he is initiated into society, narrative traditions in the seventeenth and eighteenth centuries increasingly allowed for middle class success stories and turned the pícaro into a literary reflection of actual rather than pretended social mobility. This roguish type of pícaro, however, arguably also marks the beginning of the relative silence of the picaresque *form*, which lasted for approximately two hundred years. This is not to say that the pícaro was entirely mute during that time. On the contrary, thematic aspects which

---

49   Mann, *Briefe 1948–1955*, 223.
50   Wicks, *Picaresque Narrative*, 323.

can be related to the picaresque continued to capture the imagination of readers and writers alike, but it is difficult to ascribe them to a specific picaresque tradition. They are rather part of a wider fascination with adventure tales that sported a rogue figure as the main character but had lost the autobiographical intricacies of the picaresque *apologia*.

A number of works in German, ranging from Christian Reuter's *Schelmuffskys wahrhafftige curiöse und sehr gefährliche Reisebeschreibung zu Wasser und Lande* (1696–7) to Joseph von Eichendorff's *Aus dem Leben eines Taugenichts* (1826) and Heine's *Aus den Memoiren des Herrn von Schnabelewobski* (1834), have been discussed as possible continuations of the picaresque. Moreover, German Romanticism was enchanted by, if not obsessed with, Spanish culture (as well as by the *Schwank*-like tales of *Münchhausen* and *Eulenspiegel* or similar kinds of folklore). Generally speaking, however, the classic pícaro did not fit particularly well into an epistemic framework that was forged by the tenets of either rationalism and Enlightenment or revolutionary politics and Romantic universalism, an environment that apparently fostered the emergence of a different kind of initiation story that pitches a human individual in new ways against society—the *Bildungsroman*: 'The focus on a harmonious ending which allows the protagonist to strike a balance between his aspirations and the given order shapes the form of the *Bildungsroman*.'[51]

Robert Alter entered this debate, yet his two influential claims are difficult to maintain. He observed that the pícaro is, 'of necessity, a fixed, undeveloping character', and, furthermore, that the *Bildungsroman* emerged predominantly due to the fact that '[f]or a writer and a reading public that hold sacred some strict ideal of social conformity and propriety, the picaresque novel is no longer a real possibility'.[52] While Lazarillo may well not develop in a modern psychological sense, he does, however, clearly present himself as somebody who is capable of learning his lessons and advancing his lot (albeit in the vicious cycle of initial confidence game and subsequent social exclusion). Alter's second claim, purporting a direct analogy between public decorum

---

51 Jacobs, 'Bildungsroman und Pikaroroman', 13; see also Koopmann, 'Pikaro in der Romantik?', 22–6.

52 Alter, *Rogue's Progress*, 31 and 114. See also Miles, 'The Pícaro's Journey', 980, who regards the 'pícaro' (as opposed to the 'confessor') as one of the two basic 'hypostatizations' of the literary hero in general: 'the nondeveloping hero, the unselfconscious adventurer or man of action'. He ignores the fact that the pícaro, from the very beginning, confesses whatever he deems beneficial to confess and integrates his confessions into the *apologia* structure. Miles's characterization of the *Bildungsheld*, by contrast, as a 'confessor' with a 'painful awareness of change and growth' (981) is closer to the pícaro than to any character in the *Bildungsroman*.

and artistic reflection, like Dunn, wrongly assumes that the social imaginary at play in a work of art inadvertently coincides with the social ideology of the day. The relation between ideology, reality and social imaginary is of a more dialectical nature.

While this traditional distinction between the picaresque and the educational novel is untenable, a more important difference should be noted. A hero who aims at reconciling his development with the social order through education, understood in an idealistic sense of self-improvement, replaces a hero who is predominantly concerned with pretending precisely this development in his life-story. In his theory of communicative action, Jürgen Habermas distinguishes two principal perspectives on society, an internal (*Teilnehmerperspektive*) and an external perspective (*Beobachterperspektive*): 'Society is conceived from the perspective of acting subjects as the lifeworld of the social group. In contrast, from the observer's perspective of someone not involved, society can be conceived only as a system of actions.'[53] The student figure of the *Bildungsroman* moves from the position (either imposed or self-inflicted) of an observer of society to the position of integration into such a specific social 'lifeworld'.[54] The pícaro, by contrast, will always remain sitting on the fence, perched on the border between different social spheres, constantly emulating *various* walks of life but never committing to *one* specific one. In other words (and befitting the nineteenth-century context), the pícaro would always readily accept any opportunity to act as a *Bildungsbürger*; he would, however, never be able or willing to become one, to identify with the perspective of an actual 'participant' in society.

If the line between the two novelistic forms is sometimes hard to draw, this is, more often than not, due to the difficulty readers have in telling apart *being* from *seeming*—or, to speak in the jargon of cultural theory, to distinguish the social nexus of delusion (*Verblendungszusammenhang*) from the deceptive trickery enacted by the picaresque hero and narrator. While critics agree that there is a considerably reduced production of the picaresque in German between 1700 and 1900, it is not quite so obvious why the episteme around 1800—the aftermath of rationalism and the Enlightenment, the reverberations of the French Revolution and the emergence of Romantic philosophy zooming in on the human

---

53 Habermas, *Theory of Communicative Action* II, 117; *Theorie kommunikativen Handelns* II, 179.

54 The idea of *Bildung* behind the German version of the educational novel is rooted in the mode of self-reflexivity, which connects individual and society, biography and history: '*Bildung* is not a pregiven form waiting to be fulfilled but rather a processual state that constantly and actively changes through reflexivity. *Bildung* is both the process of producing as well as the result of having been produced.' (Koselleck, 'Structure of *Bildung*', 175–6)

'subject' as its main focus, in combination with the powerful rise of the bourgeois and, eventually, the restorative tendencies after the Congress of Vienna—would necessarily form a conglomerate less conducive to the picaresque imagination. After all, the period qualifies as an era of crisis, if there ever was one, and provides just as many ingredients of a major socio-economic and political change as Golden Age Spain, the Thirty Years' War or Western European modernity. Guzmán's conflict between 'free will' and 'misguided inclinations' was, indeed, as virulent as ever around 1800.

Various explanations have been offered, but none seems to capture this phenomenon comprehensively. Arnold Hirsch, for example, observes an increasing 'Verbürgerlichung' of the pícaro after 1700, as if Lazarillo or Simplicissimus were not, at least partially and temporarily, successful in their bid for a middle class haven (one as a town crier, the other one as a town mayor).[55] Helmut Koopmann argues that it was not only the influence of Goethe's *Wilhelm Meisters Lehrjahre* but also Schiller's poetics that dominated (or restricted) the production of novels in the German-speaking world after 1800. Schiller, who denigrated the novel in general, regarded the *Bildungsroman* as the only *sentimentalische*, and thus self-reflexive (and acceptable), novelistic genre.[56] This may partly explain its predominance and the relative silence of other narrative forms, in particular the picaresque novel. Koopmann, however, does not manage to explain why we should regard Schiller as such a prominent critical voice for novelists around 1800. Surely, Friedrich Schlegel with his innovative meta-reflexive poetics and profound appreciation of Spanish culture would have carried some clout, at least with young novel writers.[57] And even if Koopmann were right—why would Schiller's verdict remain influential for so long? And finally, how do we explain that it is not only in German letters that the picaresque experienced a lack of attention, but across nineteenth-century Europe?

As yet, nobody has offered a comprehensive and satisfying answer to these questions. Franco Moretti may well be on the right track when he describes the nineteenth century as 'the serious century', concerned with the reconfiguration of everything human under the auspices of meritocracy and the art of social compromise: 'the enormous and unconscious collective enterprise of the *Bildungsroman* bears witness to a different solution to modern culture's contradictory nature. Far less ambitious than synthesis, this other solution is *compromise*: which

---

55 Hirsch, *Bürgertum und Barock*, 18; see also Rötzer, 'Schelmenroman und seine Nachfolge', 139–47.
56 Koopmann, 'Pikaro in der Romantik?', 30–1.
57 See, for example, Siguan Boehmer, 'Deutsche Romantik und Spanisches Barock'.

is also, not surprisingly, the novel's most celebrated theme.'[58] This certainly provides insights into the pícaro's return and his uncompromising exposure of the compromises established during 'the serious century' in what follows—the violent century.

Both the *Bildungsroman* of the nineteenth century and the revival of the picaresque in the twentieth century in German literature share a common feature which Peter Brooks finds in the modern novel in general:

> It may in fact be a defining characteristic of the modern novel (as of bourgeois society) that it takes aspiration, getting ahead, seriously, rather than simply as an object of satire (which was the case in much earlier, more aristocratically determined literature), and thus makes ambition the vehicle and emblem of Eros, that which totalizes the world as possession and progress.[59]

As we will see repeatedly in most of the novels discussed here, the modern pícaro incorporates the eroticism of ambition into his narrative, totalizing 'the world as possession and progress', a feature it shares with the *Bildungsroman*. In contrast to Goethe's bourgeois apprentice Wilhelm, however, whose ultimate goal was, as Novalis mockingly remarked, the acquisition of an 'aristocratic birth certificate' (*Adelsdiplom*), Jakob von Gunten and Felix Krull are already in the possession of such a certificate, at least so they claim.[60] Their ambitions may be equally 'erotic' and acquisitive, which roots both of them in the 'Verbürgerlichung' of the Western world, but otherwise they could not be more different. The *Bildungsheld* moves from the position of the observer to the participant and thus 'totalizes the world as possession and progress'. The modern pícaro embraces the world in his histrionic and narrative role-plays and, in the process, performs his individuality as a pseudo-autobiographical observer of his own social mimicry. Thus, he discloses the (social and economic) genealogy of the 'world as possession and progress', which the *Bildungsroman* presents as a natural or authentic way of relating to the world. This genealogical gaze defies Moretti's 'art of compromise' and is rooted in the pícaro's position as 'half-outsider', embodying a form of individuality that focuses on social adaptation, mimicry, self-fashioning and self-narration. In short, individuality in the modern picaresque is a tall tale rather than a *grand récit*. It is always bracketed by its very divisibility. Both participating in and observing society, the modern pícaro tries to have his cake and eat it.

---

58 Moretti, *The* Bildungsroman *in European Culture*, 9.
59 Brooks, *Reading for the Plot*, 39.
60 Novalis, *Das philosophisch-theoretische Werk*, 807.

2. 'Students Who Have Lost the Holy Writ': Franz Kafka's *Der Verschollene*

A Quixotic Mission for Sancho Panza

'Sancho Panza' reads one of the subtitles in Walter Benjamin's essay 'Franz Kafka. On the Tenth Anniversary of His Death'. As we might expect from this master of the enigmatic digression, the essay takes a few turns (lingering on a Hassidic story, fool figures in Kafka's writings and the little hunchback in German folk songs), underpinned with a plethora of well-hidden philosophical references, before our attention is eventually focused on Kafka's brief prose piece 'Die Wahrheit über Sancho Pansa' ('The Truth About Sancho Panza'). In this story, Kafka reads Sancho Panza as the real protagonist of Cervantes' novel, giving him credit for keeping 'his demon', Don Quixote, at a distance by feeding him romances of chivalry and adventure:

> Sancho Pansa, ein freier Mann, folgte gleichmütig, vielleicht aus einem gewissen Verantwortlichkeitsgefühl dem Don Quixote auf seinen Zügen und hatte davon eine große und nützliche Unterhaltung bis an sein Ende.

> A free man, Sancho Panza philosophically followed Don Quixote on his crusades, perhaps out of a sense of responsibility, and had of them a great and edifying entertainment to the end of his days.[1]

Benjamin embeds this inversion of the master–servant relation between Don Quixote and Sancho Panza within a discussion of student and scribe figures in Kafka's work—figures he describes as 'spokesmen for and leaders' of Kafka's 'clan of fools'.[2] For Benjamin, they are 'Schüler,

---

1   Kafka, 'Die Wahrheit über Sancho Pansa'; 'The Truth About Sancho Panza'.
2   Benjamin, 'Franz Kafka', 434/813.

denen die Schrift abhanden kam' ['students who have lost the Holy Writ'] and function as the embodiment of modernity, which he regards as 'an age of maximum alienation of men from one another'.[3] He compares their asceticism and vigilance to a 'cavalry attack' against 'forgetting' and thus relates them to his eschatological philosophy of history:[4] Sancho Panza is envisaged as a new master, who has lost his script and needs the old master, Don Quixote, to act out that very script for him. Reliant on both the protection by tradition (law) and Don Quixote's imagination (chivalrous or not), he does not live in the actual world but rather in a realm of potentiality, dedicated to imagining life in the act of reading or writing, of studying and perpetually converting 'existence into script'.[5] What Benjamin highlights here, among other things, is the position of the writer hiding behind fictional masks and simultaneously maintaining an ambiguous relationship with both the archive of tradition and the smithy of unshaped imagination.

In other words, Sancho Panza, in Benjamin's *Gedankenspiel*, does not interfere with reality, he simulates reality through Don Quixote. Together they form the two voices of the narrator and the narrated persona in any autobiography and give us a sense of the complexities of life-writing in general. Although Benjamin does not reflect on the picaresque tradition as such in his Kafka essay, his inversion of Cervantes' parody of the picaresque in the figure of Sancho Panza sheds light on the relevance of the picaresque imaginary in modern literature. (The fleeting references to figures such as Schweyk and Schlemihl underscore the validity of Benjamin's essay for this context.[6]) The notion of a histrionic self, as it is enacted in Kafka's prose piece and in Benjamin's elaboration on the fool figures (particularly in Kafka's *Der Verschollene*), is germane to the ways in which picaresque fiction dramatizes the role of the individual in modern societies.

The pícaro in the twentieth century embraces open and changeable environments, yet he also always finds himself in Sancho Panza's position of those students who have lost their 'Holy Writ', both bereft of and reliant on a tradition, a law. He may eke out an existence and even manage to climb the social ladder, but he is always acutely aware of the fact that he is on a precarious track towards justice: 'Das Recht, das nicht mehr praktiziert und nur studiert wird, das ist die Pforte der Gerechtigkeit.' ['The law which is studied but no longer practised

---

3   Ibid., 437/815; 436/814.
4   Ibid., 436/814.
5   Ibid., 437/815.
6   Ibid., 436/814.

is the gate to justice.']⁷ It is this position of moral instability and self-inhibition that marks the protagonist Karl Roßmann in Kafka's first major fragmentary novel, *Der Verschollene* (*The Man Who Disappeared*, 1912–14). And, needless to say, Franz Kafka is in the position of Sancho Panza, while the young Karl Roßmann acts as Don Quixote, at least if we follow Benjamin: Sancho Panza is the one who creates *a* world as a *total* world and, in the process, renders problematic the category of reality.

The tandem of Sancho Panza and Don Quixote embodies, for Benjamin, the Kafkaesque fool type who transforms 'existence into script' and, in the process, connects the past with the future, turns law into justice, and even nourishes the 'possibility of redemption'.⁸ This implied promise of redemption Benjamin sees dramatized in a fool figure that moves beyond the impasse of the student figure, namely the actor figure, whose many avatars in *Der Verschollene* presumably were designed to populate the unfinished final section of the novel on the Theater of Oklahoma [*sic*]. Karl Roßmann will neither be accepted as an actor into that theatre, nor can he fully identify with students such as, for example, the law student in the 'Brunelda' chapter, who, perched on a balcony, seems fully immersed in his work, swapping books 'mit Blitzesschnelle' ['with lightning speed'] and keeping his face buried in his notebook (264/177). As the reader is quickly assured after this passage, Karl starts off as a keen student at home in Europe and during his time in New York, where he takes English language and riding lessons; but then he becomes entangled in the rat race of American capitalism, dabbles with petty crime, and is eventually accepted into the universal Theater of Oklahoma—as a technician rather than an actor (311/213). In all likelihood, he dies on the way there (318/218).⁹

Kafka's literary play on Don Quixote and Sancho Panza also exposes another obsession shared with the picaresque: the quest for origin and its impossibility. Is it Sancho Panza who lures 'his demon' into the

---

7   Ibid., 437/815.

8   Ibid., 434/813.

9   Kafka's image of American society was influenced by the travelogue *Amerika: Heute und morgen* (1912) by the Czech-Jewish Socialist Arthur Holitscher, a slide-show and lecture by František Soukup, published under the title *Amerika: řada obrazů amerického života* (1912), and the novella 'Der kleine Ahasverus' by the Danish writer Johan Vilhelm Jensen, printed in *Neue Rundschau* in 1909. Kafka was also influenced by the stories of and about his 'American cousins' documented in Northey, *Kafka's Relatives*, 51–67. For detailed accounts see Born, *Kafkas Bibliothek*, 145, Hellbich, 'German Images of the United States', Jahn, *Der Verschollene*, 144–50, and Wirkner, *Kafka und die Außenwelt*. On Kafka's images of identity and alterity see Heimböckel, 'Amerika im Kopf', 137–9, and Ivanovic, 'Kafkas verstoßener Sohn', 45–47 and 57–65.

adventures through feeding him books, as Kafka seems to suggest? Or is it Don Quixote who follows his own intuition and guides Sancho Panza, the 'unbeholfene Gehilfe' ['clumsy assistant'], as Benjamin seems to suggest?[10] While Kafka's inversion and its refractions in Benjamin can be seen as a playful exchange on the nature of authorship through various narrator personae, it also lends itself to reflections on origin and creation in a broader sense. What is at stake here is the equiprimordial genealogy of autonomy and heteronomy in the modern individual. In this regard, everybody belongs to Benjamin's Kafkaesque clan of fools—whether as an actor or a technician in the Theater of Oklahoma, as a Nietzschean self-fashioner on the high wire, or as one of those students who have lost their 'Holy Writ'. The modern pícaro is the harbinger and patron saint of these actors and students, and not surprisingly, he has a story or two to tell about all of us.

The Birth of the Modern Pícaro out of Guilt

Der Verschollene, originally published by Max Brod under the title *Amerika* in 1927, follows the itinerary of Karl Roßmann, an outsider in American society and an aspirant to its way of life. His itinerary inverts the *Bildungsroman* trajectory of the Wilhelm Meister type. Goethe's hero moves through the realm of the theatre, where he experiments with his potential social and professional skills, into a 'New World', where he realizes some of this potential; Karl, by contrast, ends up in a kind of *theatrum mundi* in the middle of nowhere, after traversing an uncanny 'New World' from East to West. Karl Roßmann, whose surname means horse man or stable-boy, never masters the art of riding (or anything else, for that matter). Ousted from his Central European home, he does not succeed in giving himself a clear direction or goal in his American exile. He resembles Don Quixote sent out by his Sancho Panza (Kafka) and bereft of the protection by tradition (Benjamin's 'law'); he is the student who has lost both his 'Holy Writ' and his wits—an actor in and a student of a Chaplinesque silent movie.

Der Verschollene displays many of the prime structural features of the picaresque, which prompted Guillén to call it 'the first important picaresque novel of our time'.[11] Karl meanders (or rather stumbles) through a clearly defined social milieu to which he obtains access through certain masters and mystagogues (the stoker, the uncle, Pollunder, the cook, Brunelda, Fanny); his experiences follow an episodic Sisyphus structure of admittance and ejection (revolving around the central metaphor of the *theatrum mundi*);[12] and finally, his

---

10 Benjamin, 'Franz Kafka', 438/816.
11 Guillén, *Literature as System*, 262.
12 Cf. Wicks, *Picaresque Narrative*, 55–6.

journey is an incomplete initiation story that leads to a precarious and ambiguous social identity, vacillating between observer and participant, to use Habermas's terms again. While all these aspects clearly root Kafka's novel in a picaresque imaginary, its limited third-person narrative perspective—*personale Erzählsituation* or *erlebte Rede*—does not allow for the ambiguity of voices germane to picaresque irony and satire.

Kafka's characteristic free indirect style, which focuses exclusively on the protagonist's perception, motivation, mental activity, but replaces the 'I' by a third-person narrator, 'this rigidly located (almost imprisoned) narrative voice',[13] anticipates one of the developments I will highlight throughout the modern picaresque, namely its narcissistic voice.[14] Most modern pícaros are invested in the ambiguity of narrative voices as an extension of their social role-play and an elaborate variation on the fundamental duality of the autobiographical voice, but they also have a profound kind of solipsism in common. To speak with Kafka's Quixote story, the narrative perspective in *Der Verschollene* also indicates Karl's incapacity to turn into a fully-fledged Sancho Panza who takes charge of his own narrative voice. Karl *Roßmann* always remains Don Quixote on horseback (Rosinante), but he never learns to ride her, let alone swap his role for (or combine it with) Sancho Panza's (as many picaresque narrators do). He is in the position of the classic pícaro—abandoned by his family, cast into a hostile environment, and reliant on his own resources—yet, contrary to his Spanish predecessors, he fails to turn his homelessness into an asset, into a lever with which he could pry open the exclusion mechanisms of his social environment.

It is unclear whether the free indirect style conveys Karl's internalization of outer social mechanisms and values, or whether it dramatizes the projection of Karl's 'inwardness onto the outer world': Karl's 'unmotivated distrust, which deprives itself of its own foundation, his translation of coincidence into causality, his tendency, furthermore, to treat impressions with purely subjective relevance as if they were objective facts' are presented as direct sensory reactions.[15] Kafka's *personaler* narrator renders the relation between Karl and his environment ambiguous, suspended between the poles of internalization and projection.

Part of this narrative dramaturgy is best understood as a reflection of Franz Brentano's psychophysics and philosophy of perception. This school of thought, influential in the turn-of-the-century Habsburg Empire due to its wide dissemination at the *Gymnasium* and university

---

13 Wicks, *Picaresque Narrative*, 99.
14 See Stanzel, *Theorie des Erzählens*, chapter 6; Kobs, *Kafka: Untersuchungen*, 25–6.
15 Kobs, *Kafka: Untersuchungen*, 47.

level, was based on the assumption that it is only through our inner perceptions that we can obtain knowledge of the external world. What constitutes humans, this implies, is the way in which their brain decodes stimuli. The *personale* narrator enacts this condition through merging narrating and narrated personae in one single perspective ('Einsinnigkeit'), but moves beyond it by highlighting the discrepancies between the two through the detachment of the third person.[16] The reader is thus granted a meta-position of observing the observer (narrator) observe himself, which playfully undermines Brentano's denial of any possible position outside the stimulus–reaction pattern of the human mind.[17]

Kafka strips the picaresque hero of his psychological dimension in an environment that is metaphorically overdetermined by psychology; the absence of psychological points of reference is counterbalanced by a profusion of psychological semiosis. Instead, Kafka systematically translates the dreamlike perception of all his protagonists, suspended between the semantics of psychoanalysis on the one hand and *Bewusstseinsphilosophie* on the other, into spatial terms. Psychoanalysis emphasizes the polyvalent nature of man's interaction with his environment, while contemporary philosophy in the Habsburg Empire stressed the union of consciousness and environment (Ernst Mach), the unity of consciousness (Franz Brentano) and the analogy between physical stimulus and sense reactions (Gustav Fechner).[18] While some of this philosophy is reflected (and challenged) in the third-person narrator, whose view is strictly limited to the protagonist, psychoanalytic models of the self are reflected (and challenged) in the way Kafka projects them onto spatial topography.

Karl's is an autobiography without an 'I'. Its 'I' persona is governed by a limited third-person narrator and does not find a 'self', since it is concealed by the narrating voice which Karl proves unable to infiltrate and appropriate as his own—as his *auto*biography. He is caught up in the same kinds of social rituals and language games again and again and does not take control of his own story. At the same time, the narrated persona is the absolute centre of consciousness: 'Neither Kafka, the author, nor the narrator (that has to be postulated) vouchsafe for the existence of what is narrated. Therefore we are not in the position to say that the narrator is making a statement or wants to convey an idea, since he or she is reduced to the function of merely

---

16 Beißner, *Der Erzähler Kafka*, 28.
17 Cf. Ryan, *Vanishing Subject*, 100–6.
18 Cf. Mach, *Empfindungen*, 58–60.

recording what is happening. It is only the protagonists who see, hear, act and reflect in these poetic creations.'[19]

In this respect, *Der Verschollene* falls short of the picaresque template—a shortcoming that does, however, help us understand some of the most basic structures underlying the modern picaresque: Karl's cousins may be quicker on the uptake when it comes to learning how to trick others, but they operate within the same repetitive and circular framework; Karl may lack the skills to play the picaresque confidence game, but it is precisely this failure that allows us to observe what other first-person picaresque narrators disguise so expertly, namely the fact that their relentless pursuit of happiness and trust in self-reliance is rooted in the projection of a 'self'. At the root of most pícaros of the twentieth century, there is always a Karl Roßmann—a conformist by volition and a dissenter by guilt. *Der Verschollene* calls into question one of the basic assumptions of the picaresque narrative template, namely the idea that humans can dissociate themselves from their past genealogies and reinvent themselves. (Nobody will orchestrate the futility of this attempt better than Oskar with his drum in *Die Blechtrommel*.) The modern picaresque is as much about this vitality of self-invention as it is about the perpetual fear of failure.

Kafka's novel casts into profile a social background of mutual distrust and insecurity, pitching a comic enactment of human physicality against the backdrop of salvation-history and its travesty. This is reflected in Karl's trajectory: it begins with his expulsion and arrival in a land of opportunities (none of which he manages to seize) and leads to his disappearance in a deathscape of mountains and ravines, whose chill 'das Gesicht erschauern machte' ['made their faces shudder'] (318/218). The contradictory implications of Kafka's America—redemption and annihilation—create a mythological framework similar to the one sketched out by one of his favourite authors, Heinrich von Kleist. In 'Über das Marionettentheater', Kleist describes the existential situation of modern man as comparable to being barred from Paradise by the Cherub and doomed to undertake a potentially infinite journey: 'Doch das Paradies ist verriegelt und der Cherub hinter uns; wir müssen die Reise um die Welt machen, und sehen, ob es vielleicht von hinten irgendwo wieder offen ist.' ['Paradise, however, is barred and the Cherub is behind us; we have to go on a journey around the globe and find out whether we may get access from behind.'][20] This constitutes, in a nutshell, one of the mythological undercurrents of the modern picaresque journey.[21]

---

19   Kobs, *Kafka: Untersuchungen*, 32.
20   Kleist, 'Marionettentheater', 429, trans. B.M.
21   Cf. Nicolai, *Kafkas Amerika-Roman*, 235–7.

Karl's journey around the world in search of Paradise is under-pinned by the dual symbolism of birth and death—what James Joyce, with tongue-in-cheek profoundness, calls 'womb, Oomb, allwombing tomb'.[22] The first days of a European in America could be compared to a rebirth, remarks Karl's fully assimilated American Uncle Jakob (46/29), and that is certainly the expectation most readers would have throughout the novel: Karl will eventually grow up, realize his radically changed situation and seize the day. Yet, his itinerary through the New World moves in circles, and every new opportunity for a 'birth' turns into yet another expulsion from Paradise. He embodies, to quote Theodor Adorno, the 'technological and collective rendition of the déjà vu experience' that marks Kafka's entire work.[23] It is this compulsive re-enactment of the biblical myth of the Fall of Man that structures the novel.

This biblical subtext and its ramifications tie together the cultural and the social dimensions of the novel in a literary topography of displacement that is governed by the oppositions of rootedness versus circulation, property versus traffic, autochthony versus allochthony. *Der Verschollene* enacts displacement by mapping failed confidence structures onto spatial alienation. George Steiner writes: 'It was the Fall of Man that added to human speech its ambiguities, its necessary secrecies, its power to dissent speculatively from the opaque coercions of reality. After the Fall, memories and dreams, which are so often messianic recollections of futurity, become the storehouse of experience and of hope.'[24] Karl, prone to Steiner's 'ambiguities' and 'coercions of reality', is so much drawn into the confidence trickery he thinks he needs to perform in order to succeed in a world of swindlers and liars, however, that he never uses the power of ambiguity to dissent from anyone or oppose anything. Yet, it is only dissent and opposition that would, according to Steiner, allow him to live up to the potential and humane quality of guilt—and thereby possibly step out of his entrenchment in perceiving himself as a fallen one. Karl's haphazard forms of dissent are always modelled on patterns of consent, his dissimulation follows patterns of simulation rather than vice versa. He relies more on the opinions of the 'Schwindeldoktoren' ['quack doctors'] (269/181) around him than on his own intuition. It is true that this marks him as Guillén's 'half-outsider', but he is a half-outsider who is not able to capitalize on the potential inherent in that position. The progressive displacement imbricated into *Der Verschollene* is also the result of Karl's inability to exploit the difference between dissent

---

22 Joyce, *Ulysses*, 60.
23 Adorno, 'Aufzeichnungen zu Kafka', 263.
24 Steiner, *No Passion Spent*, 308.

and consent in the world of American confidence trickery, the way it is exploited, for example, by the various avatars of the confidence man in Herman Melville's eponymous satire.[25] Because he fits the picaresque template only partially, Karl foreshadows that fundamental dilemma of the picaresque existence which was to prove of paramount importance for modern writers: the awareness that dissent, as a mere strategy of adaptation, is, at the end of the pícaro's long day, tantamount to consent and conformism.

Another major device of rendering displacement in Kafka's novel, apart from the mythological context, is its complex use of space. Ousted from home, Karl finds himself on an incessant move westward, seemingly embracing the American dream and the myth of the westward migration of civilization: the further away Karl moves from home, the deeper he finds himself entrenched in the power structures of his familial and cultural origins, a place from which allegedly 'nichts Gutes' ['[n]o good'] can come, as Uncle Jakob apodictically states in his epistolary edict of expulsion (97/63). It is this progressive regression that informs the uncanny effect of the novel. The uncanny is that which lost its familiarity but recurs. Karl's experience is as much about 'the other' submerged 'within'—Europe in America—as it is about the 'within' ensconced in 'the other'—America in Europe. The hinge between the two is formed by the notion of guilt and its structural equivalents in Kafka's literary universe—the patterns of compulsive repetition and the monitoring of the protagonist through the eyes of the limited third-person narrator.[26]

Yovel has demonstrated that shame and guilt are the prime motivators and agents in the Spanish picaresque narrative. These affects are rooted in the double ostracism and simultaneous social success of many *conversos* and, according to Yovel, give rise to their attempt to shed social stigma through crafting a fictitious identity as half-outsiders.[27] The classic picaresque is a mode of overcoming shame and feelings of guilt in a narrative form which is particularly suited for articulating and simultaneously concealing experiences of ostracism. The roots of the modern pícaro, as Kafka shows, can be related to a particularly European-Jewish social imaginary poised between cultural assimilation and individualistic dissimulation, yet its implications are even more wide-ranging. The modern picaresque is born out of and battles the spectres of human guilt and thus unearths the psychological, social and religious underpinnings of man's fallen state. Its hero is also born

---

25 Cf. Lindberg, *Confidence Man*, chapter 5 ('Promised Land') and Malkmus, 'Birth of the Modern Pícaro', 605–11.
26 Cf. Hiebel, 'Parabelform und Rechtsthematik', 187.
27 Yovel, 'The Birth of the Pícaro', 1317–20; *The Other Within*, 263–83.

out of the experience of shame and guilt. His is the story of an orphan, stranger, homeless traveller and social outcast, who stages his life and manipulates his narrative in a way that allows him to present himself as a self-fashioning shape-shifter. Yet, the modern pícaro dramatizes a sense of shame and guilt that interrelates psychological, social and economic dependencies. He tends to externalize internalized patterns of guilt and shame. Karl's picaresque peers may be more successful at giving birth to themselves by shedding their guilt complexes, but they will return to them nevertheless.

Occidental Disorientation

Der Verschollene begins with an arrival, and in many regards it is quite a promising one: against the odds, Karl finds himself under the protection of his influential Uncle Jakob, a senator and businessman, who prevents him from getting hopelessly lost 'in den Massenquartieren des New Yorker Ostens' ['in the cramped ghetto in the eastern part of New York'] (152/101). Yet, from the very opening scene, Karl's moves are shadowed by ambiguous, even contradictory metaphors. The entry sequence is set aboard a transatlantic ocean liner before disembarking in the harbour of New York. Kafka's Statue of Liberty famously holds a sword rather than a torch, an allusion to the Cherubim (Genesis 3.24) and an unmistakable sign of the irrevocability of Karl's fallen state:

> Als der siebzehnjährige Karl Roßmann, der von seinen armen Eltern nach Amerika geschickt worden war, weil ihn ein Dienstmädchen verführt und ein Kind von ihm bekommen hatte, in dem schon langsam gewordenen Schiff in den Hafen von Newyork einfuhr, erblickte er die schon längst beobachtete Statue der Freiheitsgöttin wie in einem plötzlich stärker gewordenen Sonnenlicht. Ihr Arm mit dem Schwert ragte wie neuerdings empor und um ihre Gestalt wehten die freien Lüfte. (9)

> As the seventeen-year-old Karl Rossmann, who had been sent to America by his unfortunate parents because a maid had seduced him and had a child by him, sailed slowly into New York harbour, he suddenly saw the Statue of Liberty, which had already been in view for some time, as though in an intenser sunlight. The sword in her hand seemed only just to have been raised aloft, and the unchained winds blew about her form. (3)

As in the biblical account, in which the Cherubim guard the eastern gates of Paradise, the Statue of Liberty—an ambiguous figure representing both the memory of Paradise lost and a reminder of the forbidden—faces ships approaching New York from the east. America signifies hope and despair, redemption and expulsion. This ambiguity is underscored by the convergence of stasis and movement that frames the scene: 'plötzlich' and 'neuerdings' are temporal adverbs at odds with the inertia associated with a statue, however dynamic its metaphorical connotations may be. Karl's lapse converges with his arrival in a realm at once hostile and hospitable, a land of paradisaical promise and inescapable death straddling the border 'between uncontained expansion [...] and containment within a scenario whose primordial conditions manage to reinscribe themselves from scene to scene'.[28]

America here seems to connote both life and death, promise and betrayal, origin and simulacrum. In Kafka's Paradise the promise of self-fulfilment and self-determination is perpetually deferred. The mythical frontier keeps on shifting westward, and so does the mythical location of salvation: New York, Butterford, Ramses, Oklahoma, California.[29] Uncle Jakob even provides his nephew with a train ticket to the West Coast, but Karl never makes use of it. This is not surprising, since the uncle's slip of tongue, locating San Francisco in 'the East', is symptomatic of a systematic confusion of occident and orient, expulsion and redemption, home and exile throughout the novel. Spatial deferral is closely related to the triangulation of the novel's characters: Karl always finds himself between 'lateral figures' (*Flankenfiguren*) such as the stoker/Schubal, Pollunder/Green, Robinson/Delamarche.[30] He lives in a country that is envisaged as a place where humans can neither live nor die.

Scholars such as Giuliano Baioni and Scott Spector have argued that the spatial imagery of Old versus New World functions as a projection of the predicament of Habsburgian and Prague Jewish identity between *Ostjudentum* and *Westjudentum*.[31] Joseph Metz reads *Der Verschollene* as a literary reflection of 'the popular American trope of "Zion in the West"', culminating in what he calls the 'Yiddish' Theater of Oklahoma and pitched against Western mainstream culture and Ashkenazi assimilation.[32] Karl's move west, according to this reading, is a return to his Eastern Jewish communal identity. The fundamental question recurs in numerous variations: where is the frontier between

---

28   Sussman, *Metaphor*, 71.
29   The place-name Butterford is associated with the land of milk and honey and related to the name of Franz Butterbaum (to whom Karl foolishly entrusts his suitcase on the ship). Karl never arrives at Butterford, but he finds himself in possession of his suitcase again when he is expelled by his uncle.
30   Nicolai, *Kafkas Amerika-Roman*, 105.
31   Cf. Baioni, *Kafka: Literatur und Judentum* and Spector, *Prague Territories*.
32   Metz, 'Zion in the West', 669.

the orient and the occident, between home and exile?[33] Karl's situation is imagined as a co-habitation between two impossible poles, the return to Paradise and perpetual exile. Both of these merge in the image of the West, in an American theatre of millenarian projections. Karl has never lost Paradise, nor will he ever be able to regain it. By abandoning his hero in this kind of limbo, Kafka subverts, as John Zilcosky has shown, the turn-of-the-century 'fantasy of *Selbstfindung*'.[34] Caged in his particular narrative mode of consciousness, Karl can resort to neither the omniscience of a detached narrator nor the self-assertive voice of a first-person narrator.

The Ramses scene is of particular interest in our context. The symbolical affinity to the site of servitude and the exodus of the Israelites from Egypt is evident. (Genesis 47.11; Exodus 1.11) The name Ramses evokes the ancient Egyptian kings and is a place in the eastern delta of the Nile, from where the Israelites embarked on their exodus from Egypt. The cities Pithom and Ramses were built to store the fruit of the enslaved Israelites' labour, a detail reflected in the immense storage rooms of the Hotel Occidental (121–4/79–82). These various references to the biblical story, which relate Karl to the figure of Joseph in Egypt, are also connected with the biblical Ya'akov. A visionary figure who wrestles with the angel and is named 'Israel' afterwards (Genesis 32), Ya'akov is turned into a travesty as Uncle Jakob and the liftboy Giacomo. Karl himself is addressed as 'Herr Jakob' (62/39) by Klara at Pollunder's villa and finds himself wrestling with her (74–5/46–8). Later on he ends up in an even less enviable situation in which the not-so-angelic Valkyrie figure Brunelda 'drückte Karl noch fester ans Geländer, er hätte mit ihr raufen müssen, um sich von ihr zu befreien' ['pressed Karl even harder against the railing, he would have had to fight her to get free of her']. (255/171)

Karl gravitates towards Ramses, the place of enslavement, rather than breaking free from the Egyptian bondage. The biblical exodus in Kafka's novel appears in a decisively absurd light: Karl, incapable of escaping his abusers, the sadomasochistic triangle around Brunelda, flees together with them into even deeper bondage: 'Sie waren übereingekommen, die *Auswanderung* noch in der Nacht zu bewerkstelligen, um in den Gassen kein Aufsehen zu erregen, das bei Tag unvermeidlich gewesen wäre' ['They had agreed to arrange the *exodus*

---

33 See also Sokel's distinction between the ambiguous categories of 'Innerlichkeit' (Europe, stoker, procrastination, authenticity) and 'Außenwelt' (America, uncle, decision-making, alienation), *Tragik und Ironie*, 311–19. Sokel also points out that the opposite spatial concepts of order (America) and labyrinth (Europe) are subject to a gradual convergence throughout the novel (321–5).

34 Zilcosky, *Kafka's Travels*, 42.

for night-time, to attract none of the attention in the street which would have been inevitable by day'] (289/197, emphasis added). This converging of opposite dynamics (exodus versus bondage; liberty versus dependence) underlines the structural element of circularity dominating the entire novel. Once Karl approaches a new border, the previous one is internalized rather than confronted—borders between Europe and America, between rural and urban space, between East and West. The characters around him invite 'Karl into their world only to expel him from it into another set of foreign circumstances'.[35] The accumulation of similar experiences of expulsion and stigmatization drive Karl further away from a sense of origin.

Karl always finds himself restricted and reduced to the transitional dynamic of traffic, since he can neither return home nor make exile a permanent new home for himself; not even the realm of circulation, *locus classicus* of the picaresque, however, provides a sense of identity. He is not successful in either of the two main areas of circulation grafted on top of the spatial westward dynamic: economic exchange and sexuality. The pícaro traditionally embraces erotic, economic and geographic mobility; Karl, however, is not capable of propelling this dual dynamic in a way that would serve him. He is a *Roßmann*, horse and man—the emblematic centaur satyr, yet lacking the satirist's wits.

Father Trouble: Triangulating the Picaresque Initiation

Der Verschollene is an extreme departure from the *Bildungsroman* and its ultimate parody—a 'Verirrungsroman'.[36] Whereas most picaresque novels poke fun at the *Bildungsroman* tradition in one way or another, they at least adhere to some sense of experiential development, albeit in a non-idealistic and more functional manner. Lazarillo gleans all kinds of tricks from his masters as he traverses society and comes to know its ropes, finding his way around beggars, clerics and merchants; Felix Krull, although he claims otherwise, largely relies on the instruction by various masters to find his position in the world of confidence trickery. This rudimentary sense of development within the episodic structure of the picaresque has often been exploited as a travesty of the concept of *Bildung*. *Der Verschollene*, however, takes the episodic structure to extremes and inverts the concept of individual development through social integration. The novel is not only circular, like many picaresque novels, but also excessively repetitive. The narrative always returns to the very moment of transgression and compulsively translates that moment into an endless semiosis of spatial metaphors. On a figural level, we can observe a similar dynamic with regard to another

---

35 Anderson, *Kafka's Clothes*, 106.
36 Zilcosky, *Kafka's Travels*, 54.

characteristically picaresque feature, the pícaro's rite of passage into a corrupted society.

Karl is expelled from home by his parents, because he was seduced by a maid and fathered a child with her. (Premature fatherhood connects Karl with Wilhelm in Goethe's landmark novel.) During the passage, he seeks protection in the interior of the ship, where the stoker Schubal seems to offer both paternal protection and homoerotic appeal. The conflicting role models and expectations combined in the stoker—lover and father—are indicative of Karl's inner frontiers, which he is unable to transgress without feeling pangs of guilt. Scholarship has largely ignored the obvious fact that Karl is the father of a child and was possibly sent to America to avoid paying alimony.[37] This is even more surprising since the life story of the father of Therese, the head cook's servant, reads like a variation on Karl's story:

> [Therese] war ein uneheliches Kind, ihr Vater war Baupolier und hatte die Mutter und das Kind aus Pommern sich nachkommen lassen, aber als hätte er damit seine Pflicht erfüllt oder als hätte er andere Menschen erwartet als die abgearbeitete Frau und das schwache Kind, die er an der Landungsstelle in Empfang nahm, war er bald nach ihrer Ankunft ohne viel Erklärung nach Kanada ausgewandert, [...]. (152)

> [Therese] was an illegitimate child, her father was a builder's foreman, and had sent for the child and her mother from Pomerania, but then as though that represented the limit of his obligation, or he had expected other people than the exhausted woman and sickly child he greeted at the harbour, he had emigrated to Canada shortly after their arrival, [...]. (101)

The three terms 'illegitimate child', 'builder's foreman' and 'Pomerania' establish a link between the life stories of Karl and Therese's father: both have illegitimate children, are associated with work in construction (Karl wants to become an engineer and ends up as a technician), and come from the eastern fringe of the German-speaking world around 1900 (Pomerania and Bohemia respectively). The trial scene complicates the picture by introducing an inverted oedipal reference. The mother figure of the head cook in the hotel is indirectly associated with Johanna Brummer, the maid who abused her position by raping Karl. This link is corroborated by the overtones of a mother–daughter

---

37   A notable exception is Kittler, 'Dead Beat Father'.

relationship between the chief cook and Therese, both of whom seem to embody Karl's split affinity to certain women as mothers and lovers.[38]

This figural centrepiece of the novel re-enacts the power triangulation in Karl's family and dramatizes Karl's existence as a never-ending rite of passage. Originally dominated by a paternal principle, these triangular power relations are then destroyed by the same paternal principle (or an agent who internalized that principle). The actual photograph which Karl took with him on his journey reminds him of another one that shows him together with his parents: '[…] Vater und Mutter sahen ihn dort scharf an, während er nach dem Auftrag des Photographen den Apparat hatte anschauen müssen'. ['[…] his father and mother were both glaring at him, while he had been instructed by the photographer to look into the camera'.] (106/69) His memory of the triangular relationship in the past, marked by austere parental authority, shifts to his contemplation of a photograph of him and his mother, taken in the absence of his father.

Karl's position is determined by two elements. First, the authority of the father seems to have waned. Once outside his and the uncle's rule, Karl does not seem to be able to reconnect with his past or engage in a dialogue with his parents:

Desto genauer sah er die vor ihm liegende [Photographie] an und suchte von verschiedenen Seiten den Blick des Vaters aufzu-fangen. Aber der Vater wollte […] nicht lebendiger werden, sein waagrechter starker Schnurrbart sah der Wirklichkeit auch gar nicht ähnlich, […]. (106)

The more minutely he now examined the one [photograph] in front of him and tried to catch his father's gaze from various angles. But try as he might, […] his father refused to become any more alive, his heavy horizontal moustache didn't look anything like the real thing, […]. (69)

Second, his mother provokes conflicting feelings in Karl. The photograph elicits an almost unbearable sense of her presence in him that forces him to avert his gaze. When he returns to the image, 'fiel ihm die Hand der Mutter auf, die ganz vorne an der Lehne des Fauteuils herabhing, zum Küssen nahe'. ['he was struck by his mother's hand, dangling from an armrest in the very foreground of the picture, close enough to kiss'.] (106/69) This emotional response is followed by the question whether he should contact his parents again. Then he accuses himself of having found his real home in the gutter

---

38 Cf. Sokel, 'Zwischen Drohung und Errettung', 256–7.

and in self-imposed exile. Karl's combination of emotional excitability, feelings of love and eroticism with a self-denigrating sense of guilt also dominates the trial scene in the hotel. It shows him pushing through a potentially endless series of initiations into the picaresque world of American capitalism, whose guilt structure mirrors his psycho-sexual economy of desire.

The hotel trial episode duplicates the pattern of a malevolent, authoritarian and alienated father figure (head waiter) and a benevolent, supportive, sympathetic mother figure (head cook). The final tableau of the scene returns to the configuration of the first photograph that shows his parents joining forces in an erotic gesture:

Die Oberköchin schloss die Augen, sie wollte damit Karl beruhigen. Während er sich zum Abschied verbeugte, sah er flüchtig, wie der Oberkellner die Hand der Oberköchin wie im Geheimen umfasste und mit ihr spielte. (196)[39]

The Head Cook closed her eyes, she did it to soothe Karl. As he bowed in farewell, he just caught a glimpse of the Head Waiter's hand discreetly taking the Head Cook's hand and playing with it. (130)

As much as he is excluded from the gaze of his father, Karl is also removed from his mother, whose posture suggests a certain intimacy, especially in the image of her relaxed, dangling hand. At the same time she seems to be requesting submission. The whole scene re-enacts Karl's loss of his father and stages his confrontation with the unconscious insight that he has lost his mother, too.

Eroticism is dramatized as part of a power game. In this context Karl appears as a victim, while most modern pícaros also show either abusive sexual tendencies or a playful engagement with sexuality. While most picaresque heroes use sexuality to forge, or rather mimic, an identity, Karl's sexual experiences (with Therese and Brunelda), however limited, do not initiate him into life, they hurl him back into a vicious cycle of guilt. If Karl's picaresque cousins do present themselves as successful apprentices of the eroticism of power, they will, however, never quite manage to patch up Karl's predicament of innocent guilt.

---

39 The name of the head cook, Grete Mitzelbach, is a tongue-in-cheek allusion to the pornographic novel *Josephine Muzenbacher oder die Geschichte einer wienerischen Dirne von ihr selbst erzählt* (1906) by Felix Salten, cf. Politzer, *Kafka*, 212. Similarly, Fanny in the Oklahoma fragment can be related to John Cleland's *Memoirs of a Woman of Pleasure* (called 'Fanny Hill' after the protagonist) (1748–9).

The oedipal aspect hinted at in the photograph is reinforced by the separation between the head cook and Therese. Therese appears at the trial before the head cook. The reader never learns the reasons for her nocturnal absence, and there are no further explanations why the erotic associations of her appearance seem to correspond with Karl's state of mind, which is described as 'ermattet':

> Karl war so ermattet, dass er kaum grüßte, als er zu seinem Staunen [...] Therese leichenblass, unordentlich angezogen, mit lose aufgesteckten Haaren hereinschlüpfen sah. Im Augenblick war sie bei ihm und flüsterte: 'Weiß es schon die Oberköchin?' (183)

> Karl was so exhausted that he could barely manage a greeting, when, to his amazement, he saw a ghostly pale Therese slip into the room [...], untidily dressed and with loose, piled-up hair. In an instant she was at his side, whispering: 'Does the Head Cook know?' (121–2)

Therese's allusive question and the tiny word 'es', lost in translation, suggest an erotic encounter between them. The head cook, who has just left to make sure that Karl's money is in safe hands and that he will have a place to go to and a perspective for the future, corroborates that impression by insinuating: 'Pension Brenner—Du warst doch schon mehrmals mit Therese dort.' ['Pension Brenner—you've been there several times with Therese.'] (194/129) Obviously, Therese does not perceive the whole scene as a farewell, she rather regards herself as a companion for Karl's future. She seems to be a secret part of him, be it as mother, lover or daughter, apparently fulfilling the promise of the photograph, yet exacerbating his feeling of guilt. It is this moment of perpetually reinstated guilt and shame around which the novel revolves. Karl may be a servant of many masters, he may have an elective affinity to the Benjaminian student on the balcony (263/177), yet he does not take the picaresque opportunity to position himself outside the social power play into which he invests so much.

After Karl's first few days in America, the uncle remarks about this power play:

> Die ersten Tage eines Europäers in Amerika seien ja einer Geburt vergleichbar und wenn man sich hier auch, damit nur Karl keine unnötige Angst habe, rascher eingewöhne als wenn man vom Jenseits in die menschliche Welt eintrete, so müsse man sich doch vor Augen halten, daß das erste *Urteil* immer auf schwachen Füßen stehe und daß man sich dadurch nicht vielleicht alle

künftigen *Urteile*, mit deren Hilfe man ja hier sein Leben weiter-
führen wolle, in Unordnung bringen lassen dürfe. (46, emphases
added)

The first days of a European in America were like a new birth,
and while Karl shouldn't be afraid, one did get used to things
here faster than when entering the human world from beyond,
he should bear in mind that his own initial *impression* did stand
on rather shaky feet, and he shouldn't allow them any undue
influence over subsequent *judgements*, with the help of which,
after all, he meant to live his life. (29, emphases added)

This passage introduces the notion of trust in a new context and
relates it implicitly to the concept of 'Urteil', which can be translated
as sensual impression, judgement or verdict, providing the basic
notions of prejudice and stereotype underpinning the novel.[40] Uncle
Jakob's advice is a variation on the blind master's lesson in *Lazarillo de
Tormes*, who smashes Lazarillo's head against the bull sculpture, a rude
awakening designed to hammer home a double message: don't get
fooled, and do fool the world, because it wants to be fooled. Yet, Karl's
'Urteil' stands 'on shaky feet' and continuously calls him back into the
regressive-repetitive logic in which the spatio-temporal framework of
the entire narrative is rooted. His 'judgements' about his American
environment are always immediately absorbed by the 'verdicts' passed
by the paternal authorities, or, as Deleuze and Guattari phrase it: 'The
memory blocks desire, makes mere carbon copies of it, fixes it with
strata, cuts it off from all its connections.'[41] Kafka's specific brand
of free indirect style is crucial in rendering this process of memory
repetition, these 'carbon copies'. It never allows Karl to transcend his
own limited perspective and make these 'connections' or engage with
his environment in an active way, which was to be so typical of subsequent picaresque novels featuring a first-person narrator.

It is only towards the end, in the final fragments of the novel, that
Karl's American socialization appears in a different light. Here, Kafka
creates a projection screen for the fantasy of a fatherless world—a
utopian 'impossible non-identity' that constructs family and culture
through the son rather than the father.[42] This aspect of the Oklahama
fragment anticipates the subtext of narcissism and the motif of parricide,

---

40 The motif of 'Urteil' connects this passage to the first chapter ('Der Heizer'),
    which Kafka intended to publish with the stories 'Das Urteil' and 'Die
    Verwandlung' under the title *Söhne*, see Wolff, *Briefwechsel*, 29.
41 Deleuze and Guattari, *Kafka. Toward a Minor Literature*, 4.
42 Keller, 'Verkehrte Akkulturation', 230.

both of which were to become so vital in much of modern picaresque fiction. The Theater of Oklahama is designed as a contrast to the *Bildungsroman* institution of the bourgeois theatre that prepares for life in society through play and experiment; it proves, however, to be the refusal and perpetual deferral of any initiation—a theatre that is only referred to in theatrical gestures. (Maybe the student Joseph Mendel, singled out in Benjamin's reading of Kafka's fool figures, is witnessing the incident in the novel that comes closest to a solution of Karl's father trouble: the masses congregating in the streets are canvassing and lobbying for the election, rather than appointment, of a judge, the quintessential Kafkaesque father figure.)

Oklahama

Uncle Jakob rules over a world of perpetual circulation, a kind of 'commissioning and forwarding business', a

> Zwischenhandel, der aber die Waren nicht etwa von den Producenten zu den Konsumenten oder vielleicht zu den Händlern vermittelte, sondern welcher die Vermittlung aller Waren und Urprodukte für die großen Fabrikskartelle und zwischen ihnen besorgte. (53–4)

> The actual business consisted of intermediated trade, but not delivering goods from producers to consumers or even to retailers, but the supplying of goods and raw materials to the great factory cartels, and from one cartel to another. (34)

This business is all about administering the kind of capitalism Kafka's sources about the United States projected as typically 'American' and tended to criticize severely. It is 'an economy which is marked by the fact that it incorporates circulation into the process of production'[43]— a world in which there is no room for Benjamin's fools, students and actors. This bureaucratic apparatus may also, as Metz argues, be associated with the industrial world into which many Ashkenazi Jews assimilated in Western Europe and the United States. The Theater of Oklahama, by contrast, could be seen as representing Eastern Jewish life, the world of the Hassidim, Yiddish theatre, language and culture, which had a particularly strong appeal for Kafka during the production of *Der Verschollene*, especially through his friendship with the Yiddish actor Yitzhak Löwy. Although Karl fails miserably in his attempt to integrate into mainstream American culture, Metz points out, 'his alternative integration into the (Yiddish) theater of the (pseudo-)west

---

43   Vogl, *Ort der Gewalt*, 113.

and his return to the oldest East through the newest, is far from tragic: by becoming Negro/Löwy (both Yitzhak and Mother), Karl/Kafka finally realizes his "authentic" Jewish self, his idealized locus of self-identification.'[44] Karl is in the assimilated realm outside the (Jewish) Law, he has lost his 'holy Writ' and he does not have the strength of the pícaros or Benjaminian fools of the novel, the students and actors (Robinson, Delamarche, Renell) who translate their existences into scripts and create identities by performing them. Yet, through luck or a picaresque hoax he participates in the universal script of the Theater of Oklahama, not knowing whether it is a holy Writ (the 'o' is replaced by the 'a', conflating alpha and omega, beginning and end of the world as a stage) or merely a film script. After all, Karl may never be able to reach the Theater; all we learn about it is restricted to the enormous apparatus on the race track designed to recruit 'everybody' for the Theater.

Metz discloses an important Zionist subtext in *Der Verschollene*, but it is worth reminding ourselves that this is only one subtext among others. Kafka may encourage the reader to conceive of the Oklahama masses as Eastern Jewish *luftmentshen* and of Karl's journey as a literary reflection of the Jewish exile (*galut*). Yet, the immediate context of the 'Zwischenhandel' passage cited above is embedded in a metaphorical nexus of mechanical devices (administration, desk, nativity) and works against Metz's neat classifications. With the most overtly self-reflexive metaphor of the novel—the American writing desk with its numerous compartments and intricate mechanisms—Kafka continues a sequence of images designed to anticipate the artifice of the Theater of Oklahama: 'außerdem war an der Seite ein Regulator und man konnte durch Drehen an der Kurbel die verschiedensten Umstellungen und Neueinrichtungen der Fächer nach Belieben und Bedarf erreichen' ['but even better than that, it had an adjuster at the side, so that by turning a handle one could rearrange and adjust the compartments in whatever way one wanted or needed'] (47/29).

This metaphor of writing as a process of assemblage and reshuffling triggers memories of childhood in Karl, images of nativity scenes (with life-size figures, still popular in the Czech lands): by turning a crank, an old man makes the three Magi follow the star haltingly towards the 'befangenen Leben im Stall' ['shy life in the holy stable'] (48/30). In the two related images of the desk and the mechanical nativity scene as well as the preceding description of the uncle's inflated business, Kafka conflates three realms in a manner that casts doubt on attempts such as Metz's to enlist Kafka for specific agendas: modern capitalism,

---

44 Metz, 'Zion in the West', 669–70 (referring to the fact that Kafka's mother's maiden name was Löwy).

messianic expectation and the act of writing. The concepts of self-redemption (uncle, American capitalism), religious revelation and art as surrogate religion are subjected to a scathing critique in this mock imagery—a critique that also has implications for an interpretation of the Theater of Oklahama. This conflation of puppet player with uncle and omnipotent God shows Karl's new home and exile as always already marked by the old mechanisms of ideological and material power. His life will always be a 'befangene[s] Leben' in the holy stable, a life in exile, and his enthusiastic engaging with stories of redemption (such as the nativity scenes) will eventually be silenced by the mother, who 'ihm den Mund zuhielt' ['put her hand over his mouth'] (48/30).

The Theater maintains a complex relation to these three interconnected realms. It does not have creators or producers, nor does it seem to attract spectators, it focuses solely on the act of acting without a script. It functions as a symbol which combines the figural opposition of Karl and his uncle in the conflation of their different trajectories. Ultimately, the metaphorical structure of the novel seems to suggest, the difference between ubiquitous connectedness and isolation is not substantial in a world of 'Zwischenhandel', which is also a satirical reference to the merchant father in *Wilhelm Meisters Lehrjahre*. Goethe's protagonist frees himself from the expectations of his father and experiments with his identity in the realm of theatre. Kafka picks up on this and subverts any implied teleological concept: Karl goes through the 'Zwischenhandel', fails and ends up in the Theater as a technician rather than an actor. Yet, in its utopian world that could just mean that any technician is an actor and vice versa. After all, the Theater extends an unconditional acceptance to all applicants.[45]

Kafka took the idea of Oklahoma as the destination for his hero from the travelogue by Arthur Holitscher. Oklahoma, the first state in the nineteenth century to force native Americans into reservations (on the infamous 'Trail of Tears') and the location of a short-lived emancipation for Afro-Americans (e.g. the 'Negro Wall Street' in Tulla) before a mass lynching in 1921, is featured there by a photograph with the sarcastic title 'Idyll aus Oklahama', which shows a lynched Afro-American and

---

45 The Theater could also be a reference to one of Nietzsche's discussions of histri-onics, namely a passage in *Die fröhliche Wissenschaft*, where Nietzsche ruminates about the trust in role-play as a social merit. He singles out the 'American faith' (*Amerikaner-Glaube*), a kind of self-confidence that is 'ungefähr jeder Rolle gewachsen' ['is up to playing any role']—a position in which 'jeder mit sich versucht, improvisiert, neu versucht, mit Lust versucht, wo alle Natur aufhört und Kunst wird […].'—'everyone experiments with himself, improvises, experiments again, enjoys experimenting, where all nature ends and becomes art […].' *Die fröhliche Wissenschaft*, 596; *Gay Science*, 216 (§ 356).

a white mob.[46] Oklahama is in all likelihood a deliberate reproduction of Holitscher's typographical error in the caption of his photograph about the lynching. Whether intended or not, replacing the 'o' with an 'a' (alpha, aleph) fits into Kafka's topography of origin and its codification as law and authority. John Zilcosky stresses in this context that Kafka, by using Oklahoma as an ambiguous spatial reference, attempts 'to move beyond the binary of utopia/dystopia. Instead, he constructs a self that grows increasingly exotic to itself—to the point of its own final silencing.'[47]

As Carolin Duttlinger has shown, this iconographic reference to Holitscher is linked to the depiction of an image featuring a lavishly decorated theatre box that evokes Abraham Lincoln's assassination by John Wilkes Booth in the Ford's Theater in Washington in 1865:[48]

Dieses Bild stellte die Loge des Präsidenten der Vereinigten Staaten dar. Beim ersten Anblick konnte man denken, es sei nicht eine Loge, sondern die Bühne, so weit geschwungen ragte die Brüstung in den freien Raum. […] Man konnte sich in dieser Loge kaum einen Menschen vorstellen, so selbstherrlich sah alles aus. (314)

This picture showed the box of the President of the United States. At first sight, one might think it wasn't a box at all, but the stage, so far did the curved balustrades jut out into empty space. […] It was hardly possible to imagine people in this box, so sumptuously self-sufficient did it look. (215)

This image, with its oblique historical index, is presented as one of a series of pictures of the Theater (313/215) and encourages us to read the Theater as a miniature version of America as 'selbstherrlich', a space where patriarchal power still reigns, even in the absence of a father *imago*, even after the mythical parricide. The killing of the father figure takes place on a loge that looks like the stage of a theatre. Again, due to the narrative mode, the reader is uncertain whether Karl maps his fears and desires onto an American motif or whether an American anxiety imprints itself on Karl's imagination. After all, Karl does not realize that the photograph is a reference to Lincoln's assassination.

The photographic subtext with its theme of violent death ties together the main strands of the novel. Both the autonomy of the self and the patriarchal authority of the political leader are metaphorically

46 Cf. Holitscher, *Amerika*, 278.
47 Zilcosky, *Kafka's Travels*, 68.
48 Duttlinger, 'Photography', 442–4.

annihilated. The desired overcoming of the oedipal configuration of the Old World, epitomized by Karl gazing at the photograph of his parents, leads to a spectacle without obvious authority and anarchy (New World). Whatever untenable European clichés about America may be at stake in this scene and elsewhere in the book, everything seems to point towards the fact that the American dream is satirically subverted as a fake Paradise with violent undercurrents.

Bernhard Greiner writes: 'Thus, all the signs nourished and produced by the recruitment apparatus of the Theater do not refer to anything. The actions of the recruitment apparatus are nothing else but a mere "as if"; they are simply theatre—a theatre that can only authenticate its connection with the Theater of Oklahoma by consisting of the same "stuff"—theatricality [...].'[49] This dual 'theatricality' also supports the picaresque theme of circularity; Karl moves from master to master, all figures of authority, without being able to learn any lessons. He is neither able to present a fake linearity of his walk of life as a success story nor does he perceive his detachment as independence.

The power of Kafka's novel 'to deterritorialize and disfigure America's identifying signs, to un-name and silence the name', reflects on the impossibility of its inhabitants to progress. Kafka's pícaro is a frontier dweller between absence and presence, incapable of either drawing on the identity models of his past or following 'America's identifying signs'.[50] His self-silencing culminates when he calls himself 'Negro', the underprivileged outcast. At the same time, his final self-defacement is more complex than it seems. Horst Seferens points out that the Oklahama fragment forms a double contrast to the rest of the novel: its community is all-inclusive rather than an endless rat race. Karl, however, begins acting in the calculating manner characteristic of that very rat race, or, put differently, he is on his way to becoming a pícaro. As soon as he is able to shed the straightjacket of society, Karl acts according to the internalized principles of that very society.[51] Seferens relates this mechanism to the theory that human existence under capitalism is tantamount to a perpetual initiation—or, to use Adorno and Horkheimer: 'Life in the late capitalist era is a constant initiation rite. Everyone must show that he wholly identifies himself with the power which is belabouring him.'[52] Karl tends to interpret everything compulsively as a trial exacting self-defence on his part. If the Theater stands for redemption, Karl is not ready for it; if it is an

---

49 Greiner, 'Im Umkreis von Ramses', 654.
50 Anderson, *Kafka's Clothes*, 105.
51 Seferens, 'Das "Wunder der Integration"', 582.
52 Adorno and Horkheimer, *Dialectic of Enlightenment*, 153.

extension of corporate America, Karl will either perish or become one of its angels, blowing the 'Lärmtrompeten des Nichts' ['alarm trumpets of the void'].[53]

Space (the race track) is often connected with traffic (the race) in the topography of Kafka's America: Whether in the form of corridors, lifts or streets, traffic defines spatial entities in Karl's *theatrum mundi*:

> Aus den Straßen, wo das Publikum in großer unverhüllter Furcht vor Verspätung im fliegenden Schritt und in Fahrzeugen, die zu möglichster Eile gebracht waren, zu den *Theatern* drängte, kamen sie durch *Übergangsbezirke* in die Vorstädte, wo ihr Automobil durch Polizeileute zu Pferd immer wieder in Seitenstraßen gewiesen wurde, da die großen Straßen von den demonstrierenden Metallarbeitern, die im Streik standen, besetzt waren, und nur der notwendigste Wagenverkehr an den *Kreuzungsstellen* gestattet werden konnte. (60, emphases added)

> From the streets where people, showing an open fear of arriving late, hurried their steps and drew up outside theatres in speeding vehicles, they passed some *transitional areas* and then reached the suburbs, where their car kept being diverted off on to side-streets by mounted policemen, as the main thoroughfares were all occupied by striking metalworkers, and only the most essential traffic could be allowed to pass at the *crossroads*. (38, emphases added)

New York's theatres are linked to the 'transition districts' (between centre and suburbs) and 'intersections', thus linking the metaphorical race track (theatre, Oklahama) with the actual race (which is lacking in the Oklahama fragment). We are on the way to Mr Pollunder's villa outside New York—the stage on which the lips of Mr Pollunder morph, in a dreamlike fashion, into his daughter Klara's voluptuous red lips (64/40), on which Mr Green emerges as an authoritarian father figure,[54] on which Karl wrestles with Klara (72–5/46–8) and will eventually be expelled from the family (96–7/62–3). The experience of exchange and role change is intertwined with the negative experience of loss and expulsion. Karl then 'marches' to Ramses and ends up in Clayton, where he is hired by the Theater and boards the train to Oklahama. *Clay*ton is directly related to Ramses and Jewish servantship through the biblical reference to the hard labour 'in brick and mortar' (Exodus

---

53 Kafka, *Tagebücher 1914–1923*, 149; *Diaries*, 175.
54 Mr Green's declamation of the uncle's letter is an inversion of Abbé's *Lehrbrief*, the central rite of passage in *Wilhelm Meister's Lehrjahre*.

1.13–14). Karl arrives in Clayton as Roßmann and leaves as 'Negro'; symbolically he turns from a defeated Egypt ('*Roß* und *Mann* hat er ins Meer gestürzt' is Luther's translation of Exodus 15.1, describing the Pharaoh's retreat) to a serf, possibly reversing the exodus story of the Sinai. Whatever the implications of the names, Karl gets lost during his exodus—he is the lost Roß-Mann who does not reach the Sinai, the locus of the Law.[55]

Conclusion

In the final fragment of *Der Verschollene*, the rail journey, invariably signifying death for 'Roß und Mann', emerges in a new light: Karl and Giacomo, his alter ego, travel through a landscape dominated by high mountains:

> Bläulichschwarze Steinmassen giengen in spitzen Keilen bis an den Zug heran, man beugte sich aus dem Fenster und suchte vergebens ihre Gipfel, dunkle schmale zerrissene Täler öffneten sich […]. (318)

> Blue-black formations of rock approached the train in sharp wedges, they leaned out of the window and tried in vain to see the peaks, narrow dark cloven valleys opened […]. (217)

The ambiguity between demise and sublime transcendence, between the opaque Red Sea reference (implying the defeat of the Pharaoh's troops) and the Mosaic hope for the divine Law (a travesty of which we find in the promise of Oklahama), ought to be seen in conjunction with Karl's picaresque vacillation between self-assertion and disenfranchisement.[56]

Kafka explores a dead-end of picaresque fiction. At the core of proactive modern pícaros such as Thomas Mann's Felix Krull and Saul Bellow's Augie March there is always the repetitiveness and self-induced passivity of the desperate Karl Roßmann, who constantly observes himself, yet cannot sustain and utilize the detached position he gains in the process. However cleverly he navigates through the

---

55 Cf. Greiner, 'Im Umkreis von Ramses', 656.

56 This ambiguity is also highlighted by the names: the brothers Franz (Kafka) and Karl (Roßmann) Mohr (cf. 'Negro') in Friedrich Schiller's *Die Räuber* epitomize the duality of victimhood and self-assertion, see Ivanovic, 'Kafkas verstoßener Sohn', 52–3. See also the discrepancy between Karl's diary entry in which he states that 'Roßmann und K. [from *Der Proceß*], der Schuldlose und der Schuldige' were both 'unterschiedslos strafweise umgebracht' (*Tagebücher 1914–1923*, 101) and Brod's testimony that Kafka designed Roßmann's final journey to lead to 'freedom' and a reunion with his family ('Nachwort').

challenges of the modern world, the pícaro knows that he is prone to Karl's sense of dislocation. He is an observer of himself, and he observes his fellow human beings observe him as an excluded person, thus anticipating other people's judgement within the logic of his economy of guilt. He always runs the risk of replicating the effects of exclusion, of turning from an impresario into a clown—a risk epitomized by Karl, who has neither quite learned his lessons from the 'Schwindeldoktoren' nor mastered the picaresque rites of passage. Gerhard Kurz notes that 'Karl [...] incessantly reflects on the way he acts and his situation, in order to dominate it and those people involved in it. He never calls himself into doubt.'[57] While he may well do the former, he certainly does not refrain from the latter: he continuously calls himself into doubt. (He does so in ways that are markedly different from other pícaros, for whom self-doubt is not an impediment but a productive stratagem to gain the sympathy of the reader.) The following instance, for example, shows how the typical convergence of third-person narrator and first-person perspective dramatizes doubt: 'Delamarche war einverstanden und nur Karl glaubte zu der Bemerkung verpflichtet zu sein, dass er genug Geld habe um das Nachtlager für alle auch in einem Hotel zu bezahlen.' ['Delamarche agreed with him, and only Karl felt obliged to reveal that he had enough money to pay for them all to stay in the hotel.'] (119/78) The 'nur' is revealing: it is 'only' Karl, in a society of confidence tricksters, who has not managed to turn the confidence game into a game, who still manages his stigma in accordance with inner compulsions rather than in anticipation of external pressures. He is the only one who 'calls himself into doubt' in an existential or psychological sense; the other characters seem completely free of this compulsion (e.g. Uncle Jakob) or they play with it in a self-distancing fashion (e.g. Delamarche). In this sense, Karl remains the uninitiated pícaro in a perpetual rite of passage, for he 'does not understand life and is right about it', as Kurt Tucholsky once remarked.[58]

Kafka's cipher of America anticipates the ambiguity of the modern picaresque condition—the imbrication of individuality in a social and economic nexus from which it was wrested to begin with. While many modern picaresque heroes revel exuberantly in the exhilaration of ludic self-fashioning, there is a tendency in the German tradition that continues to return to Karl Roßmann. Kafka's creation reminds us that at the root of this exhilaration and freedom of self-expression and self-invention, there is an ineradicable residuum of guilt and debt. Karl is the unconscious of Felix Krull and his peers. Kafka's Sancho Panza

---

57   Kurz, *Traum-Schrecken*, 153.
58   Tucholsky, 'Auf dem Nachttisch', 45.

does not seem to know the direction any more into which he once sent his 'Roß und Reiter'—Don Quixote on his Rosinante, or Karl Roßmann on his transatlantic steamer.

3. Students Who Have Lost Their Teachers: Robert Walser's *Jakob von Gunten*

Yet Another Quixotic Mission

When *Jakob von Gunten. Ein Tagebuch*, one of Kafka's favourite novels, was published in 1909, the critic Josef Hofmiller of the *Süddeutsche Monatshefte* did not mince his words: 'Rambling scribblings of this kind, without any verve or gusto, are unbearable.'[1] One may take issue with this apodictic verdict, but it is certainly not wildly inappropriate for evaluating a picaresque novel. Its weaker exemplars have often been accused of exactly that: lack of direction, conceptual clarity and linguistic cohesion. In spite of the formal economy and rhetorical precision of some of its best works, picaresque fiction has, more often than not, been reproved for a certain propensity to formal sloppiness and stylistic syncretism. Yet, Hofmiller's judgement did not meet with unanimous agreement. Efraim Frisch, for example, writes in the *Neue Rundschau* about a sense of dreamlike elation and simultaneous disorientation that marked his reading experience. Walser, according to Frisch, both comforts and disturbs the reader, he dissolves and displaces social and psychic structures in order to show their uncanny omnipresence.[2] This, by contrast, is not the kind of critique one would expect in the review of a picaresque novel. And yet, Frisch's reading touches precisely on the picaresque nature of *Jakob von Gunten*—its play with absence and presence, death and birth.

In his diary, the narrator-protagonist Jakob pens an impossible *creatio ex nihilo*: the reader witnesses Jakob's narrative self-generation as a character after he transformed Fräulein Benjamenta, both mother and lover figure, into a dead image (145–7/120–2) to facilitate his 'self-birth'

---

1   'Jakob von Gunten. Gedichte', in Kerr, *Über Robert Walser* I, 51.
2   Cf. 'Ein Jüngling. Jakob von Gunten', in Kerr, *Über Robert Walser* I, 70–5.

in a performative speech act.[3] In an ironic and light-hearted fashion, he leads the reader (and himself) through the maze of his observations and dreamscapes, ultimately celebrating himself as absolutely autonomous. He thus reverses the trajectory of the quest story: rather than working towards some kind of goal, Jakob cultivates the art of procrastination in the servant school Institute Benjamenta, which gradually disintegrates on the pages of his diary. Through writing he claims to assert himself, to move himself out of the Institute into a realm of freedom: 'Mich bindet nichts, verpflichtet nichts, zu sagen "Wie wär's, wenn ich—" Nein, es gibt nichts mehr zu wären und zu wennen.' ['Nothing's keeping me, nothing obliges me to say: "How would it be if … " No, there's nothing left to be woulding and iffing about.'] (164/136)

Jakob generates himself as an independent character by devouring and deconstructing the Institute in this dream-text. The very institution that is designed to change him from an aristocrat into a servant is repeatedly enacted as the figment of his imagination. The Institute is turned into the proscenium of a family and initiation story. Jakob struggles through various avatars of father, mother and brother, before he ventures out into the world, with a tamed father figure as companion and without a pen to record (and manipulate) the experiences ahead of him. The final dream, in which Jakob imagines himself in the desert together with the director of the Institute, Herr Benjamenta, is an extended fantasy of self-sufficiency (and redemption). The episode is underpinned by references to Don Quixote.[4] The director features in this dream as a knight on horseback, clad in noble armour, his gaze directed towards 'die Ferne, ins Leben' ['into the distance, out and down into life'] (162/134). They get involved in various kinds of enterprises, including a revolution in India. The narrator exclaims enthusiastically:

> Das Leben prangte vor unsern weitausschauenden Blicken wie ein Baum mit Zweigen und Ästen. Und wie stunden wir fest. Und durch Gefahren und Erkenntnisse wateten wir wie in eiskaltem, aber unserer Hitze wohltuendem Flußwasser. Ich war immer der Knappe, und der Vorsteher war der Ritter. (163)

> Life was flourishing before our far-seeing gaze, like a tree with branches and twigs. And how steadfast we were! And through dangers and experiences we waded as through icy waters that

---

3   Liebrand, 'Jakob von Guntens Maskeraden', 350.

4   In a letter to Frieda Mermet, dating from 30 June 1918, Walser calls Cervantes' mock epic 'the greatest novel in world literature', see *Briefe*, 133–5. Elsewhere Walser relates the notion of servanthood to *Don Quixote*, see 'Tobold (II)', 227.

were a balm to our heat. I was always the Squire and the Principal was the Knight. (135)

The reference to Don Quixote is less straightforward than it seems. There are a number of indicators that point towards a blurry distinction between the apprentice and the knight. While the dream only indirectly refers to the possible duplication of one character, Jakob's ironic portrayal of the quixotic figure mockingly puts a distance between observer and observed and indicates that they may, in fact, be only two personae of the same person—Jakob as Don Quixote and Sancho Panza:

Und nicht einmal den Kopf bog er nach mir. Mir scheinbar zuliebe rollte jetzt der Traum, als wenn er ein Wagen gewesen wäre, Stück um Stück weiter, und da befanden wir uns, ich und 'dieser Mensch', natürlich niemand anders als Herr Benjamenta, mitten in der Wüste. (162)

And he didn't even turn his head. For my benefit, it seems, the dream now rolled on, bit by bit, like a wagon, and then we found ourselves, I and 'This Person', naturally no other than Herr Benjamenta, in the middle of the desert. (134)

The fixed direction of the head, the ambiguous phrasing of 'mir scheinbar zuliebe', the ironic bracketing of 'dieser Mensch'—all this points towards a dream logic of displacement that suggests a latent identity of ego and persona. The knight in the dream is very much staged as a mask of the apprentice, the mask through which Jakob perceives what he narrates as reality. He subjects himself to the institutionalized gaze of his school, which he, at the same time, claims to have created (or dreamed) himself. Accordingly, Jakob and Herr Benjamenta never seem to look at each other or interact. Rather, Don Quixote acts as Sancho Panza's mask, an inversion of the conventional roles that is reminiscent of Kafka's quixotic reading of Sancho Panza. This aspect is further underscored when, at the moment of awakening, the director is asleep and Jakob, imagining himself as self-sufficient, takes the active part by reversing the positions in this oedipal play between the roles of father and son. Both Kafka and Walser (as meta-narrators) wittily allude to the drama of authorship behind Cervantes' protagonists, thus undermining it as a necessary fiction of individuality that can never fully disguise the fact that acts of creation (including selfhood) are always derivative. As Martin Walser has shown, Jakob's sense of self-reliance is paradoxically rooted in his ironic self-deprecation; eventually he abandons both the school and his diary as a fully narrated individual who claims to have written himself into life and *hors du texte*.[5]

The phrase 'dieser Mensch' is probably also a parodic reference to the biblical *ecce homo*, Pontius Pilate's mocking of Christ, and questions the potential hopes of redemption associated with any father figure. (It may also be a parody of Nietzsche's self-apotheosis in *Ecce Homo. Wie man wird, was man ist*.) As in Kafka, Sancho Panza follows Don Quixote after manipulating him. Jakob only accepts Benjamenta after he bows down as an 'entthronter Herrscher' ['dethroned ruler'] (157/130). At the end, he even has to wake him up, so that Jakob can lead him into the desert. He takes over the surrogate father's position through the act of imagination. Sancho Panza is imagined as the creator and Don Quixote as the created figure. This also corroborates an interpretation of Jakob as perched between fantasies of omnipotence and self-annihilation as conflicting forces shaping the precarious nature of male gender constructions around 1900. His picaresque ruminations are an imaginative correlative for contemporary male gender roles: they are challenged and shaped by both authoritarianism and meritocracy, on the one hand, and the playfulness of artistic self-invention that is able to transcend narcissism in an oblivious 'Turnen oder Tanzen' ['gymnastics or dancing'] (63/51).[6]

Jakob's self-fashioning as a servant and his expression of fears and hopes in the form of dreams mirror an episodic structure in which he only seems to react to external pressure and adversities, yet in fact creates, in his own mind, a laboratory for imagining the self as a self-sufficient monad. It is this motif of *creatio ex nihilo* that was to prove one of the most powerful ingredients in the re-creation of the picaresque in German-language literatures. What makes *Jakob von Gunten* such a rewarding novel in our context has to do with one aspect in particular: the novel employs a rhetoric of understatement (*tiefstapeln*) that is linked to the theme of servanthood, which in turn is used to play a confidence game (*hochstapeln*) with the reader. I argue that *Jakob von Gunten* encapsulates a combination of *tiefstapeln* and *hochstapeln* that is characteristic of the modern picaresque. The extreme narcissistic totality inherent in Jakob's project of self-creation (his impossible project of self-reliance through self-annihilation), also highlights a limitation of the picaresque form that differs from the repetitive circularity in *Der Verschollene*. It shows self-absorption to be both symptomatic of modern depersonalization and a potential form of resistance against it by dramatizing the vacillation between the

---

5   Cf. Martin Walser, *Selbstbewußtsein und Ironie*, 149–52.
6   On the structure and motif of dance in Walser see Utz, *Tanz auf den Rändern*, chapter 11.

Institute's gradual disintegration and Jakob's fantasies of total power, or, to phrase it in his spatial metaphors, between an increasingly empty centre (the Institute) and his self-creation from the social fringe, 'von g(anz)unten'.

It is on this level of the histrionics of selfhood that I refute Michael Pleister, who argues that *Jakob von Gunten* is not a picaresque novel on the grounds that it does not feature the following aspects: the motif of low descent; perpetual change of place and profession, episodic structure; proactive agency of the protagonist; satirical exposure of social deficiencies.[7] I will show that all these aspects are, in fact, present in the novel, focused by the negotiation between *Hochstapler* and *Tiefstapler* personae and the kind of narrative meta-reflexivity that turns this diary into a picaresque self-parody.

The *Tiefstapler*: The Servant As Ruler

Jakob von Gunten epitomizes a crisis of paternal authority, both with regard to a past feudal hierarchy, reflected by von Gunten's name and pedigree (and by a few objects displayed in the Institute, such as a sword and an iron helmet), and with regard to the modern nuclear family. Jakob is dismissive of his family ties. (22/18) The renunciation of the family as well as the absence of fathers are common themes in the picaresque tradition. The classic pícaro is often an orphan and has to deal with step or surrogate fathers. What is seen as a stigma in society—his dubious social origin—is, however, also one of the pícaro's major assets: he forges his own identity outside a predestined social trajectory. Paradoxically, Jakob is not in the orphaned position of the classic pícaro, he yet has to attain that status, and that is why he enters the Institute Benjamenta. He even metaphorically kills his surrogate mother in the *Dienerschule* and attempts to educate himself independently of his parents, as if he was an orphan:

Nein, nie nehme ich je Hilfe (Geld) von den zärtlich verehrten Eltern an. Mein verletzter Stolz würde mich aufs Krankenlager werfen, und futsch wären die Träume von einer selbsterrungenen Lebenslaufbahn, vernichtet für immer diese mir in der Brust brennenden Selbsterziehungspläne. (69)

No, never shall I accept help (money) from the parents whom I so tenderly respect. My injured pride would fling me onto a sickbed and bang would go all my dreams of an independent life, destroyed forever these ardently cherished plans for self-education. (57)

---

7   Pleister, 'Utopie oder Resignation?', 99.

These ideals of self-exploration and self-education Jakob intends to pursue actively in the Institute, yet, at the same time, it is the very deconstruction of that Institute in the dreamscape of his diary which ultimately allows him to envisage the self in terms of exploration and education. In the *Dienerschule* two metaphorical spaces converge: it represents both low (servanthood) and high social life (Jakob's alleged heritage). His family is reduplicated in the main figures: Jakob's three picaresque masters are the father figure Herr Benjamenta, the mother figure 'Fräulein' Benjamenta and the brother figure Kraus. This nuclear family configuration is undermined by the fact that the director and the Fräulein are siblings and by the biblical subtext that marks Kraus (the Joseph figure) as Ya'akov's son and Benjamin's brother. The master–servant theme is refracted on various levels. Most importantly, Jakob describes his relation to the Fräulein as one of love, while his relation to the director appears to be dominated by competition and ultimately reconciliation (a constellation reminiscent of Goethe's *Wilhelm Meister*).[8]

This paradoxical position of the Institute (which proves most useful for him in its dysfunctional state and ultimate demise) is reflected in the novel's formal and thematic dialectic of serving and ruling. Dieter Borchmeyer describes servanthood in *Jakob von Gunten* as 'a disguised form of ruling'.[9] We do not have to agree with Borchmeyer's interpretation of *Jakob von Gunten* as a deliberate counterpoint to Nietzsche's *Antichrist* to appreciate the fact that Walser loosely refers to Nietzsche's concept of a human who manages to overcome nihilism by himself, the *Übermensch*.[10] Yet, servanthood in Walser does not only function as a 'consciously anachronistic opposition against [...] rationalized modern society',[11] it is also a picaresque strategy of asserting individuality in a hostile environment. For Jakob, humility is a way of inventing himself outside 'the world of possession and progress' into which the modern novel, according to Brooks, tends to implicate its heroes, as discussed in Chapter One. In this regard, *Jakob von Gunten* is not only an obvious parody of the bourgeois ethos of self-advancement in the *Bildungsroman*, but also an intricate parody of social mimicry in the picaresque novel. By radically reducing his social circles, Jakob is eventually able to imagine himself as moving from text into life. Jakob's diary dramatizes two concurrent processes. By annihilating himself through the persona of the servant, Jakob asserts himself beyond the conflicting claims of autonomy and heteronomy. At the same time, Jakob destroys the very

---

8   Cf. Greven, *Existenz*, 87.
9   Borchmeyer, *Dienst und Herrschaft*, 1.
10   Ibid., 62–76; see also Reginster, *Affirmation of Life*, 103–6.
11   Ibid., 2.

institution which allows him to erase the social genealogy of his self, the Institute Benjamenta and its labyrinth of 'inner chambers', and thus metaphorically erases his family.[12]

Jakob may well represent an antithesis to Nietzsche's invective against Christianity, yet he also joins, as many modern German pícaros do, in Nietzsche's celebration of the aesthetic man—he who is capable of embracing appearance (*Schein*) in life:

> Schein ist für mich das Wirkende und Lebende selber, das soweit in seiner Selbstverspottung geht, mich fühlen zu lassen, dass hier Schein und Irrlicht und Geistertanz und nichts Mehr ist,—dass unter allen diesen Träumenden auch ich, der 'Erkennende', meinen Tanz tanze, dass der Erkennende ein Mittel ist, den irdischen Tanz in die Länge zu ziehen und insofern zu den Festordnern des Daseins gehört, und dass die erhabene Consequenz und Verbundenheit aller Erkenntnisse vielleicht das höchste Mittel ist und sein wird, die Allgemeinheit der Träumerei und die Allverständlichkeit aller dieser Träumenden unter einander und eben damit *die Dauer des Traumes aufrecht zu erhalten.*

> To me, appearance is the active and living itself, which goes so far in its self-mockery that it makes me feel that there is appearance and a will-o'-the-wisp and a dance of spirits and nothing else—that among all these dreamers, even I, the 'knower', am dancing my dance; that the one who comes to know is a means of prolonging the earthly dance and thus is one of the masters of ceremony of existence, and that the sublime consistency and interrelatedness of all knowledge may be and will be the highest means to *sustain* the universality of dreaming, the mutual comprehension of all dreamers, and thereby also *the duration of the dream.*[13]

Jakob plays this game of 'self-mockery', even if his servanthood is pitched against Nietzsche's transvaluation of values. His entire diary spins out the tale of a sleepwalker who, over and over again, has to prevent himself from waking up. He dramatizes his dreams as extended moments of 'knowledge' and yet, at the same time, draws attention to the fact that delaying the moment of awakening is only an act of playing 'the masters of ceremony of existence'. Kraus, the

---

12 Cf. Bloemen, 'Durch die "inneren Gemächer"', 60–6. Martin Walser's groundbreaking study on irony in *Jakob von Gunten* falls short of acknowledging this; it reduces individuality to its socio-psychological dimension, see *Selbstbewußtsein und Ironie*, 141–3.

13 Nietzsche, *Die fröhliche Wissenschaft*, 417; *Gay Science*, 63–4 (§54).

model student and brother figure, remarks about Jakob as a dreamer and his dreamscapes (and their Nietzschean duality of creation and self-awareness):

> […] du gehörst zu denen, die sich, so wertlos sie sein mögen, über gute Lehren erhaben vorkommen wollen. Ich weiß es schon, schweig nur. Du willst in mir einen sturen Pädagogen und Rechthaber erblickt haben. Geh mir. Und was fühlst du denn, du und deinesgleichen, Pralhanse, was ihr seid, was ernst-sein und achtsam-sein eigentlich sagen will? Du bildest dir auf deine springerische und tänzerische Leichtfertigkeit ganz gewiß, und mit ohne Zweifel ebenso viel Recht, nicht wahr, Königreiche ein? Du Tänzer, o ich durchschaue dich. (138)

> […] you're one of those worthless fellows who think they're above the rules. I know. You needn't say anything. You think I'm a grumpy pedagogue and dogmatist. Well, I'm not. And what do you and your sort, big mouths, what do you suppose it really means to be serious and attentive? You imagine you're king, just because you can leap and dance around, definitely and quite rightfully, without a doubt, don't you? Oh, I can see through you, you dancer. (115)

And he continues a little later: 'Weißt du was, Jakob, Herr des Daseins: laß mich in Ruhe. Ziehe auf Eroberungen. Ich bin überzeugt, es fallen dir welche vor die Füße, und du wirst sie nur aufzulesen brauchen.' ['Do you know something, Jakob, lord of life: let me be. Go and make your conquests! I'm certain a few will fall at your feet, and they'll be there for the picking.'] (139/115) This 'lord of life'—or 'master of ceremonies'—is, Kraus implies, the product of boastful rhetorical 'carelessness'. Whether or not we take Kraus's comment seriously as a form of criticism, he certainly offers an accurate description of Jakob as a Nietzschean dancer who is at home in the realm of appearances.

As much as Jakob ironically overdetermines himself with references to a Christ-like ethos of serving, he first and foremost 'draws on this model of service […] to pervert it for his own ends', as Rochelle Tobias notes: 'Service does not require a sacrifice on his part. On the contrary, it elevates and enlarges him by allowing him to become a being that no one notices and consequently is not confined to any one place. Nowhere in particular, Jakob is potentially everywhere. This reversal informs every aspect of a servant's life, including his time or temporality.'[14] The epitome of Christian charity is treasured not so much for its altruism

---

14   Tobias, 'Double Fiction', 297.

but for the freedom it bestows on the charitable person who is not acting within the confines of social obligations: 'Jemandem, den man nicht kennt und der einen nichts angeht, einen Dienst erweisen, das ist reizend, das läßt in göttlich nebelhafte Paradiese blicken.' ['To be of service to somebody whom one does not know, and who has nothing to do with one, that is charming, it gives one a glimpse into divine and misty paradises.'] (23/18) This captures Jakob's notion of serving in a nutshell: the servant is free in that he chooses the master. His logic takes the master–servant dialectics out of its socio-political context and transposes it into the aesthetic sphere.

Serving in Walser's novel is not tantamount to an attitude of humility, it is predominantly the deliberate attempt to exert willpower, to subject one's fate to an exercise of will in a picaresque role-switching between master and servant, father and son, creator and creature. In this sense, Jakob cannot avoid the logic of meritocracy, even if he frequently takes pleasure in a good rant against its effects. The attempt to engineer oneself through becoming a servant ultimately equals the psychology of asceticism and its hidden claims to moral supremacy. By renouncing something one hopes to make oneself worthy of an ideal. It is this notion of asceticism in *Jakob von Gunten* that underlies its ambiguous image of aristocracy. On the one hand, Jakob clearly shows an anti-aristocratic affect; on the other, he calls himself an aristocratic 'Abkömmling' ('descendant') as opposed to the meritocratic 'Emporkömmling' ('upstart'). (117/97) The pride he takes in becoming a servant is both an ascetic gesture directed against the buzz and depersonalized structures of modern life and, at the same time, the perpetuation of an anachronistic sense of community, which he sees embodied by Kraus:

Ja, man wird Kraus nie achten, und gerade das, daß er ohne Achtung zu genießen dahinleben wird, das ist ja das Wundervolle und Planvolle, das An-den-Schöpfer-Mahnende. Gott gibt der Welt einen Kraus, um ihr gleichsam ein tiefes unauflösbares Rätsel aufzugeben. Nun, und das Rätsel wird nie begriffen werden, denn siehe: man gibt sich gar nicht einmal die Mühe es zu lösen, [...]. Kraus ist ein echtes Gott-Werk, ein Nichts, ein Diener. (81)

Yes, nobody will ever pay any attention to Kraus, and precisely this, his going on living without enjoying attention, that is the wonderful thing, which seems to be part of a plan, the sign of the Creator. God gives a Kraus to this world, in order to entrust to it, as it were, a deep, insoluble riddle. And the riddle will never be understood, for look: people don't even try to solve it, [...]. Kraus is a genuine work of God, a nothing, a servant. (67)

Kraus is described in terms of the mystical experience of indistinctness, not affected by the *principium individuationis* of space and time that breaks the entity of life into fragments. He is marked by an utter lack of will in his sense of serving, he does not even attract any curiosity in his fellow humans to understand the 'enigma' of his servanthood. In this mystical seclusion, Kraus combines the features Jakob persistently strives for and envisages for himself: a quasi-messianic otherworldliness ('und das Rätsel wird nie begriffen werden' refers to the Messiah in John 1.10, as Luther translates it: 'Er ist kommen in die Welt und die Welt hat ihn nicht erkannt'), creatureliness ('Gott-Werk'), absence ('ein Nichts'), and the ethos of humility expressed in the Sermon on the Mount ('ein Diener').

Kraus is envisaged by Jakob as the perfect servant, who has internalized the lessons of the Institute and turned the annihilation of the self into an art without perceiving it as such. For Jakob, by contrast, self-annihilation is an exercise of self-reflection and, consequently, of willpower. The perpetual rhetorical and narrative self-dramatization of Jakob as 'zero' and servant and underdog I call *tiefstapeln*, as opposed to *hochstapeln*. We will, however, see in the course of this discussion that the modern picaresque novel systematically blurs the distinction between *hochstapeln* and *tiefstapeln*.

Jakob follows Kraus, but only rhetorically. The light touch of his ironic diary entries forms a stark antithesis and outlines the development of the entire novel: while the narrator proclaims his admiration for Kraus, he also distances himself through his artistry. While he purports to strive for Kraus's mystic self-annihilation, Jakob rather sees himself as an interpreter of the inscrutable 'enigma'—an enigma created by Jakob himself in the first place.[15] Again, we find the characteristic circularity which allows the narrator to inaugurate himself as the creator behind the 'Gott-Werk'. This is most clearly sketched out in one of the central dreams of the novel. Fräulein Benjamenta leads Jakob into the 'inneren Gemächer', the inner chambers (97–103). In a pun on *Gemach* (*n.* chamber, *adj.* slow, gentle) and *Ungemach* (*n.* trouble), she comments on Jakob's painful initiation:[16]

Hörst du, wie es zornig einherdonnert und -rollt? Das ist das Ungemach. Du hast jetzt in einem Gemach Ruhe genossen. Nun wird das Ungemach über dich herabregnen und Zweifel und Unruhe werden dich durchnässen. (102)

---

15   On this dialectical relation see also Martin Walser, *Selbstbewußtsein und Ironie*, 135–9.

16   On the etymology of 'Gemach' see Bloemen, 'Durch die "inneren Gemächer"', 60–1.

Listen, can't you hear their angry thunder, they're coming. This room is the chamber of calamity. You have had your repose in it. Now calamity will rain down on you and doubt and restlessness will drench you through. (85)

Walser's diary novel vacillates between a dreamscape of ironic omnipotence and the initiation story of loss (represented by the gradual disintegration of the Institute). Before Jakob enters the inner chambers he notes: 'Es war mir, als sei ich zu Hause. Nein, es war mir, als sei ich noch nicht geboren, als schwämme ich in etwas Vor-Gebürtigem.' ['I felt as if I were at home. No, it was as if I hadn't yet been born, as if I were swimming in some element before birth.'] (95/79) And a similar metaphor is used during the following initiation dream:

> [...] kaum hatte sie zu Ende gesprochen, da schwamm ich in einem dickflüssigen, höchst unangenehmen Strom von Zweifel. Durch und durch entmutigt, wagte ich gar nicht, mich umzuschauen, ob sie noch neben mir sei. Nein, die Lehrerin, die Hervorzauberin all dieser Erscheinungen und Zustände, war verschwunden. Ich schwamm ganz allein. (102)

> [...] she had hardly finished when I was swimming in a gluey and most unpleasant river of doubt. Thoroughly disheartened, I didn't care to look around to see if she was still near to me. No, the instructress, the enchantress who had conjured up all these visions and states, had disappeared. I was swimming all alone. (85)

Before this experience of loss, Fräulein Benjamenta opens the inner chambers into an open ice rink, from where they are observing the stars together. She warns him against falling in love with freedom, 'denn nur momentelang, nicht länger, hält man sich in den Gegenden der Freiheit auf' ['for one can only be in the realm of freedom for a moment, no longer'] (101/84). This exposition of the nature of freedom is followed by an ambiguous passage that insinuates sexual consummation with its pun on *Lust* and *Lustigkeit*: 'so sanken wir von der erklommenen Höhe und Lustigkeit in etwas Müdes und Trauliches hinunter' ['we sank from our summit of happiness down into a place that was tired and cosy'] (101/84). This dramaturgy of opposites—cosmic space and inner chambers, freedom and restriction, ecstasy and melancholy, *Ungemach* and *Gemächer*—makes evident that the rhetoric of servanthood and the histrionics of *tiefstapeln* are intimately linked up with fantasies of artistic self-creation and the *Hochstapler*'s ludic approach to appearances.[17]

Family Trouble: Territorializing Zero

Before Fräulein Benjamenta dies, Jakob writes: 'Jedenfalls gehorche ich Fräulein und schweige über diese Geschichte. Ihr gehorchen dürfen! So lange ich ihr gehorche, ist sie am Leben.' ['Anyway, I shall obey the Fräulein and say nothing about this. To be allowed to obey her! As long as I obey her, she will live.'] (135/112) After her death, Jakob claims that he is carrying with him 'her' law. These internalized laws, embodied by Fräulein Benjamenta, would live on in him and in Herr Benjamenta when they embark on their final journey—and the same, we can assume, holds true for the exercise of self-assertion through writing a diary, even after the diary is closed. The laws of human self-reflection and self-knowledge and their limitations through certain cultural practices (such as writing, autobiography, diary) live on as modes of perception shaping the way in which humans engage with their environments. The metaphorical relation between Fräulein Benjamenta's life and Jakob's text is the central phantasm of this diary.

Typically the pícaro picks up the pen in the last chapter and starts chapter one. Here, Jakob claims to abandon writing altogether in order to engage with the world and return to the land of the fore-fathers: 'Aber weg jetzt mit der Feder.' ['But now I'll throw away my pen!'] (164/136) Whether this is a tongue-in-cheek exclamation or supposed to be taken seriously is impossible to determine—the readers are at the mercy of the diarist and his volatile inclinations. Jakob writes himself out of his origins, into the zone of 'zero': 'Und wenn ich zerschelle und verderbe, was bricht und verdirbt dann? Eine Null. Ich einzelner Mensch bin nur eine Null.' ['And if I am smashed to pieces and go to ruin, what is being smashed and ruined? A zero. The individual me is only a zero.'] (164/136) One metaphor of origin, the pen, is replaced by another, the desert as the ancestral land. Abandoning his pen, Jakob claims to have achieved a new state of independence and self-sufficiency. The reader can never determine whether or not Jakob's role as *Tiefstapler* and servant are simply the trick of a *Hochstapler*—self-assertion as the ultimate confidence game. It remains unclear whether the final move is a diarist's confidence trick with the reader or a move *hors du texte*, a liberation from the infinite regress of a paradoxical self-annihilating

---

17   See Liebrand, 'Spielkonfigurationen', 347–9, for a psychological reading based on Deleuze; see Bloemen, 'Durch die "inneren Gemächer"', 54–60, for a post-structuralist reading.

self-absorption. In both cases, the reader is an integral part of the narrative set-up and its implied dialogical structure. As Tobias notes, 'Jakob would have us believe that he retreats from the very pages of the book we hold in our hands to emerge on the other side of writing, that is, in life as someone we fail to acknowledge. The two instruments he uses in this undertaking are his pen and us. We, the readers, are the necessary witnesses to his passing into eternal life.'[18]

The ending of most picaresque novels is a flight into the security of textual self-legitimization: the pícaro writes himself back into his story with the aim of manipulating it in the face of particular charges against him. Jakob, by contrast, pens a self-parody: he writes himself out of his pseudo-biography in a way that can also be read as a hidden response to his brother, the accomplished artist and parvenu, who works in the metropolis. The brother represents the failure of kinship bonds in modern society, something Jakob, in his contradictory manner, both endorses and detests. (53/43) In ascribing the realm of bourgeois values to his brother, Jakob claims the genuinely aristocratic attitude. As mentioned above, he draws a clear distinction between a 'descendant' and an 'upstart'; in the context of his strained relationship with his brother, this can be read as part of a defiant *apologia* addressed to the brother:

> Ich vergesse nie, daß ich ein Abkömmling bin, der nun von unten, von ganz unten anfängt, ohne doch die Eigenschaften, die nötig sind, emporzugelangen, zu besitzen. […] Ich habe gar keine Emporkömmlingstugenden. Ich bin manchmal frech, aber nur aus Laune. Der Emporkömmling aber ist von einer permanenten bescheiden-tuenden Frechheit, oder von einer frechen, fortwährend frechen Unbedeutendheitsgebärde. (117)

> I never forget that I'm a descendant beginning from all the way down, without having the qualities which one needs if one is going to rise to the top. […] I have none of the virtues of an upstart. I'm cheeky sometimes, but only as a passing mood. The upstart's cheekiness is a permanent shaming of modesty, or his gesture is that of cheeky, permanently cheeky insignificance. (97)

This passage refers to two different subtexts of Jakob's diary. First, it creates an artificial opposition between Jakob, the self-appointed *Abkömmling*, and his brother, the *Emporkömmling*. Second, in playing

---

18   Tobias, 'Double Fiction', 301.

with the self-image of the *Tiefstapler* as a *Hochstapler*, Jakob himself prepares the ground for the very critique that Kraus, the brother figure, launches against him a little later, as cited above: Jakob here is discredited as a bragger ('Pralhans') who acts as the lord of life ('Herr des Daseins'). By ironically debunking himself, by blurring the boundaries between *Tiefstapler* and *Hochstapler*, Jakob anticipates Kraus's critique, which thus sounds like a mere echo of Jakob's own voice.

A third subtext of this figural dichotomy is related to the motif of the metropolis. Jakob enacts his narrative persona in opposition to the modern urban character, which he describes in the following terms:

> Es herrscht unter diesen Kreisen der fortschrittlichen Bildung eine kaum zu übersehende und mißzuverstehende Müdigkeit. Nicht die formelle Blasiertheit etwa des Adels von Abstammung, nein, eine wahrhafte, eine ganz wahre, auf höherer und lebhafterer Empfindung beruhende Müdigkeit, die Müdigkeit des gesunden-ungesunden Menschen. Sie sind alle gebildet, aber achten sie einander? (116)

> In these circles of progressive culture there's a fairly obvious and unmistakable fatigue. Not the formal blasé-ness, say, of an aristocrat of birth, no, but a genuine, a completely authentic fatigue of the healthy-unhealthy person. They're all cultivated, but do they respect one another? (96)

In an earlier passage, Jakob, by contrast, presents himself as the epitome of the very 'tiredness' he criticizes in this passage, thus undermining yet again the distinction between aristocrat and parvenu:

> Bin ich der geborene Großstädter? Sehr leicht möglich. Ich lasse mich fast nie betäuben oder überraschen. Etwas unsagbar Kühles ist trotz der Aufregungen, die mich überfallen können, an mir. Ich habe die Provinz in sechs Tagen abgestreift. (40)

> Am I a born city dweller? It's quite possible. I hardly ever get stunned or surprised. There's something unspeakably cool about me, in spite of the excitements that can attack me. (33)

Jakob's servanthood and *Tiefstapelei* are also a form of self-dramatization as a successful parvenu marked by what Georg Simmel describes as the blasé attitude of the modern metropolitan dweller.[19] He

---

19 Simmel, 'Großstädte und das Geistesleben', 117–19; 'Metropolis and Mental Life', 175–6.

cultivates this attitude naturally due to his social detachment as both aristocrat and servant. The *Tiefstapler* hides a *Hochstapler* who eludes the mundane trials and tribulations of modernity.

'Nichtstun und dennoch Haltung beobachten, das fordert Energie, der Schaffende hat es dagegen leicht.' ['To do nothing and yet maintain one's bearing, that requires energy, a person doing something has an easy time in comparison.'] (71/58) This is not only a reference to dandysme, it also highlights the paradox inherent in Jakob's rejection of bourgeois life. As much as he wants to escape the modern compulsion to excel in one or several social subsystems, so does his intellectual rigour and poetic craftsmanship betray his will to succeed and prove himself as the better 'Schaffende'. His diary may be full of invectives against meritocracy, yet, as always, the text is interlaced with many counter-examples. It is only a few diary entries after his brother's endorsement of money and its economic (and other) merits that Jakob himself begins to fantasize about the value of money and its elective affinity to the picaresque mode of living (74–7/61–3). His brother Johann, however, seems to be increasingly infected by Jakob's inclination to contradictory statements. He encourages him to earn 'viel, viel Geld' ['lots and lots of money'], only to conclude that he should stay poor, since rich people these days 'sind die wahren Verhungerten' ['are the really starving people'] (67–8/55). Johann's contradictory statements point at the Janus-faced character of money. Simmel, who published his *Philosophy of Money* in 1900, similarly elaborates on the dual nature of money.[20] According to him, money allows both unlimited circulation and complete annihilation of value, since it attaches virtual value to certain goods and services rather than to some quality inherent in these goods and services; at the same time, money facilitates accumulation, which then facilitates investment on a large scale. Metaphorically, Jakob claims this double nature of money and its structural duality of nullity and absolute exchangeability for himself. His self-annihilation may pay off in the end, yet it does not solve anything, least of all his family trouble; it rather dramatizes his reliance on (or identity with) his brother in the very act of setting himself apart from him.

Jakob's position is marked by a 'dual eccentricity'.[21] He is both an outsider at the fringe of society and a stranger to himself, approaching the self from the eccentric vantage points of narrative self-annihilation (*Tiefstapelei*) or self-creation (*Hochstapelei*). In this position he eludes the bourgeois distinction between public and private realms. He does not separate a realm in which role-play is deemed conventional (the

---

20 See, for example, Simmel, *Philosophie des Geldes*, 160–8.
21 Fuchs, *Dramaturgie des Narrentums*, 147.

public sphere) from a realm that is demarcated as authentic (the private sphere). In the Institute Benjamenta the two spheres converge in a complex allegory of the nuclear family. As shown above, the family roles in the Institute are fluid, exchangeable and even reversible, yet, at the same time, they are rigid and uncompromising, marked by fixed power structures. In a seminal diary entry, Jakob writes about the moment when Herr Benjamenta works himself into a fit and nearly kills him:

> Der Vorsteher kam in eine unbeschreibliche Wut hinein. Er glich einem Simson, jenem Mann aus der Geschichte Palästinas, der an den Säulen eines hohen, menschenerfüllten Hauses rüttelte, bis der festliche, lüsterne Palast, bis der steinerne Triumph, bis die Bosheit zusammenstürzte. (142)

> The Principal got so angry, it was indescribable. He was like Samson, that man in the history of Palestine who shook the pillars of a tall house full of people till the festive, wanton palace, till the stone triumph, till naughtiness itself came tumbling down. (118)

Jakob modifies his comparison of the Institute with a 'palace', yet then goes on to spell out the Samson reference by turning Benjamenta into a biblical revenge figure who, for no obvious reason, takes it out on Jakob, but eventually breaks out in fits of laughter about the entire incident. This demonstration of paternal power leads to a childish fantasy about parental authority which is projected onto the brother figure Kraus. The father's punishment converges with the brother's solidarity:

> Wenn doch nur Kraus käme. Mir ist doch ein wenig bange. Wie nett wäre es, wenn der gute Kraus käme und mir wieder ein wenig, wie schon so oft, die Leviten läse. Ich möchte ein wenig ausgeschimpft, abgekanzelt, verknurrt und verdonnert werden, das würde mir unsagbar wohltun. Bin ich ein Kind? (143)

> If only Kraus would come! I'm still a bit scared. How nice it would be if dear Kraus would come and give me a scolding, as he often does, out of his Book of Commandments. I'd like to be scolded a little, told off, condemned and sentenced, that would do me no end of good. Am I childish? (119)

This blurring of roles can be related to a deeper underlying issue, namely the connection between a specific family structure and the context of modern capitalist and industrial society. Gilles Deleuze and Félix

Guattari have devised, in their attempt to cross-fertilize philosophy and psychoanalysis, a language for describing certain connections in capitalist societies between the modern nuclear family and the tendency to homogenize life through one quantifiable measure of exchange—money and capital. In their genealogy of capitalism, they describe the dual effect of what they term deterritorialization and (re)territorialization. Capitalism, they argue, unravels petrified structures and decodes fixed codes (deterritorialization), yet only to ultimately subject this new potential for change and innovation to the code of capital and the exchangeability of any aspect of life (reterritorialization). It fosters the proliferation of anything that is new; yet, this drive for innovation and its deterritorializing challenges for society are always rooted in the value system of money as the code of exchange. This dynamic, Deleuze and Guattari assert, contains innovation within those power structures it originally set out to overcome (in order to facilitate innovation): the quantification of life through money.[22] They illustrate their theory by using the example of the Oedipus complex, which, they claim, is not a universal incest taboo, but rather a direct result of capitalist relations of production as they manifest themselves in family relations: 'a fixed conjugation between individuated persons, in which desire is subordinated to reproduction, leads to the filiation of new individuals by exclusive disjunction. Gestation, birth and growth become more than just the production and emission of a set of desiring-machines [i.e. a psyche that is modelled on social relations]: the child is separated from the mother's body by means of the socially imposed prohibitions which found their separate identities.'[23] In other words, the family organizes the child's desire in a way that reproduces capitalist structures of production and consumption, namely the extension of the paternal authority and the displaced repetition of desire for one's mother.[24]

Jakob von Gunten renders a world of perpetual territorialization, that is, modes of establishing a symbolical code and narrative for the nuclear family. At the same time, the novel presents us with the dynamics of deterritorialization, that is, 'schizoid' modes of breaking down the structure and validity of these established codes. Eventually, Jakob and Benjamenta venture off into the desert, but it is unclear what defines their relationship. Are they father and son or master and servant (in these cases it would be unclear who is who, due to the power changes mentioned above and the biblical name associations explored below), or do they merge in one narcissistic body with the two personae of Don Quixote and Sancho Panza, as suggested above? Jakob's family diary

22 Deleuze and Guattari, *Anti-Oedipus*, 370.
23 Goodchild, *Politics of Desire*, 88.
24 Deleuze and Guattari, *Anti-Oedipus*, 123–33.

enacts the drama of the nuclear family in capitalism, as Deleuze and Guattari define it: Jakob extends and inherits the paternal authority and organizes his erotic desire around the Oedipal taboo and the ensuing dynamic of attraction and prohibition. Yet, at the same time, the very ambiguity of the picaresque narrative and its unclear addressee (maybe the brother who has broken away from the claustrophobia of the family), not to speak of the dream-like displacement between Jakob's (unknown) actual and his (omnipresent) surrogate family in the Institute, counter the cyclical structure of (re)territorialization. The picaresque narrative constantly instils semiotic and hermeneutical insecurity into the representation of desire and keeps the signification processes open-ended rather than contained in a fixed logic.

The Catcher of the Heel

A closer look at names allows us to further explore Jakob's family troubles. The biblical name Ya'akov means 'the one who catches/holds the heel'. Genesis and Hosea relate the story of Ya'akov struggling for the birthright with his twin brother in his mother's womb. As he was about to lose the fight, he went, in vain, after Esau's heels to prevent him from becoming the first-born. Later Esau trades his birthright for a pottage of lentils (maybe he wanted to forfeit his birthright, thus dissociating himself from his people after God declared that they would be enslaved for four hundred years before being able to return to their homelands). When their father Isaac, nearly blind, lies down on his deathbed and wants to bestow his paternal blessing on his first-born, Ya'akov impersonates Esau and deceives their father into giving him the blessing which is Esau's privilege. Hence the association of Ya'akov with deception. (Genesis 25.24–34, 27.1–40)

This biblical subtext makes clear that the name Jakob von Gunten does not only constitute a contrast between the aristocratic 'von' and the implied humility of 'g(anz) unten', but also a dialectical relationship between the fighter and the servant. Jakob, the shape-shifter, both fights and serves his father, both dissociates himself from his brother and, at the same time, identifies with him, and, last but not least, also resembles Joseph, the proverbial biblical dream interpreter (and Ya'akov's favourite son). The narcissistic totalization of the self, which is the mark of many modern picaresque novels, is mapped onto two of the most central biblical stories about deception, and the fraternal conflicts between Esau and Ya'akov and between Joseph and his brothers.

The dream sequences in Walser's novel are fantasies about power, dominance and (male) self-assertion. They reframe Jakob's picaresque strategy and recode, in a Deleuzian sense, his rhetoric of servanthood: Jakob's self-mastery in how he claims to abdicate the ways of the world is mirrored in the dreams, which do not necessarily decode reality but show its otherwise hidden mechanisms. There is no clear distinction between Jakob's dreams and the rest of his diary: his servanthood, which appears as complicity with a petit bourgeois ethos, turns out to be a ludic dissolution of any social structure in a rhetoric of self-annihilation, while his dreams with their destructive force of creative fantasies appear much closer to the social code of the newly emerged metropolis.

In the orgy dream in the middle of the novel, for example, Jakob presides over a banquet, during which he kills his enemies and revels in sadism. Then various allegorical embodiments of virtues defile in front of him and succumb to him, partly in an overtly erotic fashion. After deflowering 'Virtue', he conjures God: 'Ich schrie: "Was? Auch du?" Und erwachte schweißtriefend.' ['I shouted: "What? You too?" And I woke up, dripping with sweat […].'] (88–9/73) This oblique reference to Ya'akov's wrestling with the divine figure is yet another inversion of the Ya'akov/Esau/Joseph story. Ya'akov fears Esau's revenge for stealing Isaac's paternal blessing from Esau with a trick. The night before Ya'akov expects an attack from Esau's small army, he spends in prayer when a figure, whose identity remains unclear, descends upon him and wrestles with him till dawn. The struggle remains undecided, but before the angel, as he is popularly imagined, leaves the scene, he inflicts a wound on the tendon of Ya'akov's thigh, Ya'akov then asks for a blessing and is told that he should bear the name Israel (the one who fights with God) henceforth. The next day, Esau and Ya'akov decide to reconcile.

Jakob's dream turns the hierarchy upside down: Jakob summons God by 'whistling' (88/73). The underlying irony here is the fact that the epiphanic figure may not even be God; biblical exegesis allows an interpretation of this ominous figure as either one of Esau's soldiers, Esau's guardian angel or God himself. The Ya'akov story creates an extended subtext in the novel and is one of the devices that connects the dream sequences with other diary entries. Jakob's surrogate family in the Institute is part of this subtext: Herr Benjamenta is both a father figure and a reference to Ya'akov's youngest son Benjamin. Fräulein Benjamenta is both mother and lover for Jakob and thus refers to the biblical figures of Rebekah and Rachel. Kraus, a kind of surrogate father (143/119) and personification of the Institute's superego (28/23), is directly related to Joseph (78/64–5), and thus, in biblical terms, Ya'akov's favourite son, although he takes on the position of Jakob's brother. In all cases, we can observe a deliberate overdetermination of Jakob. Every single figure around him is associated with mutually exclusive family roles. The biblical context deepens Jakob's family trouble.

What Walser achieves by ascribing a parodic biblical typology to his characters is twofold. First, he creates a tension between the narrator and the author persona. The biblical subtext is the only one that exhibits a certain level of organizational cohesion that points beyond the narrator to an author persona. Second, the biblical subtext works against any narrative tendencies to disambiguate the relationship between the involved characters, the family tableau of *Jakob von Gunten*; in doing so, it contributes to the ongoing process of deterritorialization. The ironic identification, for example, of the biblical model character Joseph (who has considerable appeal for women) with Kraus, who suffers from pimples and does not exactly share Joseph's attractive features, organizational skills and expertise as dream interpreter, does have the effect of comic relief; but it also creates further disorientation. If we take into account that Joseph was sent into slavery in Egypt by his brothers at the age of 17, because they were suspicious of his dreams, in which he figures as king over them, the episode appears in a different light. (Genesis 37–50)

Just as the biblical genealogy in Walser's novel between Jakob and Herr Benjamenta is inverted, so is the genealogy between Jakob and Kraus, who features both as Ya'akov's son Joseph, as Ya'akov himself, and as Ya'akov's brother. The biblical subtext, on the one hand, serves as a subtextual device to enact Jakob's dissolution of individuality as an immersion into alternative identities; the perpetual inversion of father–son relations supports his rhetorical self-projection as someone who creates identity *ex nihilo*. Servanthood, on the other hand, is also Jakob's mode of avoiding battle, the wrestling with his brother, his angel or his God. The mythological figure who befits him best is probably Odysseus' son Telemachos, 'the one who stays away from the battle', and his modern incarnation, James Joyce's Stephen Dedalus.

The moments of struggle in the novel are unexpected and sudden. They punctuate an incalculable fluctuation between acceptance and dismissal. In Jakob's case, this structure can be found with regard to the metropolis, the Institute and the inner chambers. He perpetually decodes conventional social bonds (and bondages) and deterritorializes power relations imposed upon him. Jakob's diary decodes what he perceives as an extreme form of meritocracy governed by excessive competition that forces him to be on his guard all the time. Metaphorically, he arms himself against 'den unheimlichen Überrumpler, den heimlichen Dieb'—'the awful ambush, the servant thief' (115/96). The casual play with *heimlich* versus *unheimlich* (homely/furtive/secret versus uncanny) relates the dialectic of coding versus decoding to the psycho-analytic categories of conscious versus unconscious. While Jakob implicitly claims that he is decoding the code of meritocracy, in particular in the various sequences about his brother Johann, the psychoanalytic phrasing suggests that there will also be a re-emergence of the coding, in Deleuzian terms: a reinstating of the nuclear family power structures. Manfred Engel's claim that Jakob 'breaks' with his family and the aristocratic tradition is misleading, since the very act of breaking is only conveyed in the ambiguous picaresque rhetoric of a decoding that also affirms the code.[25]

Pondering on his prospects as a future servant, for example, Jakob muses: 'Ah, man muß auftreten. Wer sich mit gemessenem Anstand in die Brust zu werfen weiß, der wird als Herr behandelt. Man muß Situationen zu beherrschen lernen.' ['Ah, one must play the part. A person who can throw his chest out is treated like a gentleman. One must learn to dominate situations.'] (60/49) The next diary entry shows Jakob demanding from Herr Benjamenta that he should put more effort into finding him a position. The director's brusque denial of responsibility triggers a storm of protest in Jakob, who retreats to his little cell, where he immerses himself in the Institute's textbook and revels in the fantasy that the Institute is 'das Vorzimmer zu den Wohnräumen und Prunksälen des ausgedehnten Lebens' ['the antechamber to the drawing rooms and palatial halls of life at large'] (64–5/53). Then, suddenly, he finds his brother in a dense crowd, who, at a café, praises Jakob's humility and 'zero' existence (66/54). Only a little later, his brother encourages him to accumulate money, which, in turn, evokes Jakob's daydreams about a 'selbsterrungene Lebenslaufbahn' ['an independent life'] and 'Selbsterziehungspläne' ['plans for self-education'] (69/55). It is unclear whether he taps into his brother's affirmation of humility or his materialism. The entire scene describes the perpetual process of territorialization and deterritorialization in a cascade of contradicting statements about the individual in relation to modern society and materialism. Jakob vacillates between ascetic self-sufficiency and money as the 'vollkommen idealen Wert' ['completely ideal value']: '[i]ch möchte reich sein und den Kopf zerschmettert haben' ['I would like to be rich and smash my head in'] (74/61). Claudia Liebrand has coined the phrase 'subversion through mimicry' to capture the effects of Jakob's rhetoric of self-contradiction.[26]

Jakob seems to be suspended between the 'Zögling' Kraus, the epitome of the servant and an old order, and his brother, the epitome of the parvenu and the modern world. These two figures stand allegorically for his position between a paternal law or coherent symbolical code to decipher the world and its perpetual dissolution. What makes *Jakob von Gunten* such a unique example of the modern picaresque is the fact that this paternal law cannot easily be attributed to anyone

---

25 Engel, 'Aussenwelt und Innenwelt', 536.
26 Liebrand, 'Jakob von Guntens Maskeraden', 346.

or anything, it is always occupied by shifting signifiers. The constant changes between authority and powerlessness, aloofness and submissiveness, distance and affinity ultimately lead to an excessive semiosis, tantamount to the nullification of meaning. Jakob, the 'zero' character, stages himself as someone who eludes the territorializing effects of meritocracy and capitalism by laying bare their inherent mechanisms in what I call a family diary. The picaresque format makes it impossible to determine whether this disclosure is part of the diegetic *Tiefstapelei* or part of its extradiegetic meta-reflection, or self-parody. We may agree with Hans Hiebel, who characterizes the novel as a 'transcendental buffoonery', yet his conclusion that it therefore amounts to a 'play with nothing, designed to destroy meaning', is flawed.[27] Jakob's hilarious diary exposes psycho-economic mechanisms without reflecting them, steering clear of the discursive fallacies and temptations of meaning. The novel does not 'destroy' meaning; rather, to apply some of its metaphors, the narrator plays and dances with meaning. And he does so, as Benjamin remarks, 'for wholly Epicurean reasons'; Jakob and many Walser protagonists want to 'enjoy themselves, and in this respect they display a quite exceptional ingenuity. Furthermore, they also display a quite exceptional nobility. And a quite exceptional legitimacy. For no one enjoys like a convalescent.'[28]

Conclusion

At the beginning of his family diary, Jakob declares that he has nothing to expect from the future: 'Eines weiß ich bestimmt: ich werde eine reizende, kugelrunde Null im späteren Leben sein.' ['But one thing I do know for certain: in later life I shall be a charming, utterly spherical zero.'] (8/6) In the last entry of the diary he returns to this motif: 'Und wenn ich zerschelle und verderbe, was bricht und verdirbt dann? Eine Null. Ich einzelner Mensch bin nur eine Null.' ['And if I am smashed to pieces and go to ruin, what is being smashed and ruined? A zero. The individual me is only a zero.'] (164/136) The initial 'zero' is directed towards the future; it is mentioned in a series of predictions none of which is likely to come true, culminating in the tongue-in-cheek complaint: 'Seit ich hier im Institut Benjamenta bin, habe ich es bereits fertiggebracht, mir zum Rätsel zu werden.' ['Since I have been at the Benjamenta Institute I have already contrived to become a mystery to myself.'] (7/5) The itinerary of the novel is a circular movement, demarcated by the framing zero, which moves from self-doubt ('Rätsel') to

---

27 Hiebel, 'Zerstörung der Signifikanz', 253. See also Geulen, 'Autorität und Kontingenz', 817–18.

28 Benjamin, 'Robert Walser', 351–2/259 ('Denn niemand genießt wie der Genesende'.)

self-annihilation, and ultimately the symbolical self-birth that reinstates the original existential mystery.

Peter Utz suggests that the zero metaphor is the central *gestalt* governing the text, a 'periphery around an unwritten center'.[29] This 'Nullstelle' is both the metaphorical place of narcissistic self-invention and the psycho-economic body of Jakob, the discursive self he cannot dominate through his narrative. Towards the end of the novel, the protagonist turns from a fixation on the 'inner chambers'—the epitome of the zero metaphor—to the desert which is imagined as a pure existence, 'belebt von einer kühlen, ich möchte sagen, großartigen Zufriedenheit'—'animated by a cool, I might say splendid, contentment'. (162/134) This feeling, however, is marked by a certain ambiguity—an ambiguity that permeates much of modern picaresque fiction. The final move into the desert, comparable to Karl Roßmann's journey into the dustbowl of Oklahoma through a mountainscape, can be interpreted either as the reflection of a delusory idea of freedom or as a liberation from solipsism that facilitates a new sense of community. Jakob counters the annihilation posited against him by accepting, even affirming it. As will emerge from the ensuing discussion, most of the modern German pícaros dramatize this ambiguity, yet choose not to decide between delusion and potential liberation.

The way Jakob stages the death of the (figurative) mother and elicits the final confession from the father figure (Herr Benjamenta admits that he has actually never presided over the Institute) allows him to take, as the humble servant he purports to be, the adopted father's position and thereby engender his own origin—a literary act of self-fashioning that reflects Nietzsche's notion of the aesthetic man. All this turns Walser's novel into a surprisingly typical example of picaresque fiction, including the components Pleister was missing: Jakob pursues his 'low descent'; he drives his (pseudo)autobiography to the point of perpetual 'change' (for example, in the final desert scene); he 'proactively' self-fashions (and debunks) himself as a *Tiefstapler*, satirically exposing 'social deficiencies' around him (embodied, for example, by his brother and the metropolis).[30] Two important aspects of the novel, however, work against its reception as a picaresque novel in the eye of the reader. First, *Jakob von Gunten* does not feature the antagonism between a picaresque hero and a world that wants to be deceived. And second, he does not follow the typical episodic journey through diverse strata of society under the guidance of various masters. Jakob's master–servant dialectics is tied in with his family trouble. It is part of his attempt to constitute himself as an autonomous individual outside

---

29   Utz, 'Walsers *Jakob von Gunten*', 494.
30   Pleister, 'Utopie oder Resignation?', 99.

the patriarchal laws of his family and the Institute. The narrative totalization of this fictitious autonomy in Walser's *Jakob von Gunten* I would like to call, with Utz, the narcissistic 'Nullstelle' of modern picaresque fiction in German—'Nullstelle' as a double entendre connoting both an empty template and a kind of 'square one'. It operates as a hidden point of reference and default position that is always present when the modern pícaro travels, yet not necessarily manifest in his narrative.[31]

While Kafka's default position of the modern picaresque is the repetitive circulation of the modern individual around the absence of a home (and its intertwining with guilt), Walser's default position is the delusory presence of a home in a dreamscape that totalizes the world in a narcissistic autobiography—in the kind of dreamscape that, according to Nietzsche, haunts everybody: '—ich bin plötzlich mitten in diesem Traume erwacht, aber nur zum Bewusstsein, dass ich eben träume und dass ich weiterträumen *muss*, um nicht zu Grunde zu gehen: wie der Nachtwandler weiterträumen *muss*, um nicht hinabzustürzen'. ['I suddenly awoke in the middle of this dream, but only to the consciousness that I am dreaming and that I must go on dreaming lest I perish—as the sleepwalker has to go on dreaming in order to avoid falling down.'][32] The sleepwalker metaphor offers the best connection between these two default positions, encompassing both the profoundly disturbing and the hilariously playful aspects of the picaresque figure. The distinction between dream and nightmare becomes obsolete for a novelistic form whose foundation, manifest or not, is the circular structure of guilt and the self-reduplication of the narcissistic self.

---

31 The term 'Nullstelle' is used by Peter Utz in order to elucidate his idea that Walser systematically undermines any hermeneutical attempt to decipher linguistic codes, see 'Walsers *Jakob von Gunten*', 488.

32 Nietzsche, *Die fröhliche Wissenschaft*, 417; *Gay Science*, 63 (§54).

Picaresque Topoi I
Tertium Datur: Between Autonomy and Self-Preservation

In his lecture 'Des Espaces Autres' ('Of Other Spaces'), Michel Foucault, never shy of sweeping yet hauntingly accurate generalizations, proclaimed the twentieth century to be 'the epoch of space': 'We are in the epoch of simultaneity: we are in the epoch of juxtaposition, the epoch of the near and far, of the side-by-side, of the dispersed. We are at a moment, I believe, when our experience of the world is less that of a long life developing through time than that of a network that connects points and intersects with its own skein.'[1] The acceleration of mobility as well as the explosion of knowledge in modern meritocracies makes space, according to him, the key category in organizing social inter-action and individual development. While he regards time as being entirely dissociated from its religious roots in salvation history through the developments of the nineteenth century (a highly contestable theory, given early twentieth century progressivism and messianic strains in certain veins of Marxist politics and capitalist technocracy), he diagnoses a dual drift in modern conceptualizations of space.

On the one hand, lives are still being governed by binary oppositions that Foucault regards as rooted in notions of the sacred, 'oppositions [...] between private space and public space, between family space and social space, between cultural space and useful space, between the space of leisure and that of work. All these are still nurtured by the hidden presence of the sacred.' On the other hand, he stresses that modernity is also marked by the high productivity of alter-native spaces, namely utopias (imaginary spaces without territorial roots) and what he terms 'heterotopias'—both of which he defines as spaces 'which are linked with all other [social spaces], which however

---

1   Foucault, 'Of Other Spaces', 22.

contradict all the other sites'.[2] He shows that heterotopias of *crisis* are constituents of any society (sites of birth, initiation, death), but marginalized in technocratic meritocracies, which are increasingly marked by heterotopias of *deviation* (hospital, asylum, prison, retirement home). There are, however, also heterotopias that are neither particularly ancient nor modern, the garden, for example, or the theatre, both delimiting a site that combines several spatial frames that would otherwise be incompatible, for example vegetation zones in a garden or social strata on the theatre stage. Both Karl Roßmann and Jakob von Gunten combine elements of acting out these incompatibilities on the stages of Amerika and the Institut Benjamenta respectively, which can be related to Foucault's heterotopias of deviation. Both the Institute and the Theater of Oklahama are marked by a coalescence of utopian liberating energies and the oppressive forces of surveillance or self-monitoring associated with a prison or an asylum (or a reservation for ethnic minorities). Both aspects—the emancipating and the restricting one—form a spatial correlative for the social agency of the modern pícaro in general.

Heterotopias are both related to many social subsystems and, most importantly, tend to regenerate the power structures organizing those subsystems. They do, however, not reduplicate the exact same structures and can potentially mobilize subversive energies or help facilitate change. This is what Foucault means by calling heterotopias sites 'which are linked with all other [social spaces], which however contradict all the other sites'. The Theater of Oklahama (judging from the little we learn about it) and the Institut Benjamenta are certainly microcosms that reflect and even resemble their broader social contexts and their psycho-economic power relations (as far as we can tell, being limited to the inside perspectives of the *personale* narrator or a narcissistic first-person narrator, respectively). They do, however, also 'contradict all the other sites', that is to say, they offer an imaginary, maybe even utopian, potential that differs from, for instance, the business of Karl's uncle or the art circles that lionize Jakob's brother.

Other typical modern heterotopias are related to archives, museums and libraries, or, particularly pertinent for the next novel under scrutiny here, 'the mode of the festival'.[3] Sites such as gambling halls, circuses and brothels, designed to create distractions and delusions, are favourite spots for the pícaro to engage with society. Felix Krull's itinerary from the demimonde of Paris, culminating in Andromache's circus stunts, to the natural history museum of Professor Kuckuck in Lisbon reflects Foucault's doubly utopian nature of the heterotopian

---

2   Ibid., 23; 24.
3   Ibid., 26.

space, namely the connection with the physiological exuberance of life, on the one hand, and the delusion of mastery through form, on the other. Both celebrating art in Paris (the high-wire artistry of Andromache) and charting evolutionary history in Lisbon (the scientific system of Professor Kuckuck) are rendered as attempts to master life through form. Individual life is being dissolved in the continuum of human identities (the Paris demimonde) or the evolution of life in general (the chain of being in Professor Kuckuck's natural philosophy).

New York, Frankfurt, Paris, Lisbon, Tel Aviv, Berlin and Danzig (Gdańsk): the narrators discussed in this study lure us into heterotopias that are often embedded in the modern city—museums and libraries, theatres and brothels, prisons and *Dienerschulen*. As outcasts, outlaws and pariahs of these newly emerged centres of social differentiation, the modern pícaros tend to travel the fault-line between individuation and reification. An accelerated exchange of goods and increased mobility do not necessarily (only) provide a higher degree of individual refinement, but they also create new dependencies, namely on money and its power of convertibility between highly disparate units. The simultaneous hypertrophy, scarcity and ephemeral character of interaction in the modern city requires and shapes characters who arc capable of transmitting an effective picture of their own character and position in as short a time as possible. The pícaros of this study often learn how to cultivate the appearance of 'individuality' in some of these heterotopian spaces.

I would like to explore some of the epistemological underpinnings of this picaresque chronotope, a term I use in Mikhail Bakhtin's sense that human perception is marked by 'the intrinsic connectedness of temporal and spatial relationships' and that various literary genres develop different ways of dramatizing this epistemological inseparability of space and time.[4] As the discussion of Kafka has shown, the picaresque connects these two elements predominantly through acceleration and circulation, categories which are given prominence in most investigations of modernity. Charles Baudelaire's influential definition, for example,—'By "modernity" I mean the ephemeral, the fugitive, the contingent, the half of art whose other half is the eternal and the immutable.'[5]—provides a number of useful keywords. Modernity here is defined by its compulsive dissociation from tradition through innovation. Baudelaire confronts us with the predicament of a culture that emphatically stresses transitoriness and seeks its centre of

---

4   Bakhtin, *The Dialogic Imagination*, 84.
5   Baudelaire, 'The Painter of Modern Life', 13 (*Œuvres complètes* II, 695: 'La modernité, c'est le transitoire, le fugitif, le contingent, la moitié de l'art, dont l'autre moitié est l'eternel et l'immuable.')

gravity by projecting itself into the future. In this dynamic, Baudelaire regards the artist as a detached observer who can make transparent the eternal recurrence of life through the perpetual metamorphosis of art, ultimately by re-enacting 'the immense transformation of matter and energy that modern science and technology [...] have brought about'.[6] He historicizes beauty as transient and ephemeral, while the moment of epiphany takes on essentialist qualities and is envisaged as the mode of eternal transformation.[7] The paradigmatic character of Baudelaire's ideas lies in his radical notion of the present as dissociated from the past. Modernity is, as Jürgen Habermas explains with reference to Baudelaire, defined by a classicism of the new (*modernus*), which orients itself towards a projected contingent future and glorifies the present.[8]

Walter Benjamin, in his reading of Baudelaire's literary rendition of the modern metropolis, characterizes urban perception of time as a series of continuous shocks and, more precisely, as 'the *tertium* in which experience and automatic reflex converge'.[9] Benjamin here presents a reading of *choque* that conceptualizes the human as someone who both *resists* and *is shaped* by 'the ephemeral, the fugitive, the contingent'. The *choque* reaction highlights the degree to which the modern city dweller is conditioned by automatic reflexes; but it is also highlighted as a force that activates experience, rooted in individual memory. In other words, *choque* triggers a conflicting reaction between alienation and identity affirmation, it dramatizes the individual as both reactive and active—overwhelmed by contingency and, at the same time, capable of accessing and resorting to the resource of individual experience.[10]

Benjamin's concept of a *tertium datur* as a given third category between 'automatic reflex' and 'experience', between alienation and identity, locates the origin of the sensual patterns through which we perceive our social (urban) reality outside the logic of cause and effect. We can never be quite sure whether our reactions to our quickly changing environments are conditioned responses or rooted in experience and individual memory.

The convergence between 'automatic reflex' and 'experience' situates the modern individual's sense of time within concrete moments of

---

6   Berman, *All That Is Solid Melts Into Air*, 145.

7   See, for example, 'La Fontaine de Sang', *Les Fleurs du mal*, in: *Œuvres complètes* I, 115.

8   Cf. Habermas, *Moderne*, 33–8.

9   Benjamin, handwritten notes on his Baudelaire essay (Benjamin-Archiv, Ms 7), *Gesammelte Schriften* I.3, 1172 ('der Chock als das *tertium*, in dem das Erlebnis und der Automatismus zusammenkommen'), trans. B. M.

10 Cf. Benjamin, *Charles Baudelaire*, 608.

experience in concrete spaces.[11] The coalescence of identity and alien-ation in these moments of *choque* are dramatized frequently in the modern picaresque. Even Karl Roßmann, who is a newcomer to New York and only watches the metropolis from the safety of Herr Pollunder's car, has contradictory reactions to urban masses: exposed to the massive 'unverhüllte Furcht vor Verspätung' ['open fear of arriving late'] of frantic theatre goers, he nevertheless feels drawn to the 'Masse, deren Gesang einheitlicher war, als der einer einzigen Menschenstimme' ['their massed voices more in unison than a single human voice'].[12] Most modern pícaros, including Karl on his subse-quent journey through America, do not perceive the city from inside a car; they experience it viscerally as simultaneity of alienation and familiarity. Felix Krull, for example, is the epitome of the picaresque character who presents every *choque* as the miraculous product of his own will, patching over the rift between identity and alienation which Benjamin describes as inherent in the *choque*.

The modern pícaro does not follow a dialectical pattern, but rather exemplifies a mediating principle between various social spheres. The picaresque narrative eludes the notion of progress in an emphatic sense and performs mobility rather than development. Felix Krull, for example, travels throughout Europe but he never experiences Goethe's ideal of *Bildung*, which characterizes so many of Mann's other literary characters (albeit always with an ironic twist). The pícaro shows that the gallery of modern life consists of frames without pictures. He becomes an expert in cultural practices precisely by ignoring their original context and social genealogy. By sticking to the rules that various social circles impose on individuals, and, at the same time, by infringing on the boundaries between these social sub-systems, he diverts social and material resources for himself. Felix is a master of adjusting himself, through imitation or mimicry ('Nachahmung'), to whatever a continuously changing environment demands from him. At the same time, he lays claim to absolute creativity by virtue of his imagination ('Phantasie').[13] As a picaresque narrator, he thus yokes together heteronomy and autonomy. He mimics others and, by the same token, uses his narrative to imagine himself as self-engendered.

By appropriating the two predominant effects of modernity—individualism ('experience' in Benjamin's terms) and anonymity ('automatic reflexes')—in the double persona of self-assertive shape-shifter and silenced underdog, and by turning these components of modern human existence into an asset through social role-play, the

---

11   Cf. Mattenklott, 'Physiognomisches Denken', 146.
12   Kafka, *Der Verschollene*, 60; *The Man Who Disappeared*, 38.
13   Mann, *Felix Krull*, 194 and 32 (265 and 43).

modern pícaro seemingly embraces, but inadvertently undermines freedom as a condition of social evolution. Charles Taylor defines freedom as 'one of the central properties of the humans who consent to and thus constitute society, and it is inscribed in their condition as the artificers who build their own social world, as against being born into one that already has its own normal form.'[14] Modern pícaros such as Felix Krull lay claim to this agency of 'the artificers who build their own social world'. By eluding social ideologies and inhabiting heterotopias, they propel the evolution of new social worlds. At the same time, however, they also expose the rootedness of this creative potential in impression management. Individuality as a confidence trick with oneself is both self-empowerment and self-delusion, it both participates in an emphatic notion of freedom (such as Taylor's) and dissolves it in the exposure of its theatrical nature:

> Ich begann mit der Darstellung meines Befindens nicht erst vor Zuschauern, sondern bereits für mich allein, sobald der Entschluss, an diesem Tage *mir selbst und der Freiheit zu gehören*, ganz einfach durch den Gang der Minuten zur unabänderlichen Notwendigkeit geworden.

> I did not at first produce my symptoms for an audience, but for myself alone. On a certain day when *my need for freedom and the possession of my own soul* had become overpowering, my decision was made and became irrevocable through the simple passage of time.[15]

Felix sketches out the contradictory rootedness of individuality in freedom and an irrevocable decision ('Freiheit' and 'Notwendigkeit'); at the same time, he epitomizes the convergence of active (imagination) and reactive (mimicry) elements in a mode that Benjamin describes in terms of a *tertium datur* logic. As in Walser, freedom here is imagined as a performative act of self-aestheticization that gives the modern picaresque a specific gender inflection. The freedom of the self as a predominantly artistic effect is, as the following chapter will show, also a male phantasm of modernism. Given this, the absence of a female voice in this literary exploration of the modern condition may not be that unexpected after all. This absence does, however, mean that the heroes discussed in this study only zoom in on *a* modern condition rather than *the* modern condition.

---

14 Taylor, *Social Imaginaries*, 80.
15 Mann, *Felix Krull*, 29/40 (emphasis added).

This contradictory rootedness of the modern (male) individual is also reflected in the notion of money as the defining metaphor of social exchange, a topic that formed a prominent subtext in our discussion of Walser. Pícaros as diverse as Karl Roßmann and Felix Krull travel along avenues of monetary circulation, living on and scrounging off this abstract agent of transmission and convertibility, and, in the process, they adopt some of its traits, at least on a metaphorical level (and even Jakob von Gunten in his servant persona nourishes veritable fantasies of monetary omnipotence). Simmel's analysis of modernity as an ongoing process that is marked by the absolute character of flexibility finds its central metaphor in the protean adaptability of money as the principle of circulation. Money, as analysed in his various writings on the matter, binds together a reality ever more prone to the dissociation between an ideal potential and various arbitrary appearances.[16] The money economy is, according to Simmel, the perfect example of a culture that—as an objectified form of creativity—has turned against culture.[17]

Through money the formal autonomy of objectified culture, embodied in production and exchange, can easily be mistaken as 'natural' rather than as a product of a social contract and cultural imaginaries. Simmel points out a paradox: what he terms the 'objec-tified' form of culture, antagonistic to human creativity, also potentially incites new creativity. Money, the agent of this objectification, facili-tates self-distancing, and thus self-enhancement and individuation. However, he stresses that this may come at a high price: 'If money thus becomes the common denominator for all values of life, if the question is no longer what they [people] are worth but how much they are worth, then their individuality is diminished.'[18]

The picaresque shape-shifter is an imaginative correlative for money as an abstract agency, as Simmel uses it: '[M]oney "represents pure interaction in its purest form; it makes comprehensible the most abstract concept; it is an individual thing whose essential significance is to reach beyond individualities". It is "the pure form of exchange-ability" in the developed economy.'[19] Money stands for everything and anything in modern capitalist societies, but is constantly in jeopardy of

---

16 Cf. Frisby, 'Theorie der Moderne', 27–31.

17 For a critique of Simmel's subject/object division and its rootedness in Kantianism, see Ötsch, 'Objekt, Subjekt und Wert', 274–6 and 288–91.

18 Simmel, 'On the Psychology of Money', 238; 'Zur Psychologie des Geldes', 57: 'wenn das Geld so zum Generalnenner aller möglichen Lebenswerte wird, wenn nicht mehr die Frage ist, was sie wert sind, sondern wieviel sie wert sind, so verringert sich ihre Individualität.' See also 'Großstädte und das Geistesleben', 121–2; 'Metropolis and Mental Life', 178–9.

19 Frisby, *Simmel*, 100, quoting Simmel's *Philosophy of Money* passim.

devaluation due to its volatile nature as a symbol for shifting market correlations.[20] It is marked by an increasing drift towards exchange value, as opposed to use value: money, according to Simmel, 'is more to us than simply a random piece of possession, since it obeys us without reserve; yet it is less to us than simply a random piece of possession, since it lacks any kind of content that could be appropriated merely by virtue of the form of a possession. We own it more intensely than anything else, and we have less of it than compared to anything else.'[21]

Ultimately, money, for Simmel, possesses the paradoxical tendency to both impede and foster individuality.[22] It both *is* and *symbolizes* Taylor's freedom, underpinning the emergence of modern society and the modern individual as a self-reflexive subject—the freedom to consent or dissent, and the freedom to create one's own social world. The discrepancy of *to be* and *to symbolize* operates as the guiding *Kippfigur* of the modern individual—between liberation and disenfranchisement. And that individual autonomy always comes with the awareness of its ultimate lack of foundation, an awareness which expresses itself through the drive for self-preservation that marks the modern pícaro. He constantly runs the risk of seeing all his pretensions, impostures and masquerades disintegrate. The values he adopts and mimics can easily turn into devalued papers on the stock market of social codes. He is, economically speaking, in the position of potential exchangeability before actual exchange.[23]

Like Hermes, the Olympian god of boundaries and those travellers who transgress them, the pícaro is a messenger figure. Unlike Hermes, however, he does not translate divine into human language, but rather manipulates the expert knowledge he gleans from one group of people for his dealings with another. His acts of translation are confidence tricks and as such both facilitate and hamper exchange, depending on the situation and his aims—a duality which the Olympian demigod Hermes, with whom the pícaro is often associated, also expresses in his dual patronage over cunning thieves and successful merchants. His Roman name Mercurius, after all, derives from *merx*, the Latin word for commerce or merchandise. The pícaro functions both as Hermes and parasite, as the mediator of messages and the eavesdropper who benefits from secret knowledge he gathers as a go-between, spy or conspirator.[24] By producing semiotic excess and interference in the way

---

20 Cf. Gray, *Money Matters*, 346–56.
21 Simmel, *Philosophie des Geldes*, 349.
22 Simmel, 'On the Psychology of Money', 242–3 ('Zur Psychologie des Geldes', 64).
23 Cf. Simmel, *Philosophie des Geldes*, 161.
24 Cf. Serres, *Parasite*, 32–3.

he conducts his confidence trickery, the pícaro also creates the condition for the possibility of systemic limitation and self-(re)generation, in other words, meaning—the by-product of his relentless drive for self-preservation.

The pícaro as a literary figure is not subversive by definition. He is subversive and conformist at the same time, both a victim and the most proficient exploiter of his victimhood. Modern picaresque fiction does not only reveal the bigotry, sycophancy and mendaciousness of society in the form of a modern social satire, it also exemplifies the genealogy of the modern individual and its economic, social, psychological and epistemological ramifications. Both Kafka's Karl Roßmann and Walser's Jakob von Gunten are good examples of this dual structure, and Mann's Felix Krull, to whom we will now turn, adds even more rhetorical finesse to it. Walser and Mann, in particular, show that the modern pícaro, in rendering himself autobiographical, reaches beyond the binary opposition of individual versus society and, in the process, demonstrates the rootedness of humans in a *tertium datur* which they then can claim as the territory of 'freedom'. The pícaro stages himself in performative acts, laying claim to an autonomy he does not possess, yet the way he communicates these performative acts extradiegetically undermines the diegetic coherence of that claim. By fathering and faking identities, the pícaro both asserts and exposes, both is and symbolizes, the predicament of the modern individual: autonomy and the simultaneous awareness that this autonomy is based on an uncontrollable foundation, as Dieter Henrich elucidates: '[…] he who needs to preserve himself knows for a fact that he does not have the foundation of himself within himself […]'.[25] This drive for self-preservation (*Selbsterhaltung*) and the related awareness of the precarious nature of human autonomy constitute the vertebra of the modern picaresque.

---

25 Henrich, 'Grundstruktur der modernen Philosophie', 111.

4. The Confidence Man as Shape-Shifter: Thomas Mann's *Bekenntnisse des Hochstaplers Felix Krull*

Between Totality and Void: Narcissus

In the third book of *Metamorphoses*, Ovid narrates the story of the handsome young man Narcissus, son of the river-god Cephisus and the nymph Liriope, who is desired by many young men and women but resists all temptations. The rejected nymph Echo is consumed by her unrequited love for Narcissus and only survives in the form of her voice.[1] Narcissus, however, incapable of affection and empathy, falls in love with his own mirror image in the water instead and, dying, turns into a narcissus flower.[2] The rich history of Western adaptations of this mythological motif revolves around the issues of self-affection and self-delusion.[3] As the discussion of Walser's *Jakob von Gunten* has demonstrated, the modern successor of the polymorphous shape-shifter of the trickster myth and the dextrous petty criminal of the Spanish Golden Age taps into the Narcissus myth—be it as an iconographic reference, an anthropological subtext, or a meta-narrative metaphor.

The very notion of perpetual self-transformation, which lies at the heart of the picaresque stratagem, is essentially narcissistic. The ludic or ascetic exercises of self-voidance in Walser and Kafka are forms of narcissistic self-fashioning: the incessant repetition of self-denigration ultimately annihilates any form of essence. Ovid exclaims: 'credule, quid frustra simulacra fugacia captas? / quod petis, est nusquam; quod amas, avertere, perdes!' ['O fondly foolish boy, why vainly seek to clasp a fleeting image? What you seek is nowhere; but turn yourself

---

1   Ovid, *Metamorphoses* III, 339–510.
2   Ibid., 425–33.
3   Cf. Orlowsky, *Narziß und Narzißmus*, 57–65.

away, and the object of your love will be no more.']⁴ This reflection on the fragility and the derivative nature of the human self and its fundamental structure of self-affection is part of how the modern pícaro narrates himself—how he projects an identity that he does not possess.

Thomas Mann's *Bekenntnisse des Hochstaplers Felix Krull* (*Confessions of Felix Krull, Confidence Man*, 1913/54), whose second (yet still fragmentary) version was published exactly 400 years after *Lazarillo de Tormes*, taps into Walser's combination of the narcissistic with the picaresque narrative, but his protagonist approaches life from the opposite angle: as a *Hochstapler* rather than a *Tiefstapler*. Felix is engaged in a narcissistic self-apotheosis and constantly prone to turning into a mere hollow man; his metamorphoses are 'a divine comedy about man's universal dream of being "reborn"'.⁵ And it is this element which makes him—witness and victim of the economic boom and bust period of late Wilhelmine Germany, which drives his father into bankruptcy and suicide—a *homo ludens*, an experimenter with the opportunities and risks of these changes. Even the fact that he ends up in prison and conceives of his 'confessions' behind bars is not rendered as an endpoint, but rather as a transition —yet another stage in a series of metamorphoses.⁶ (Mann envisaged Felix, in fact, jotting down his memoirs while enjoying his retirement in London, but he never finished that part.)⁷

This chapter explores how *Felix Krull* translates experience into a precarious balance between playful self-invention and narcissism and thereby dramatizes the primordial dichotomy of the modern picaresque between autonomy and self-preservation. By interrelating the subtexts of narcissism and an aesthetics of play in Mann's novel, and by contextualizing both within the picaresque framework, I shall illuminate some of the fundamental features of the modern pícaro as shape-shifter.

Totalized Desire: Felix the *Glückskind*

Felix rises by the virtue of his charm, chutzpah and relentless self-fashioning through established circles of the European aristocracy in the Belle Époque, opening doors for himself by mimicking languages,

---

4   Ovid, *Metamorphoses* III, 432–3.

5   Lubich, '*Felix Krull*', 211.

6   Felix' confessions blur the theological boundary between creed (*confessio fidei*) and confession (*confessio peccati*). His *confessio fidei* is, of course, an inversion of the trust in God: Felix trusts in the world's desire to be deceived.

7   Cf. Wysling, *Dokumente und Untersuchungen*, 149; Schonfield, *Art and Its Uses*, 176, note 5.

customs and social decorum, by adopting other people's identities and by cultivating what he calls an erotic attitude towards the world. Both a fairy-tale *Glückskind* and a criminal confidence man, he sets out to defend his vision of the world as the best of all possible worlds. He vacillates between the simulation of various roles and self-deception. His simulation of illness, for example, when he wants to skip school or avoid being drafted, is a kind of self-deception: by simulating illness, he performs, yet never lives, the experience of identity (which would imply accepting human suffering and mortality). In his 'confessions', Felix disguises his profound discomfort with mortality behind the mask of androgynous perfection.

Felix sings the praise of 'deceit' (*Betrug*) at the beginning of the novel in what sounds like the creed of all confidence men:[8]

> Nur der Betrug hat Aussicht auf Erfolg und lebensvolle Wirklichkeit, der den Namen des Betrugs nicht durchaus verdient, sondern nichts ist als die Ausstattung einer lebendigen, aber nicht völlig ins Reich des Wirklichen eingetretenen Wahrheit mit denjenigen materiellen Merkmalen, deren sie bedarf, um von der Welt erkannt und gewürdigt zu werden. (29)

> Only one kind of lie has a chance of being effective: that which in no way deserves to be called deceit, but is the product of a lively imagination which has not yet entered wholly into the realm of the actual and acquired those tangible signs by which alone it can be appraised at its proper worth. (39)

Felix here suggests a social conduct which can best be described as mimicry. He sees himself as somebody who furnishes ('Ausstattung') the eidetic realm of *potentiality* ('Wahrheit'), which the English translation rather insufficiently renders as 'imagination', with certain 'tangible signs' of *actuality* ('materielle Merkmale'). He fashions himself as a Prospero of the realm of essence. In order to maintain this role-play, however, he is reliant on those 'tangible signs' he has to borrow from the world in his endeavour to secure acknowledgement by this very world. These features are the product of his mimicry and bear the signature of an experience that has never been 'wholly' rooted in 'the realm of the actual'.

---

8   For detailed information about the most important *Hochstapler* of his time, Georges Manolescu, and the influence of his memoirs *Ein Fürst der Diebe* on Thomas Mann see Wysling, *Narzissmus*, 153–70. On Mann's reception of the *Hochstapler* craze in the early twentieth century see Sprecher, 'Das grobe Muster' and Porombka, *Felix Krulls Erben*.

Felix claims to nourish 'alle Möglichkeiten der Welt in mir'—to be universally disposed in his 'endowments and possessed of every possible potentiality' (115/157). Reality for him consists of mutually exchangeable elements sprung from his narcissistic imagination. I would like to caution against the widespread assertion in criticism that the textual play with human imagination is solely based 'on the presupposition that [Felix'] self is fully developed'.[9] Instead, I suggest that Felix is also a Narcissus figure who couches his shortcomings in the language of past fulfilment and universal gratification. This turns him into a symptom of the 'complexity crisis' of modern consciousness and challenges readings that reduce Felix to a symbol of mature creativity.[10] The beginning sets the key for the entire novel:

> Allein, da alles, was ich mitzuteilen habe, sich aus meinen eigensten und unmittelbarsten Erfahrungen, Irrtümern und Leidenschaften zusammensetzt, und ich also meinen Stoff vollkommen beherrsche, so könnte jeder Zweifel höchstens den mir zu Gebote stehenden Takt und Anstand des Ausdrucks betreffen, und in diesen Dingen geben regelmäßige und wohlbeendete Studien nach meiner Meinung weit weniger den Ausschlag, als natürliche Begabung und eine gute Kinderstube. (5)

> But since everything I have to record derives from my own immediate experience, errors, and passions, and since I am therefore in complete command of my material, the doubt can apply only to my tact and propriety of expression, and in my view these are less the product of study than of natural talent and a good home environment. (7)

These introductory sentences are an exposition of Felix' obsession with simulation. His direct exposure to the world and 'immediate experience' consists of social mimicry and does not seem to result from a direct engagement with reality. Unashamedly declaring the smattering of knowledge he resorts to as a sign of 'natural talent', Felix entangles the reader in the kind of confidence game he plays with most of his fellow humans. As a narrated persona, he presents himself as the archetypal fairy tale *Glückskind*, endowed with effortless talent and *at one with* the world; as a narrator persona, often palpable through the ironic tone of the slight exaggerations and the stylistic polish, Felix, however, presents himself as somebody *on top of* the world. Much of the joy of reading this novel derives from the fact that the narrator manages

---

9   Renner, *Lebens-Werk*, 381; cf. also Beddow, *'Felix Krull'*, 243.
10 Sloterdijk, *Kritik der zynischen Vernunft* II, 851.

to speak to various expectations of his audience and readership at the same time. We admire Felix' naivety of paneroticism, we admire his shrewdness in deceiving others, and we admire his willingness to allow us a peek behind the scenes of his narrative construction; in short: we revel in the way Felix is crafting his implied reader.

Felix writes 'confessions' rather than '*the* confessions' of Felix Krull, and thus displays a certain degree of arbitrariness: I am providing, he seems to imply, the reader with *one* random version or selection of my confessions and I could not care less about a full account that shows remorse and asks for atonement. He claims to be 'in complete command' of his subject matter, his own life, and to comprehend it in its entirety and intuitively.[11] While Karl cuts a poor figure against the theatrical backdrop of Kafka's America, Felix embraces the theatrical gesture and freely manoeuvres in front of and behind the scenes, actively appropriating the roles offered to him. Yet, behind that performative brilliance, there is always that which the Theater of Oklahoma exhibits openly (and possibly transcends in a utopian space): the shabbiness and ramshackle nature of the social play with appearances. When his father introduces him, for example, to the hugely popular actor Müller-Rosé, who is in the process of taking off his make-up behind the scenes after a performance, Felix famously experiences a shock of recognition:

An einem schmutzigen Tisch und vor einem staubigen und beklecksten Spiegel saß Müller-Rosé, nichts weiter am Leibe als eine Unterhose aus grauem Trikot. [...] Die eine Hälfte des Gesichts war noch bedeckt mit jener rosa Schicht, die sein Antlitz vorhin so wächsern idealisch hatte erscheinen lassen, jetzt aber lächerlich rotgelb gegen die käsige Fahlheit der anderen, schon entfärbten Gesichtshälfte abstach. [...] Unsere Fähigkeit zum Ekel ist, wie ich anmerken möchte, desto größer, je lebhafter unsere Begierde ist, das heißt: je inbrünstiger wir eigentlich der Welt und ihren Darbietungen anhangen. (24–5)

Müller-Rosé was seated at a grubby dressing-table in front of a dusty, speckled mirror. He had nothing on but a pair of grey cotton drawers [...]. Half of his countenance still had the rosy coating that had made him radiant on the stage but now looked merely pink and silly in contrast to the cheese-like pallor of his natural complexion [...]. Our capacity for disgust, let me observe, is in proportion to our desires; that is, in proportion to the intensity of our attachments to the things of this world. (34)

---

11   Cf. Renner, *Lebens-Werk*, 405.

Müller-Rosé is a model of socially sanctioned confidence trickery and embodies the picaresque leitmotif of *mundus vult decipi—ergo decipiatur* (the world wants to be deceived—and so it is deceived), which Mann associated with the novel.[12] Felix' feeling of disgust and revulsion makes him focus even more on simulation and artistry as a form of coping with life, to which he is tied by 'desire', or rather 'concupiscence' ('Begierde'). He wants to turn art into absolute nature and nature into absolute art by monopolizing the principles of play and simulation. Recognizing the central mechanisms of human life and society, death and its masquerade, Felix turns into the *Glückskind* without a past, who treads the line between 'Scheinglück und Glücksschein', between deceptive happiness and the appearance of happiness.[13] The artist-charlatan as passive *Glückskind* is combined with the figure of Hermes as the ultimate mythic mediator, the epitome of active agency. In the face of the acceleration of experience in the modern world, Felix focuses on experiencing potentiality in the heterotopias of the varieté in Paris and the museum in Lisbon rather than exposing himself to the topography of modern metropolitan experience.[14] By exerting the demiurgic powers of human creativity in his narrative self-invention, he attempts to encapsulate the totality of human experience. This artistic *Hochstapelei* is mirrored in one of the most important subtexts of the novel, Schopenhauer's philosophy—a subtext that allows us to connect the aspects of desire and play.

Representing the Will: Felix the Hermes Messenger

Felix Krull was originally planned as a novel about Arthur Schopenhauer's Maya motif. The Sanskrit term Maya, denoting deception, illusion, sorcery, was used by Schopenhauer to express his idea that humans are, with regard to their perception of reality, restricted to the realm of representation/idea (*Vorstellung*) as opposed to the inconceivable trans-individual will (*Wille*).[15] In many of Mann's earlier novellas and novels, death and sleep offer a way to break through that Maya veil, dissolving the *principium individuationis* through a unification with the 'will' and life at large.[16] Schopenhauer radically dissociates poetic from divine intuition, thus challenging the idealistic equation of poetic inspiration and the autonomous individual as subject. *Felix Krull* is in many

---

12 Cf. Wysling, *Narzissmus*, 417, Schonfield, *Art and Its Uses*, 84–9, and Sebastian, 'Pikareske Parodie', 138. On the Schopenhauerian background of this scene see Appel, *Naivität und Lebenskunst*, 88–9.

13 Wysling, *Narzissmus*, 10.

14 On related psychoanalytic implications of Narcissus see Rank, 'Narcissism and the Double'.

15 Cf. Schopenhauer, *Die Welt als Wille und Vorstellung* I, § 37.

16 Cf. ibid., § 18, § 70.

respects the product of this anti-idealistic impulse. The conscription scene (71–84/95–115), in which Felix fakes a fit in order to avoid being drafted, is the most iconic rendition of a precarious vacillation between creation and mimicry, self-invention and self-deceit, in Nietzsche's terms artist (*Künstler*) and acrobat (*Artist*).[17]

Felix as the fairy-tale *Glückskind* is related to the spheres of sleep and polymorphous eroticism, driven by a desire to embrace the world in a kind of mystical union. The power of his imagination is related to the power of his erotic engagement and creates an excess of social contact without affiliation or, in Freud's terms, object love.[18] Felix does not engage in real relationships and only entertains fleeting liaisons. In 'On Narcissism: An Introduction' Freud relates this inability to establish libidinal object bonds to narcissism.[19] He distinguishes between a primary phase, in which love of the self and love of anything outside the self are differentiated, and a secondary phase, in which object libido is turned into self-libido. It is the regressive development during this secondary phase that Freud describes as narcissism. In *Felix Krull*, this regressive element of self-affection is conflated with a panerotic embrace of the world. Felix presents his environment as an obliging servant who never ceases to tend to his narcissistic desires, and he is more than willing to return these favours. Felix' Prospero qualities, his omnipotent versatile faculty of imagination, is not—as Hans Wysling suggests—'the rescue of Narcissus'.[20] Imagination for Felix is rather a Greek gift. It is true that it allows him to free himself from the limitations of his environment and the illusion of the Maya veil of representation (which, according to Schopenhauer, governs human individuation). At the same time, however, imagination for Felix is always also a posing of the self that betrays its derivative nature.

The strengthening of the picaresque structure in the reworking of *Felix Krull* (1951–54), compared to the earlier version from 1910–13, shows that Mann, while celebrating the picaresque versatility of imagination, took a rather pessimistic view of artistic self-liberation towards the end of his life, stressing the symbiotic relationship between the artist as a confidence man and the consumers of art.[21] The manner in which he capitalizes on picaresque structural elements as a reaction to this crisis has been a blind spot in the extensive, yet fairly repetitive,

---

17   Cf. Nietzsche, *Die fröhliche Wissenschaft*, 595–7; *Gay Science*, 215–17 (§ 356).
18   Cf. Freud, 'Der Dichter und das Phantasieren'.
19   Freud, 'Narzißmus'.
20   Wysling, *Narzissmus*, 104.
21   See, for example, Mann's letter to Oskar Seidlin from 10 September 1951, *Briefe 1948–1955*, 223.

secondary literature on the novel.[22] Just as much as Felix enacts himself by transgressing Schopenhauer's boundary between representation and will, the picaresque context points back to the world of representation. *Mundus vult decipi, ergo decipiatur*—he is both victim and instigator of this game, suspended between two poles: he transcends the realm of representation through *imagination* while being embedded in this very realm through his confidence man *rhetoric*.

In the Hermes figure, who figures as a mediator between diverse realms of life in ancient mythology, Mann saw a way out of the deadlock into which Schopenhauer's concept of the irremediable circularity of history had lured him. The Hermes figure entertains an elective affinity with Eros and Aphrodite and features as a mythological figure of love, burglary and commerce. He is also the inventor of the lyre, associated with Apollo. Felix, too, combines these qualities in one persona. The quintessential Hermes figure in *Felix Krull* is Professor Kuckuck, who takes Felix on the classic trip to Hades (*katabasis*) and shows him the evolutionary metamorphosis of life, the Schopenhauerian Tartaros and Faust's realm of the Mothers.[23] His 'Allsympathie' acknowledges distinctions in the given actual world only in so far as they are an expression of potentiality; by the same token, however, he praises actuality and mortality as the precondition for pan-eroticism:

> Sein sei nicht Wohlsein; es sei Lust und Last, und alles raumzeitliche Sein, alle Materie habe teil [...] an dieser Lust, dieser Last, an der Empfindung, welche den Menschen, den Träger der wachsten Empfindung, zur Allsympathie lade. (216)

> Being was not Well-Being; it was joy and labour, and all Being in space-time, all matter, partook if only in deepest sleep in this joy and this labour, this perception that disposed Man, possessor of the most awakened consciousness, to universal sympathy. (295)

This inversion of essence and substance, potentiality and actuality, theory and experience creates a paradoxical configuration, which is reflected in the picaresque narrative double strategy: by presenting himself as exposed to a wide range of experiences and by simultaneously playing the self-observer who is capable of analysing the derivative character of these experiences, Felix addresses modern

---

22 A characteristic example is Renner, *Lebens-Werk*, 383, who argues that Mann dropped the picaresque in favour of the Maya template in order to foreground issues of artistic self-reflection.

23 On the alleged antihumanism and concepts of the post-human in *Felix Krull* and the Kuckuck figure see Cha, 'Karnevaleskes Tier-Werden'.

social expectations of credibility: one has to be *both* 'authentic' and sceptical to be credible.

As the narrated persona, Felix performs his self-authentication, his creation *ex nihilo*. As the narrating persona, he simultaneously contextualizes this very creation, the picaresque individual, as a performative construction—as a manifestation of Schopenhauer's concept of representation (which is precisely what he aims to conceal). By revealing the narrated picaresque persona as derivative, the picaresque narrator persona automatically adopts a gesture of authenticity through the authority of a meta-self. By taking on this insoluble paradox, Felix opens up an infinite regress. The paradox of his narcissism between self-debunking and self-fashioning finds its structural equivalent in the picaresque confession or *apologia*, which is by the same token its most poignant parody.[24]

Narcissism in *Felix Krull* is closely linked to androgyny.[25] One hermaphroditic epiphany occurs as early as in the Frankfurt episode, where Felix describes a 'Geschwisterpaar' ['a brother and sister'] in terms of his yearning for union (64–5/89). Likewise, Andromache, the high-wire circus performer (and a direct reference to, and critique of, Nietzsche's metaphorical depiction of the human as a rope dancer in *Zarathustra*), is described as an asexual, 'vom Menschlichen ausgeschlossener Leib' (151), a body 'untainted by humanity' (207), and embodies an ascetic ideal of sublimation.[26] In Professor Kuckuck's daughter Zouzou, Felix' infatuation with the 'Ungleich-Zwiefache' ['the double-but-dissimilar'] (224/305) takes on a passionate nature. Again, Zouzou is part of a double image (with her mother Senhora Maria Pia), and reminiscent of Persephone and her mother Artemis (Demeter) and the reunification of mother and daughter on the Eleusian Fields: 'Krull's encounter with Kuckuck is tantamount to an encounter with the father of the ancient Gods, his acceptance into Kuckuck's family is an acceptance into the Olympian family and almost leads to a new abduction of Persephone, but instead ends up in the surprising final holy wedding.'[27]

In their virginity and androgyny, or motherhood, as the case may be, Zouzou and Maria Pia are opposites; as a double image they

---

24 Many investigations of *Felix Krull* and its unreliable narrator fall short of the full implications of the topic since they ignore the picaresque narrative foundations of confession and *apologia*, most recently Kablitz, 'Der *unreliable narrator* und die Struktur der Fiktion'.

25 Freud also made a controversial connection between narcissism and homoeroticism, which forms a further subtext in Mann's novel. See Freud, 'Narzißmus', 54; 'On Narcissism', 44–5.

26 Cf. Nietzsche, *Zarathustra*, I, §§ 3–4.

27 Wysling, *Narzissmus*, 265.

complement each other and together form the mythical image of mother-virgin, the 'mythic womb and tomb of all life',[28] the pagan Great Mother, who gives birth to, loves and devours her son. Maria Pia's appearance in the final section of the book prevents the rape of Persephone. She unites the qualities of mother and daughter and is overdetermined by the imagery of eros and death. What is more, she is fascinated by the bullfighter Ribeiro, who is the male counterpart of Andromache in the way he exposes himself to death. After the bullfight, however, it is Felix and Maria Pia who are united in the raptures of erotic love in the very last scene of the fragmentary novel. As Maria Pia's mimetic desire, incited and mediated through the bullfighter Ribeiro, shows, love in *Felix Krull* is dissociated from Freud's libidinal object bond; it precedes this psycho-sexual developmental stage and testifies to the interrelation between all humans, represented by the mock pantheon and the mythic wedding under the auspices of the quintessential Hermes figure Professor Kuckuck. Gods and men are united in the realm of perpetual metamorphosis and love, in the interstitial realm of Hermes, the divine 'half-outsider'.

Playing Dear Purchase: Felix the *Urkind*

During the second phase of composing *Felix Krull* in the early 1950s, Mann was reading extensively on the so-called *Urkind* mythology in the writings of Karl Kerényi and Carl Gustav Jung. In the light of these investigations, the infantile Felix does not simply appear to be going through a passing psychological stage; his metaphorical naivety is rather the constitutive feature of his artistic nature. As the pre-individual *Urkind*, Felix follows Hermes' footsteps again, the god of thieves and tricksters and the champion of artists. Implicitly referring to Nietzsche's claim that life is only justified as an aesthetic project, Mann introduces the artist as a player.[29] 'In my memories there is no clear-cut boundary between a child's play and an artistic exercise',[30] he once noted and thereby set the tone for his literary elaboration on this affinity of play and art. Felix is a *homo ludens* on various levels sketched out above: in his mutual enactment of self-apotheosis and self-debunking; in the self-fashioning of his polymorphous sexuality and its embedding in narcissistic self-affection.

The notion of play in an aesthetic and literary context conjures the argument of Friedrich Schiller's aesthetic treatise *Über die Erziehung des Menschen* (*On the Aesthetic Education of Man*). These epistolary essays

---

28   Lubich, '*Felix Krull*', 207.

29   Nietzsche, *Geburt der Tragödie*, 47; *Birth of Tragedy*, 8.

30   Mann, *Nachträge*, 131 ('Zwischen Kinderspiel und Kunstübung ist in meiner Erinnerung kein Bruch, keine scharfe Grenze.'), trans. B.M.

are an investigation of the connection between sensual perception (*aisthesis*) and freedom, and form part of a political philosophy. The main goal is to overcome the dichotomy between the sensual and the spiritual nature of humans. Humans, according to Schiller, are subject to two drives, the 'sense drive' (*sinnlicher Trieb*), which works towards metamorphosis and sensual presence, and the 'formal drive' (*Formtrieb*), which brings out the demiurgic creative energy of humans and focuses on the human cognitive faculties. Schiller maintains that neither of these two drives should become predominant and they should ideally sublate one another. Their permanent mutual balance is an unattainable goal, but the temporary experience of being able to bring together these two drives in a 'vollständige Anschauung', a complete intuition of their human nature, results in a temporary third drive, the 'Spieltrieb':[31]

> In demselben Maße, als er den Empfindungen und Affekten ihren dynamischen Einfluss nimmt, wird er sie mit Ideen der Vernunft in Übereinstimmung bringen, und in demselben Maße, als er den Gesetzen der Vernunft ihre moralische Nötigung benimmt, wird er sie mit dem Interesse der Sinne versöhnen.

> To the extent that it deprives feelings and passions of their dynamic power, it will bring them into harmony with the idea of reason; and to the extent that it deprives the laws of reason of their moral compulsion, it will reconcile them with the interests of the senses.[32]

In the fifteenth letter Schiller analyses play as a precondition of being human: '[…] der Mensch spielt nur, wo er in voller Bedeutung des Worts Mensch ist, und *er ist nur da ganz Mensch, wo er spielt*' ['man only plays when he is in the fullest sense of the word a human being, and *he is only fully a human being when he plays*'].[33]

Play for Schiller means an aesthetic state, in which humans experience themselves as a symbolic self-representation in the form of an ideal. (The background of Schiller's claim is Kant's dualism of the human dependence on both natural and moral law.) This kind of aesthetic freedom between active production and passive perception is both a utopia and a concrete educational goal, which is to say that seeking it is a moral duty even though it is unattainable as a permanent

---

31 Schiller, *Ästhetische Erziehung*, 612; *Aesthetic Education*, 95–7.
32 Ibid., 613–14/99.
33 Ibid., 618/106.

state of being.[34] Schiller's *conditio sine qua non* for the emancipation of the individual, the education of a sense of beauty and self-knowledge, remain alien to Felix, yet he mimics them as a conventionalized petit bourgeois ideal, jargon and code of conduct. Schiller's notion of disinterested play even provides a disguise for Felix' narcissism; ironically referring to his simulation of sickness as his own 'creative task', he writes:

> Ich hatte die Natur verbessert, einen Traum verwirklicht,—und wer je aus dem Nichts, aus der bloßen inneren Kenntnis und Anschauung der Dinge, kurz: aus der Phantasie, unter kühner Einsetzung seiner Person eine zwingende, wirksame Wirklichkeit zu schaffen vermochte, der kennt die wundersame und träumerische Zufriedenheit, mit der ich damals von meiner Schöpfung ausruhte. (32)

> I had improved upon nature, realized a dream; and only he who has succeeded in creating a compelling and effective reality out of nothing, out of sheer inward knowledge and contemplation—in short, out of nothing more than imagination and the daring exploitation of his own body—he alone understands the strange and dream-like satisfaction with which I rested from my creative task. (43)

Felix never disappears 'in a third [condition]',[35] as Schiller envisages it for the human being who temporarily overcomes the dichotomy between the two drives of matter and form. He is rather enmeshed in the simulation of 'Spieltrieb'. It is true that he claims to give up anything 'zugunsten des freien Traumes und Spieles' ['in favour of free play and dreams'] (172/235), yet, in fact, he does not exercise this form of play. His use of play is a calculating one, his artistic illusion is about make-believe, not about the disengagement from belief.[36] Felix seems to assert with Schiller that humans have to become 'aesthetic', before they can grasp reason, yet does not embody the full implications of this development himself.[37] While Schiller places emphasis on the value of aesthetic semblance as play, Felix presents his confidence trickery as play, or, to put it differently: he sells confidence trickery as aesthetic semblance.[38] His appropriation of an idealistic concept

---

34 Ibid., 624/125.
35 Ibid., 625/125.
36 Cf. Sharpe, *Schiller*, 164–5.
37 Schiller, *Ästhetische Erziehung*, 641; *Aesthetic Education*, 161.
38 Cf. Schulz, *Identitätsfindung und Rollenspiel*, 402.

of play (and its integration into his confidence games) may lead to a 'dream-like satisfaction', but it also dramatizes (and critiques) Schiller's problematic containment of the excluded human body: in the case of the conscription scene, for example, this becomes evident in the sickness Felix simulates and its underlying psychosomatic anamnesis. As Toni Tholen has shown, Schiller's projected unity of the two drives of matter and form erases the traces of physical life, sublating them in the *gestalt* of the perfect and whole human being (whose epitome, for Schiller, is the goddess Juno). Schiller's aesthetic play, according to Tholen, works within the logic of inclusive exclusion—between the two drives of matter and form as well as 'on the border that separates the creature from the human [...] and, at the same time, connects the creature with the human in order to "ennoble" it'.[39] It is only in this aesthetic state of play as an inclusive exclusion of the body that humans are envisaged, in Schiller's philosophy, as being able to overcome the subject/object divide, the rift between 'sensation' (*Empfindung*) and 'object' (*Gegenstand*):

> Die Schönheit ist also zwar *Gegenstand* für uns, weil die Reflexion die Bedingung ist, unter der wir eine Empfindung von ihr haben; zugleich aber ist sie ein *Zustand unsers Subjekts*, weil das Gefühl die Bedingung ist, unter der wir eine Vorstellung von ihr haben. Sie ist also zwar Form, weil wir sie betrachten, zugleich aber ist sie Leben, weil wir sie fühlen. Mit einem Wort: sie ist zugleich unser Zustand und unsere Tat.

> Beauty, then, is indeed an *object* for us, because reflection is the condition of our having any sensation of it; but it is at the same time *a state of the perceiving subject*, because feeling is a condition of our having any perception of it. Thus beauty is indeed form, because we contemplate it; but it is at the same time life, because we feel it. In a word: it is at once a state of our being and an activity we perform.[40]

This dual movement of distancing oneself from and being involved in life is mirrored in the picaresque persona of Felix, who enacts his erotic relation to the world as a gift and simultaneously appropriates life as a product of his autonomous actions:

> O Szenen der empfänglichen Welt! Nie habt ihr euch empfäng-licheren Augen dargeboten. Der Himmel weiß, warum gerade

---

39   Tholen, 'Leben und Form', 185.
40   Schiller, *Ästhetische Erziehung*, 653–4; *Aesthetic Education*, 187.

eines der Sehnsucht erregenden Bilder, die ich damals aufnahm, sich mir so tief eingesenkt hat, so fest in meiner Erinnerung haftet, daß es mich, trotz seiner Unbedeutendheit, ja Nichtigkeit, noch heute mit Entzücken erfüllt. (63)

O scenes of the beautiful world! Never have you presented yourselves to more appreciative eyes. Heaven knows why one in particular among the nostalgic pictures I stored up at that time has sunk so deeply into me and clings so persistently in my memory that despite its unimportance, its insignificance indeed, it fills me with delight even today. (87–8)

'My Memory' provides the connection between form and life in Felix' self-fashioning as an *Urkind*, endowed with an intuitive connection to life and its inherent entelechy of forms. Through memory, he claims to be able to link 'sensation' and 'object'; images and their emotional halo still establish a connection with the world that informs his actions. Felix presents himself as participating in the *'erfüllte Unendlichkeit'* [*'infinity filled with content'*] that Schiller describes as play.[41] Contrary to what Felix celebrates and enacts in this passage, however, his engagement with the world is generally marked by oblivion rather than by memory. His picaresque role changes and their narrative rendition do not only provide him with 'delightful refreshment', but also with a certain 'Ausgeblasenheit meines Innern […],—insofern nämlich, als ich alle Erinnerungen, welche meinem ungültig gewordenen Dasein angehörten, aus meiner Seele zu verbannen hatte' ['a sort of emptying out of my inmost being—that is, I had to banish from my soul all memories that belonged to my no longer valid past'] (201/275). As someone with 'der außerordentlichen Neigung und Begabung zum Schlafe' ['the extraordinary gift and passion for sleep'] (8/12), which according to the Schopenhauerian subtext of the novel indicates a certain proximity to redemption or Nirvana, Felix fashions himself as Schiller's *homo ludens*, whose memory allows him to strike the balance between observing the world (as 'object') and engaging with the world (through 'sentiment').

The novel's art of irony, in combination with the picaresque narrative framework, makes it impossible to determine whether weaving Schiller's anthropology of an ideal *homo ludens* into the fabric of Felix' exuberant rhetoric is yet another twist of the confidence man (fishing for sympathy from the bourgeois readership, who places Schiller on a pedestal) or whether the playful human being is a genuine point of reference that offers a solution for the various dilemmas of individuality

---

41   Ibid., 635/145.

under the conditions of modernity. The picaresque narrative frame and the lack of clarity as to the actual addressee of the 'confessions' strongly suggest the former. One of the latent operations of Mann's novel is more concerned with self-preservation than with any idealistic concept of human autonomy, which the textual surface so strongly suggests. Felix, by elegantly enacting Schiller's realm of play, also undermines it; he is also overdetermined by Nietzsche's charlatan and *Schein-Künstler*, simulating the aesthetic drive to the point of turning into a completely aesthetic figure himself. Play in *Felix Krull* is not only playful, it is also the product of achievement and strenuous exercise; it is, contrary to Felix' repeated claims to a panerotic sense of experience, a staged rather than an experienced ludism.[42]

Felix is incapable of perceiving a world outside the realm of his emotional economy. His approach to play is dominated by what J. Peter Stern has termed an ethics of 'dear purchase'—the idea that everything in life has to be earned from life through effort and labour, in short, the ethics of meritocracy and self-sacrifice.[43] Felix is an achiever, his skilful art of simulating and manipulating appearances is the product of disciplined willpower. Play in Thomas Mann in general and in *Felix Krull* in particular has to be seen in the context of the psychology of a rigorous work ethic; Felix' polymorphous self-invention through play is a form of self-legitimization and as such a latent form of self-accusation.[44] Felix is observing himself incessantly and introduces play as a benchmark for his own performance. He makes quite clear that his light rhetorical touch and his histrionic virtuosity—his way of observing and engaging with the world—are the product of a long process of self-discipline:

> Das Leben nämlich ist zwar keineswegs das höchste der Güter, an welches wir uns seiner Köstlichkeit wegen jedenfalls zu

---

42 I use the term *homo ludens* not in the anthropological sense popularized by the Dutch historian Johan Huizinga, but in the aesthetic sense of Schiller's letters. Huizinga, however, offers an approach which is useful for an analysis of Felix, not least since it was a widely discussed text in postwar Europe and might have had an impact on Mann's revision of *Felix Krull* in the 1950s. According to Huizinga, human nature is in equal parts characterized as *homo sapiens*, *homo faber* and *homo ludens*. Play is perceived as an ontological quality which cannot be divided into other entities and is defined by its intrinsic agonistic structure.

43 Stern, *Dear Purchase*, 382. The term 'dear purchase' (*teure[r] Kauf*) is taken from a poetic rendition of the Gospel according to Matthew by the baroque poet Andreas Gryphius (27–8) and serves to trace a long-standing theme in German literary history. See also Diederichs, *Strukturen des Schelmischen*, 48, and Jacobs, *Der deutsche Schelmenroman*, 99.

44 Cf. Wysling, *Narzissmus*, 140–3. Wysling relates Felix Krull's ethos to Schopenhauer's philosophy of suffering, Nietzsche's doctrine of the ascetic priest, Prussian militarism and the Protestant education of willpower.

klammern hätten; sondern es ist als eine uns gestellte schwere und strenge Aufgabe zu betrachten, welche mit Standhaftigkeit und Treue durchzuhalten uns unbedingt obliegt und der vor der Zeit zu entlaufen zweifellos eine liederliche Aufführung bedeutet. (48)

Life is by no means the highest good, so precious it must be clung to in all circumstances. Instead it seems to me we should regard it as a heavy and exacting task that has been assigned us, one which we have in some sense chosen and which we are absolutely obliged to carry through with loyal perseverance. (67)

Stern argues that German literature from Nietzsche to Mann is dominated by 'a morality or moral theology of strenuousness' and claims that *Felix Krull* is the first novel to 'cock a snook'[45] at this value-scheme of the 'dear purchase', the feeling that 'every inch of truth has to be wrested from oneself'.[46] It is true that Felix recreates the world as *his* world in the head of *his* implied reader in order to mirror himself and observe his own performance as play rather than duty. Yet, as *Schein-Künstler* he perpetuates the ethics of the dear purchase rather than, as Stern claims, breaking with it. In this respect, *Felix Krull* also dramatizes what Tholen has analysed as a particular feature of modern male gender roles—the conflict between a form of masculinity that is defined by hegemonic energy (and a strong ideal of duty) and one that is able to accept its createdness, fallibility and dependence on others.[47] Play has the potential to open up the latter, but, as shown above, Mann inscribes a fear of intimacy into Felix' paneroticism: Felix always runs the risk of turning into a sterile, self-absorbed Andromache figure.[18] Throughout his last novel, Mann reflects on the liberating potential of art for a re-imagination of masculinity and also draws attention to the fallacies of artistic self-invention. Felix' confidence game, refracted through its intertextual irony (a play with Mann's own author persona), blurs the boundaries between the self-delusive danger of art and its liberating potential—between a dearly purchased play and a played dear purchase.

---

45 Stern, *Dear Purchase*, 382.
46 Ibid., 22.
47 Tholen, *Verlust der Nähe*, 9–21.
48 The dichotomy creativity versus sterility is part of the Nietzschean subtext of decadence; for an illuminating discussion see Calinescu, *Five Faces of Modernity*, 171–95, esp. 183–8.

Territorializing Play: Felix the *Bildungsbürger*

The aim of Felix' con man existence is not material gain or social position. The confidence game is his way of experimenting with an hermaphroditic masculinity and maintaining freedom of spirit and mind, but it is a projected freedom and shows the fundamental irony of Nietzsche's argument, namely that the aesthetic project is *je immer schon* a project of self-legitimization and therefore neither entirely free nor purely aesthetic:[49]

> Verkleidet also war ich in jedem Fall, und die unmaskierte Wirklichkeit zwischen den beiden Erscheinungsformen, das Ich-selber-Sein, war nicht bestimmbar, weil tatsächlich nicht vorhanden. (179)

> Thus I masqueraded in both capacities and the undisguised reality behind the two appearances, the real I, could not be identified because it actually did not exist. (244)

This element of disguise permeates one prominent subtext of the novel, the parody of autobiography. Autobiography affords Felix a double framework of dissimulation: his (pseudo)autobiography is both an *apologia*, pitched against Rousseau's aesthetics of laying bare the inner self, and a parody of the nineteenth-century teleology of selfhood. Felix instead arms himself with a ludism of self-invention that renders the distinction between experience and projection ambiguous—and with it the entire discourse of authenticity.

Mann launches a double parody through Felix, the least likely and most lavishly disguised of his many *Bildungsbürger*—a parody of the confessional mode of the classic autobiography and a travesty of the *Bildungsroman*. Felix mimics, for example, the narrative tone of Goethe's autobiography, *Dichtung und Wahrheit*, playfully revelling in a comparable obsession with details and digressions. He also indulges in Goethe's tendency to talk about himself in the third person and parasitically appropriates the dignity and cultural credibility of Goethe's form of autobiography, so that it may rub off on him; this subtle form of self-parody patches over the omnipresent undercurrent of the dear purchase ethics discussed above. The gesture of Goethe's autobiographical narration is not directly parodied, but Felix the confidence man tries to appropriate the tone of this established register in order to cast his protean life into a firmly established form. In grandiloquent fashion he claims to be part of some demiurgic power:

---

49   Nietzsche, *Fröhliche Wissenschaft*, 608–9; *Gay Science*, 225–6 (§361).

Überdies ist, wo immer es sich um eine Tat handelt, in erster Linie weder an dem Was noch an dem Wie gelegen (obgleich dies letztere wichtiger ist), sondern einzig und allein an dem Wer. Was ich je getan habe, war in hervorragendem Maße *meine* Tat, nicht die von Krethi und Plethi, und obgleich ich es mir, namentlich von der bürgerlichen Gerichtsbarkeit, habe gefallen lassen müssen, dass man denselben Namen daran heftete wie an zehntausend andere, so habe ich mich doch in dem geheimnisvollen, aber unerschütterlichen Gefühl, ein *Gunstkind* der schaffenden Macht und geradezu von bevorzugtem Fleisch und Blut zu sein, innerlich stets gegen eine so unnatürliche Gleichstellung aufgelehnt. (37)

Moreover, whenever an act is in question, it is not the what nor the why that matters (though the second is the more important), but simply and solely the who. Whatever I have done or committed, it has always been first of all *my* deed, not Tom's or Dick's or Harry's: and though I have had to accept being labelled, especially by the law, with the same name as ten thousand others, I have always rebelled against such an unnatural identification in the unshakable belief that I am a *favourite* of the powers that be and actually composed of finer flesh and blood. (49, emphases added)

This rhetoric is, of course, designed to be decoded as a parodic strategy by the reader, who is constructed by that very rhetoric and implicated into the narrative as both victim and accomplice in the confidence game, as both one of the *Bildungsbürger* (who cherishes the kind of canonical literary references) and as non-conformist (who shares a good laugh with Felix, the satirist). The readers unwittingly align themselves with the narrator's implied satirical stance against the petit bourgeois mindset, which they discover, uncannily, as part of their own reader responses. This extradiegetic gesture of the satirist who moves outside his own narrative self-construction and mocks its social and cultural genealogy constitutes Felix' *Tiefstapelei*, his rhetorical self-mockery. It complements his diegetic confidence game, a fantasy of subjective autonomy and universalism, which is very much at the heart of the nineteenth-century project of bourgeois emancipation. Thus, Felix plays, on two different narrative levels, with his readers: as a philistine and as a satirist of philistinism, as a *Hochstapler* and as a *Tiefstapler*.

Many interpreters have seen this as a sign that Felix uses and utilizes society but cannot really integrate into society, which is one of the trademarks of classic picaresque fiction, distinguishing it from the *Bildungsroman*. Indeed, Felix appropriates the confidence game 'to such an extent that his (self-)manipulative capacities become both end and means', but this also implies Felix' ultimate stratagem as a confidence trickster.[50] Although Felix consistently makes claims to the effect that he finds 'die Gesellschaft reizend, so wie sie ist' ['society enchanting just as it is'] (118/160), his diegetic confidence game avoids those social categories he plays with and plays at.

Felix' freedom 'im eigenen Gleichnis leben zu dürfen' ['to live symbolically'] (84/115) is not a synthesis of disparities, as has been often suggested. It is his attempt to mould the world according to himself rather than modelling himself on what he finds in the world. By making the reader buy into the concept of aesthetic life as a supposedly deterritorialized category that can easily be reterritorialized into the trajectory of the 'adventure novel from the late bourgeois era', Felix establishes himself as a character in his narrative.[51] His self-construction is dependent upon the readers' complicity, which Felix wins by presenting himself as both *Vorbild* (model) and *Nachbild* (copy). Felix is prone to insincere self-deception in order to allow the reader to step in and, as it were, redeem him. This 'relationship of knowing collusion' entails Felix' deconstructing himself as a completely aesthetic product in order to gain the negative capability of meta-fictional credibility.[52] His 'Autohagiographie' grounds self-confidence in confidence games with the reader, thus constituting a symbiotic author–text–reader interrelation that differs significantly from the *Bildungsroman*.[53] It culminates in the various playful pseudo-repartees between narrator and reader, for example in the Frankfurt scene, in which Felix imagines the reader becoming impatient with him:

Schwärmer und Gaffer! Höre ich den Leser mir zurufen. Wo bleiben deine Abenteuer? Gedenkst du mich durch dein ganzes Buch hin mit solchen empfindsamen Quisquilien, den sogenannten Erlebnissen deiner begehrlichen Schlaffheit zu unterhalten? (65)

Dreamer and idler! I hear the reader addressing me. Where are your adventures? Do you propose to entertain me throughout your whole book with such fine-spun quiddities, the so-called experiences of your covetous idleness? (89)

Felix is his own product, a *Kunstgeschöpf*—both a *work* of art and a

---

50 Spuler, 'Notions of Freedom', 345.
51 Mann, *Briefe 1948–1955*, 223 ('Abenteuer-Roman aus dem späten bürgerlichen Zeitalter'), trans. B.M.
52 Schonfield, *Art and Its Uses*, 152.
53 Sprecher, *Felix Krull und Goethe*, 227.

creature of art—whose character is not marked by external social influences. Society is utilized as it is, it is appreciated in its appearances as a network of dissimulation. Felix' narcissism ties together his rhetorical performance as self-legitimizing *homo ludens*. He creates his implied reader as a *Bildungsbürger*, with whom he can converse, and, at the same time, as an *Anti-Bildungsbürger*, with whom he can mock the *Bildungsbürger*.

Conclusion: Deterritorializing Play

Change without transformation is a feature which has been attributed to the individual in capitalism in a long history of socio-economic critiques ranging from Marx to the Frankfurt School and from Weber to Sayer. A critique closer to the ambiguous character of change and interchangeability reflected in Mann's novel, however, leads us back to the 'Capitalism and Schizophrenia' project by Deleuze and Guattari, consisting of the two studies *Anti-Oedipus* and *A Thousand Plateaus*. Both works adopt the classic philosophical and sociological critique of capitalism, but introduce a psychological meta-reading of Freud's interpretation of the Oedipus myth to demonstrate his embeddedness in capitalist thinking patterns and the fundamental ambiguity of the capitalist system with regard to its impact on humans, both liberating and repressive. Their metaphorical use of the term schizophrenia is designed to describe a specific mode of psychic and social operations that are first facilitated and then repressed by a capitalist economy. They describe an analogy between limitless semiosis—the kind of semiosis and metaphorical exchangeability explored in *Felix Krull*— and capital as a contradictory 'multiplicity of desire' which can never be fulfilled, yet always spawns new, potentially self-destructive, desires.[54]

As Norman O. Brown has pointed out, the primary and original function of money is not trade but the creation and liquidation of debt, the fostering and assuaging of guilt.[55] As soon as one's debt is not owed to a deity upon whom humans can always project a dimension of absolute mercy, as soon as one's debt is owed to other people, it can never be completely settled. Money as an agent of debt and its liquidation functions as long as it is not fully liquidated. In order to circulate, money needs debt, in psychological terms: guilt. This context forms the background for the discussion of territories of desire in Deleuze and Guattari, that is to say, the mechanisms operated by society to govern psychological and physical impulses.[56]

---

54 Deleuze and Guattari, *Anti-Oedipus*, 112.
55 Cf. Brown, *Life against Death*, 103.
56 Cf. Foucault, *History of Sexuality*, I, 120–31.

While capital, according to Deleuze and Guattari, has an immense revolutionary potential and constantly deterritorializes desire from established structures of fixation, it also perpetually reterritorializes desire so that it favours certain objects at the expense of others, namely capital and the nuclear family, as explicated in the discussion of Walser above. Reidar Due elaborates: 'Capitalism erodes state authority because it replaces one signifying system with another. It replaces a system of codification and representation of the social realm with a purely formal system of equivalences which is not representational [money]. [...] the task of codifying desire [in capitalism] is transferred to the family and further to the individual who constructs the Oedipal subject as a mechanism of codification.'[57] Decoding speeds up the innovation of production and the turnover of consumer desires; recoding refers to the process of appropriation of the generated surplus value and creates territories of desire which exclude others. This latter process seeks to multiply what Deleuze and Guattari call 'deterritorialised schizophrenic flows'[58] and is designed to prevent circulation from coming to a halt, thereby maintaining Brown's economy of guilt within the system. Capitalism accordingly does not have exterior limits; its only interior limit is capital, which is, however, never encountered but continuously displaced by being reproduced without changing itself. In other words, the capitalist axiom of circulation is never saturated, since a new parameter can always be added and fully incorporated in the logic of monetary circulation and exchangeability— a connection anticipated by Simmel.

Deleuze and Guattari's work is an analysis of capitalism which does not reiterate the standard rhetoric of reification, rationalization and fetishization of commodity circulation, but rather aims at a more complex assessment of the psychic and social dynamics of an identity that co-emerged with capitalism. It is this heightened sense of complexity that is also at work in the mythological subtexts of *Felix Krull*. Felix embodies both aspects of de- and reterritorialization. Nietzsche's artist/acrobat, the union of the fairy-tale *Glückskind* with the mythological Hermes figure, and the anthropological trickster are all part of a network of mutually exchangeable cross-references which form an exuberant semiosis of potential meaning and its simultaneous perpetual deferral. Felix' story is endless; its fragmentary character is inherent in the confidence game it plays with the reader. He enters a series of mirror images, endlessly varied as it may seem, when his tutelary spirit, Professor Kuckuck, lectures on metamorphosis:

---

57 Due, *Deleuze*, 82.
58 Deleuze and Guattari, *Anti-Oedipus*, 75.

'Wissen Sie aber, woran sie mich erinnern?'
'Ich bitte, es mir zu sagen', antwortete ich lächelnd.
'An eine Seelilie.'
'Das klingt nicht wenig schmeichelhaft.'
'Nur weil es Ihnen wie der Name einer Blume klingt. Die Seelilie
ist aber keine Blume, sondern eine festsitzende Tierform der
Tiefsee, zum Kreis der Stachelhäuter gehörig und davon wohl
die altertümlichste Gruppe. Wir haben eine Menge Fossilien
davon. Solche an ihren Ort gebundene Tiere neigen zu blumen-
hafter Form, will sagen zu einer stern- und blütenartigen
Rundsymmetrie. Der Haarstern von heute, Nachkomme der
frühen Seelilie, sitzt nur noch in seiner Jugend an einem Stiele
im Grunde fest. Dann macht er sich frei, emanzipiert sich und
abenteuert schwimmend und kletternd an den Küsten umher.
[…]' (205)

'But do you know what you remind me of?'
'Please tell me', I replied smiling.
'A sea lily.'
'That sounds decidedly flattering.'
'Only because it sounds to you like a flower. The sea lily,
however, is not a flower but a sessile small animal of the deep
sea, belonging to the order of echinoderms and constituting
probably its oldest species. We have a quantity of fossils. Such
non-mobile animals tend to take on flower-like forms—that is
to say, circular symmetry like that of a star or a blossom. The
present-day descendant of the sea lily, the lily-star, is attached
to the ground by a stem only during its youth. After that it frees
itself, emancipates itself, and goes off adventurously swimming
and clambering along the coast. (280–1)

This ironic evolutionary vignette about Felix captures his Janus-faced
picaresque existence: he is both completely emancipated from his
original social bonds, since he has adopted the identity of Marquis de
Venosta, and, at the same time, does essentially stay fossilized, like the
sea lily with its ambiguous name. Felix' social metamorphoses refute
the generalized statements about the socio-economic implications of
the character that can be found so frequently in secondary literature.
Deterritorialization is, indeed, part of Felix' confidence game with the
reader: he reinvents himself as adventurer and dandy. At the same
time, however, Felix reterritorializes the self in a narcissistic fashion
which alienates him from any concept of organic metamorphosis or
Bildung. The confidence trickster Felix can even sell this to his reader
as the freedom, in Goethe's terms, 'Existenz auf[zu]geben, um zu

existieren' ['to give up existence in order to exist'].[59] It is this ostensible attempt to give up engineering one's existence which governs the structure of the modern pícaro as potentially infinite and circular, for individuality is envisaged as an unfinished project, something 'always still to come'.[60] Since he narrates his life in order to prove this putative lack of deliberation behind his life, he always returns to the narcissistic contradiction of claiming natural beauty through performative acts of artificial beauty. Jakob von Gunten's ascetic narcissism is always palpable underneath Felix' 'dear purchase'—his attempt to present himself as autonomous beyond the constraints of self-preservation. This potential hollowness at the core of the modern picaresque may also be one of the crucial reasons why this tradition did not offer a productive narrative template for literary explorations of female gender roles during the early twentieth century. Mann's rewriting of the *Metamorphoses* playfully de-genders the traditional male dilemma of 'loss of closeness', to use Tholen's phrase; it does, however, tie this hermaphroditic phantasm to a reflection on the precarious nature of artistic self-fashioning as a potentially new form of social isolation. Even though Felix transgresses gender boundaries, his art of transgression is underpinned by a specifically male genealogy of individuality, from Goethe's genius of life to Nietzsche's *Übermensch*. Mann may have explored the full potential of the modern picaresque, he does, however, also point to its biggest limitation.

---

59 Goethe, *Schriften zur Kunst*, 381.
60 Hamacher, 'Disgregation of the Will', 110.

Picaresque Topoi II
Third Space: A Stage for the Modern Pícaro

Pícaros often migrate between the worlds of officialdom and petty crime, between the realms of universal myth and provincial reality, and thus blur the boundaries between seeming opposites. In order to fully appreciate the stage on which these characters enact their con games it may prove useful to embed the modern obsession with the histrionic character of human life in its wider historical context. The paradigmatic change from stratum-based to meritocratic societies during the eighteenth century greatly diversified the roles available for humans in society. In particular, the second half of the eighteenth century led to a major change in what Koselleck describes as the relation between the 'space of experience' (*Erfahrungsraum*) and the 'horizon of expectation' (*Erwartungshorizont*).[1] Both categories relate to each other in a reciprocal fashion: individual and collective experiences shape the scope of expectations, whereas experience and its perception are influenced by prospects and fears projected into the future.

Experience and expectation, Koselleck argues, used to be balanced as long as new religious, political and economic developments and scientific discoveries or inventions could be integrated into existing patterns of interpretation. In the course of the eighteenth century, however, economic and technological development led to an unprecedented acceleration of social and economic life in the German-speaking world, which in turn led to the gradual replacement of cyclical concepts of time that tend to prevail in stratum-based societies. This development was, of course, not entirely new and had precursors in

---

1 Koselleck compares this period to a saddle (*Sattelzeit*), see Brunner *et al.*, *Geschichtliche Grundbegriffe*, ii–xv. See also Koselleck, *Futures Past*, 267–76 (*Vergangene Zukunft*, 349–59) and *Critique and Crisis*, 98–123 (*Kritik und Krise*, 81–103); for a critique of Koselleck's concepts see Schinkel, 'Imagination', 42–54.

the fifteenth and sixteenth centuries, fuelled by the discoveries made by the seafaring countries, by the religious, political and economic changes brought about in the North Italian cities, the Netherlands, and in the free *Reichsstädte* and the Hanseatic cities, and, last but not least, the blossoming of the arts and sciences in the wake of humanism across Europe. In the eighteenth century, the concepts of historical teleology and human perfectibility were increasingly translated into the realm of the secular.[2] Humans started to conceive of themselves as masters of their own histories and of their biographies as enterprises of gradual perfection (something not altogether unfamiliar to the proverbial Renaissance man). On a social level, the increasing dissociation of experience and expectation in the eighteenth century nourished the belief that life can be systematically monitored and engineered.

In the modern world, rationalization and its dialectic—the scientific enchantment and the utilitarian disenchantment of life—spawned a rich philosophical and imaginative concern with configurations that reach beyond binary oppositions. Every system of classification produces ambivalences in the act of establishing and maintaining systematic distinctions. Modernity, according to Zygmunt Bauman, is the failed attempt to contain reality within a system untouched by ambivalence:

> Modern mastery is the power to divide, classify and allocate—in thought, in practice, in the practice of thought and in the thought of practice. Paradoxically, it is for this reason that ambivalence is the main affliction of modernity and the most worrying of its concerns. [...] If modernity is about the production of order then ambivalence is *the waste of modernity*.[3]

Ambivalence, or 'waste', according to Bauman, is the predicament of modernity. The attempt to create, through the dominance of the human *ratio*, an anthropocentric rule over nature, on the one hand, and an absolute reliance on the individual, on the other, leads to the acceleration of a system that cannot be governed by humans any more. Or, as Simmel puts it, the accelerated 'objective' realm overtakes the 'subjective' realm and ultimately eludes control. Bauman here harks back to Simmel's work as a reflection on modernity's shift from substantive to relational social imaginaries. Simmel deals, most importantly, with a third category between what he regards as the two main

---

2   Cf. Taylor, *Social Imaginary*, 164, 194.

3   Bauman, *Modernity and Ambivalence*, 15. Bauman uses Weber's critical stance on rationalization without referring to Weber's idea of a potentially egalitarian effect of modern bureaucracies, cf. Gay, 'Weber's Bureau?', 575–87.

dynamics in modernity—the thrust towards differentiation and the concurrent thrust towards conformism. What looks like something new, a departure from tradition, may well turn out to be, Simmel argues, the product of the incessant and all-pervasive pressure towards innovation, and thus part of a conformist ideologeme of modernity. He is interested in how these two tendencies interact, what kind of social conditions they create (or prevent from emerging) and in what kind of episteme they are rooted. It is the social space of this interaction where the pícaros find their niche and habitat and which they help create.

Simmel describes the individual in modernity as the interface of overlapping group affiliations (*soziale Kreise*).[4] He is interested in showing the relationship and mutual dependence between expansion and differentiation of the social realm, on the one hand, and the evolution of individuality, on the other: 'If the radius of web affiliations within which we operate and on which we focus our attention, is extended, then we find a wider scope for the development of our individuality. As part of the whole, however, we do not have the same degree of individual qualities; the whole, as a social group, is less individual.'[5] What is at stake in this passage is the process of individual self-assertion through 'web-affiliations' as a dialectical process of alien ation and identity, resulting in diversification. This dialectical process and its creation of a third space between individuality and uniformity, is, I suggest, germane to the position of the modern pícaro, who cannot be reduced to either 'an objectification of the subject' or 'a subjectification of the object', to apply Simmel's terms.[6]

Highly differentiated societies endow humans with an enhanced sense of autonomous agency, while at the same time creating the danger that the very products of this autonomous agency may threaten autonomy. Free enterprise and free scientific exploration may serve as good examples: originally conceived of as disseminators of individual and social freedom, these ideals tend to turn into 'objectified' apparatuses that ultimately undermine the original thrust towards freedom. The acceleration of social differentiation is,

---

4   Cf. Simmel, *Über sociale Differenzierung*, 173–9 and 237–57. For comparable ideas see also 'The Web of Group-Affiliations', a translation of one of the seminal chapters of Simmel's *Soziologie*.

5   Simmel, *Über sociale Differenzierung*, 174: 'Erweitert sich der Kreis, in dem wir uns bethätigen und dem unsere Interessen gelten, so ist darin mehr Spielraum für die Entwicklung unserer Individualität; aber als Teile dieses Ganzen haben wir weniger Eigenart, dieses letztere ist als sociale Gruppe weniger individuell.' (trans. B. M.)

6   Simmel, *The Concept and Tragedy of Culture*, 58; *Der Begriff und die Tragödie der Kultur*, 390: 'im Objektivwerden des Subjekts und im Subjektivwerden des Objekts'.

according to Simmel, responsible for the 'disproportion in growth' between individual and cultural developments and ultimately leads to a paradoxical 'atrophy of individual culture through the hypertrophy of objective culture'.[7]

Picaresque fiction provides a narrative template for fathoming this duality on various levels: first, the diegetic level of interaction between pícaro and society; second, the textual level of interaction between the naive picaresque persona (narrated I) and the retrospective picaresque persona (narrating I); third, the extradiegetic level of interaction between the implied reader and the narrator as an extension of the picaresque confidence game.[8]

This threefold structure can be illustrated by using *Die Blechtrommel*. The interaction between pícaro and society is represented by the communication between Oskar Matzerath and his male nurse Bruno. While Oskar claims absolute sovereignty over his own story, it is only through Bruno that he is able to connect with society, and indeed it is Bruno who helps him put pen to paper:

> Dann, mit kühl umwickelten Händen, Füßen und Knien, mit dem Tuch auf der Stirn werde ich meinen Pfleger Bruno mit Papier und einem Bleistift ausrüsten; denn meinen Füllfederhalter verleihe ich ungern. Ob Bruno auch gut zuhören will und kann? Wird seine *Nacherzählung* auch jener Reise im Güterwagen gerecht werden, die am 12. Juni fünfundvierzig begann?

> Then, with hands, feet, and knees wrapped and cool, and a cloth on my brow, I'll give my keeper Bruno paper and pencil, for I don't like to lend out my fountain pen. Will Bruno be willing and able to listen properly? And will his *retelling* do justice to that trip in a boxcar which began on twelve June of forty-five?[9]

This asymmetric interaction is reduplicated on the narrative level between the retrospective picaresque narrator persona (the inmate of an asylum) and the naive persona he designs for himself (the three-year-old child who refuses to grow up). The retrospective persona is very much concerned with reinventing the naive persona in order to justify his walk of life; at the same time, reinventing himself as child-artist runs into problems comparable to Felix' self-fashioning.

---

7   Simmel, 'The Metropolis and Mental Life', 183–4, 'Die Großstädte und das Geistesleben', 129–30.

8   The terminology of intertextuality used here is based on Genette's typology in *Palimpsestes*, 7–16.

9   Grass, *Blechtrommel*, 551; *Tin Drum*, 400 (emphasis added).

This kind of confidence game is also played with the implied reader, who is lured into identifying herself with the satirical author persona behind the narrator persona. At no point can the reader for any sustained period of time engage with single unified perspectives; she can never fully distinguish between autobiographical confession and picaresque confidence game, historical reference and its deliberate manipulation. The degree of their complicity in the manipulative reconstruction of history and the re-invention of its protagonist(s) can never be determined.

In contrast to Simmel, Niklas Luhmann's constructivist theory views agency in modernity from the perspective of the system. According to him, the moment of differentiation is a reaction to the centrifugal and alienating forces unleashed by the meritocratic structures emerging in the eighteenth century. Stratum-based societies engender identity by embedding it in social institutions like stratum, guild and pedigree, whereas functionally differentiated meritocracies abolish this vertical structure (an idea which Luhmann borrows from Koselleck).[10] Modern society is horizontally structured as a range of subsystems which do not ascribe one single and fixed position to the individual. Participating in various social circles allows individuals to define themselves through ambition as, to quote Peter Brooks's phrase again, 'the vehicle and emblem of Eros, that which totalizes the world as possession and progress'.[11]

Luhmann goes beyond Brooks's psychological argument and seeks an explanation through understanding both society and the individual as systems. He is particularly interested in the connection between these two types of systems in modernity: according to him, the individual has to prove some kind of extrasocietal uniqueness in order to be able to participate in a functionally differentiated society. In order to enter a meritocratic society as a social value, 'individuality' needs to be extrasocietal first, that is to say, rooted in a realm of values generated outside society.[12] Otherwise 'individuality'

---

10 Koselleck, *Critique and Crisis*, chapter 11 (*Kritik und Krise*, chapter 3, iii); see also Luhmann, *Wirtschaft der Gesellschaft*, 253: 'In a functionally differentiated society there is neither a head nor a center that represents society and thus could give access to its "essence" (*Wesen*). [...] none of the functional subsystems can adopt this operational function—in this case, for example, that of the nobility —, not even politics. All functional systems set into motion a dramatic increase of their own importance and their own social effectiveness, but not a single one of them can claim to represent the society within society.'

11 Brooks, *Reading for the Plot*, 39.

12 See, for example, Luhmann, 'Individuum, Individualität, Individualismus', 160, or 'The Individuality of the Individual', 319.

would be regarded as a social effect, as the reflex of a stratum-based foundation of society, in which 'individuality' is determined by social origin. Werner Hamacher approaches the same issue from a Nietzschean viewpoint: 'Only the individual's nonidentity with itself can constitute its individuality. Measured against itself as concept, bearing, and function, the individual proves to be other, to be more—or less—than itself. [...] Individuality is unaccountable surplus.'[13] Jakob von Gunten's attempt to place himself outside society through an exercise of asceticism and self-denial can be seen as a quasi-allegorical rendition of this nexus, although his integration into society is, ironically, never spelt out (unless we read the diary or novel as a communicative act expressing the desire to integrate into society). Felix Krull also exhibits a cornucopia of rhetorical artistry to disguise the 'dear purchase' of his identity and uses the projected image of himself, this 'unaccountable surplus', as a pawn to re-enter society.

Social systems, like any other system, Luhmann reiterates, treat anything that does not operate according to their rules and regulatory codes as environment: 'living systems and conscious systems are parts of the environment of social systems, whereas social systems are part of the environment of living systems and conscious systems'.[14] Individuals ('psychic systems' in Luhmann's terms), for example, follow internal modes of operation that differ from the ones employed by social systems. This results in different modes of internal self-regulation and regeneration (Luhmann calls these modes of operation 'consciousness' for individuals and meaning-generating 'communication' for social systems).[15] Social systems are seen as applying highly specialized forms of communication: they separate themselves from their respective environments, i.e. the entirety of all other systems with incompatible codes (in the case of social systems, nature and—counter-intuitively—individuals serve as 'environments'). Like all other systems, social systems accelerate their internal differentiation, which ultimately serves the purpose of self-perpetuation (*autopoiesis*) of the system as a whole.[16]

---

13   Hamacher, 'Disgregation of the Will', 110.

14   Luhmann, 'The Individuality of the Individual', 320–1.

15   Cf. Luhmann, *Gesellschaft der Gesellschaft*, 103.

16   While Luhmann maintains that there is no communication between the various subsystems, Habermas starts his critique of system theory precisely from this point by reconstructing an intersubjective model of society with a focus on 'concrete forms of life [that] replace transcendental consciousness in its function of creating unity'. (*Philosophical Discourse of Modernity*, 326) For Habermas, the observation of distinctions is not a form of systemic closure (and *autopoiesis*), but rather a form of communicative opening that helps liberate 'concrete forms

This concept does not allow for any direct exchange or inter-action between different types of systems (and their respective internal, regulatory codes). Rather, both social and psychic systems (which are of paramount interest for us in this context) and their internal processes yield impulses and energy to their respective environments and make mutual use of their energies in order to facilitate processes of internal differentiation: '[the individual] can only exist outside society, it can only reproduce itself as a system in its own right within its environment, society—which is its necessary environment. [...] It is precisely this exclusion of the individual from the social system which subsequently enables its *re-entry* into the ideology [of a given society] *as a value*.'[17] This notion of re-entry is crucial for the understanding of the pícaro and, as I argue below, accounts for his ambivalent status as both an outlaw and an experimenter.

Social systems have to reduce external complexity in order to operate properly and avoid processing external information as internal confusion; therefore they have to increase internal complexity by virtue of differentiation processes. This reaction implements and perpetuates internal modes of communication, thus corroborating certain forms of meaning. The same holds for individuals who organize themselves by virtue of self-differentiation through reference to their own consti-tutive elements, but they cannot translate their operative mode into the one used by their environment, normally a social system.[18] Criticism has been launched against Luhmann's seemingly anti-humanist constructivism, both by social theorists such as Habermas and by cultural historians such as David Wellbery and Albrecht Koschorke.[19] In our context we are, however, less concerned with that construc-tivist superstructure than with Luhmann's exploration of the interface between social and psychic systems and the operations between social subsystems, which facilitate the process of differentiation. Irrespective of the systemic superstructure, it is these interstitial systemic positions (between society and individual, between various social subsystems) that offer a useful mode of description for the picaresque in modernity. Three components of system theory, I suggest, are helpful for our discussion: the concepts of differentiation, autopoiesis and observation.

---

of life' from purely reflexive, i.e. autopoietic, operations that lead to a 'highly abstract ego-identity'. (*Die nachholende Revolution*, 88)

17 Luhmann, 'Individuum, Individualität, Individualismus', 158–9 (emphasis added).

18 On the notion of *autopoiesis* in system theory see Beermann, 'Order from Noise'.

19 Koschorke, 'Die Grenzen des Systems' and Wellbery, 'Die Ausblendung der Genese', esp. 22.

Felix Krull, for example, as we have seen, enacts his erotic relationship with the world as an osmotic process that endows him with a never-ending stream of energy. He translates this dynamic into an incessant metamorphosis and *differentiation* of personae, ultimately encompassing all environments, both social (various strata) and natural (various stages in evolutionary history, which Professor Kuckuck relates to individual and social forms of differentiation). That is, at least, the way he stages himself in his narrative. The picaresque exuberance of role-play and histrionic virtuosity dramatizes, as shown in the previous chapter, an *autopoiesis* that functions on two levels. Diegetically, Felix' autopoietic devouring of the world disguises deep-seated doubts about the independence and autonomy of an individuality that is rooted in a 'dear purchase' logic of meritocracy; extradiegetically, Felix aligns with the implied reader he creates and addresses, with whom he *observes* and parodies his own autopoiesis as the typical product of a particular socio-economic configuration, the *Bildungsbürgertum* ethos of the Wilhelmine boom years and industrial capitalism. To speak with Luhmann, Felix moves outside the autopoietic processes of differentiation towards a second-degree position from which he (and the implied reader) observes himself straddle the systemic border between individual (the diegetic Felix) and society (Felix as a product of his stratum and time).[20] The moment Felix enacts the highest degree of individuality, as confidence man and shape-shifter in his autopoietic narrative, is also the moment when he becomes an abstract agent, the parodist of himself, the social satirist, the *Tiefstapler*, the self-observer, who cuts across 'the distinction between experience and action and the distinction between the purely psychic operations that control attention and the social operations that enact communication'.[21]

The modern picaresque hero, however, can also be read as a literary critique of constructivist attempts to conceptualize humans and society, such as the ones by Luhmann, Talcott Parsons or Peter Fuchs. Felix Krull and his peers exemplify the traffic between two systems—psychic and social systems—rather than the operative closure of one specific system. They are both the epitome of individuality in modernity and a social type, at once a fully-fledged psychological character and a multitude of personae. While they exhibit Luhmann's categories of differentiation, autopoiesis and observation, they also, by virtue of their dual agency as type and character, call into doubt the systemic boundary between

---

20   On the notion of second-degree observations see Luhmann, *Gesellschaft der Gesellschaft*, 1113–20, and *Observations on Modernity*, 9–21; see also Rasch, *Paradoxes of Differentiation*, 35–9.

21   Luhmann, *Observations on Modernity*, 47.

psychic and social systems, which is at the very core of this theory.[22] The modern pícaro both demonstrates and undercuts the reciprocity of mechanisms of inclusion and exclusion described above. By playing the double game of Simmel's participation in 'web-affiliations' and Goffman's 'impression management' as a 'half-outsider', he facilitates and reflects the differentiation of individuality *and* society as systemic entities precisely by not allowing himself to be fully ascribed to either of them.

Moreover, modern picaresque fiction combines two elements. On the one hand, the pícaro exhibits the complexity and contradictions of modern human existence and its entanglement in the contradictory claims of human nature: authentic versus derivative, original versus fake, self-reliance versus dependence. On the other hand, picaresque fiction shows and imagines a literary hybrid between type and character, who develops an intuitive understanding of this situation, appropriates it and engineers it according to his own goals. In a third step, the reader becomes the observer of the pícaro's narrative of self-legitimization. These three levels—the picaresque world, the picaresque confidence game and, finally, social satire and self-parody— are intrinsically tied up with the artistic compulsion of self-reflection in modernity. Picaresque fiction epitomizes what Linda Hutcheon has analysed as one of the major developments in twentieth-century art, and writing in particular: 'The text's own paradox is that it is both narcissistically self-reflexive and yet focused outward, oriented toward the reader.'[23]

The third space opened up by the picaresque narrative between the social and the individual, between the private and the public, dramatizes both spheres without representing them. This picaresque stage is, diegetically, a reflection of social differentiation from the perspective of the go-between and it functions, extra-diegetically, as the form for a narrative self-mockery or self-critique. The picaresque (pseudo)autobiography marks this third space as a privileged *topos* for understanding the effects of acceleration and rationalization of socio-economic and cultural differences in modern industrialized societies, or, to put it differently, for understanding the dual development of increased mobility and a 'perennially dissatisfied and restless' interiority.[24] The interstitial territory of the picaresque lifeworld is both a catalyst of

---

22 On third agencies and spaces as the seed of society in general, see the theory of double contingency, Parsons and Shils, *Theory of Action*, 16–18, and Luhmann, *Soziale Systeme*, 148–90. See also Beermann, 'Order from Noise?', 255–61, for a critique of Parsons and Luhmann.
23 Hutcheon, *Narcissistic Narrative*, 7.
24 Moretti, *The Way of the World*, 4.

these developments and, as Bauman puts it, the dumping ground for their 'waste'—for the kind of ambivalence that cannot be processed by either psychic or social systems. It is a place for both the agents and the victims of modernity, the shape-shifters and the underdogs, the *producers* of rhetorical or narrative inclusion and the *products* of social exclusion. The pícaro as a literary character is, of course, neither agent nor victim, since he dramatizes himself as both, but he occupies the interstitial systemic territory that allows us to observe, with him and through him, these processes of inclusion and exclusion. The following close reading introduces two characters who exemplify the dynamism between shape-shifter and underdog in a disconcerting double figure: Max Schulz und Itzig Finkelstein in Edgar Hilsenrath's *Der Nazi und der Friseur*.

5.   The Shape-Shifter as Underdog: Edgar Hilsenrath's *Der Nazi und der Friseur*

The Sorcery of Identity

Edgar Hilsenrath's *Der Nazi und der Friseur* (1977) dramatizes the ambivalence between the producers of inclusion and the products of exclusion in the life stories of a Jewish and a German boy, Itzig Finkelstein and Max Schulz, who are growing up in the same petit bourgeois quarter of the small German town Wieshalle.[1] Itzig, the son of a successful local barber, is a talented student at school and of 'Aryan' appearance. Max, the narrator, by contrast, grows up in a dysfunctional family, he is reliant on Itzig's help at school and resembles one of the racist caricatures of Jews in Nazi propaganda pamphlets and journals such as *Der Stürmer*. He becomes intimately acquainted with Jewish life, religion and culture. During World War Two, he kills, so he insinuates, Itzig and his entire family in a death camp in Eastern Europe. After the war he returns to Germany, makes a living as a black marketeer in Berlin and then decides to change identities, converts to Judaism, becomes a Zionist and emigrates to Palestine. There he sets up a successful barbershop and becomes involved in Zionist underground politics. Before he dies, he confesses his sins as a mass murderer to a lawyer acquaintance, with whom he also discusses eschatological issues such as guilt, atonement, divine judgement—a typical feature of the Menippean satire, one of the precursors of the picaresque. They fail to find an appropriate retribution for his guilt, and Max/Itzig is condemned to die without atonement and unredeemed.[2]

---

1   Literary predecessors of this twin situation and subsequent role changes are Mark Twain, *Puddinhead Wilson* and Günter Grass, *Hundejahre*. The novel also contains numerous parodic references to *Die Blechtrommel*.

2   Cf. Stenberg, 'Hilsenrath und der abwesende Gott' on the eschatological implications of the novel.

Although completely different in terms of narrative tone, Hilsenrath's novel echoes the characteristic narrative structure of the Spanish prototype:[3] the pseudo-autobiographical form and the encyclopaedic exploration of society, in this case that of wartime Germany or Poland and of post-war Israel.[4] Max as Itzig represents the Janus face of simulation and dissimulation in the picaresque tradition. He adopts various identities as long as they suit his aim of improving his social position. Frau Holle, his mistress in post-war Berlin, asks him about this wish to adopt new identities:

> 'Was ist das—eine andere Identität?'
> 'Wenn sich einer verwandelt', sagte Max Schulz.
> 'So wie ein Zauberkünstler', sagte Frau Holle.
> 'So ähnlich', sagte Max Schulz. (83)

> 'What's that—a different kind of identity?'
> 'That's when someone changes into someone else', said Max Schulz.
> 'Like a magician', said Frau Holle.
> 'Kind of', said Max Schulz.[5]

Hilsenrath systematically destabilizes concepts which are conventionally cast as binary oppositions, such as Jewish versus Aryan, schlemiel (or Max Nordau's *luftmentsh*) versus *Bürger* or male versus female. Frau Holle herself, obviously a reference to the protagonist of the eponymous fairy tale by the Brothers Grimm, is part of a doubly inverted play of the picaresque magician or sorcerer ('Zauberkünstler') with the categories of perpetrator and victim. She is pitched against the evil Polish witch figure Veronja, who is herself associated with the Brothers Grimm's fairy tale 'Hänsel und Gretel'. Frau Holle is portrayed as a hospitable character whereas Veronja, the victim of Nazi atrocities, literally turns into the man-eating phantasm of male castration fear. (Book Two)

Frau Holle, the wife of a dead SS officer, tells Max/Itzig that she has been raped by Russians (so she claims, but it turns out they were Americans). Her prosthetic leg metaphorically indicates both aggression and victimhood. The Veronja episode, which Max/Itzig relates to Frau Holle, can be read as a phantasmagorical spell of fear rooted in the horrors of his memory. His anxiety is connected to, or

---

3   The most precise genre classifications are satire and parable, see Lorenz, *Massenmord*, 177.

4   Cf. Bauer, *Schelmenroman*, chapter 1.

5   Trans. B. M. This passage is not part of the published English translation.

re-activated by the anxiety Frau Holle provokes with her story of an American Major, who had died in her bed from sexual exhaustion. The narrative undermines a black-and-white picture of victims and perpetrators: the widow of a Nazi official offers refuge to an alleged victim, while the victim Veronja denies this act of humaneness. The fact that Max is, however, a perpetrator rather than the victim he mimics, undercuts, by the same token, the inversion of moral evaluations dramatized by these two central female figures.

The double figure Max/Itzig is a prototypical picaresque pretender and debunker. Every attempt by the reader to obtain an unequivocal notion of the intentions of the narrator and the motivations of each narrative move is rendered vain. The reason why Max/Itzig makes his public confession in the form of his autobiography remains opaque—is there a legal authority (a 'vuestra merced', as it were) behind it or does he act out of genuine repentance or fear of divine justice? The text does not offer an answer to this question—the reader is at the mercy of an alleged mass murderer's *apologia*.

A Duck-Rabbit of a Tale

The sparse secondary literature on *Der Nazi und der Friseur* falls short of acknowledging that the novel is the picaresque self-fashioning of a shape-shifter who discovers the opportunities of adopting the under-dog's persona. It also ignores the fact that the novel lends itself to an alternative concurrent interpretation as the story of traumatic loss of a Jewish survivor, who, marked by the complex history of German-Jewish assimilation, identifies himself to an extreme degree with German culture. This traumatic persona, I argue, develops a schizoid perception of reality and his own biography during the time of the Nazi terror under a perpetual 'state of exception' (state of emergency) —not as 'an external and provisional state of factual danger', but as 'juridical rule itself'.[6] His clever and obsessive mimicry after the war warrants two diametrically opposed readings: the extreme confidence game of the SS officer as Israeli Zionist (Max as Itzig), on the one hand, and the victim of deep-rooted traumatic experiences and of severe survivor guilt (the German Itzig as the Israeli Itzig), on the other.

In its general definition, 'trauma is described as the response to an unexpected or overwhelming violent event or events that are not fully grasped as they occur, but return later in repeated flashbacks, night-mares, and other repetitive phenomena'.[7] The traumatized, according to recent scholarly attempts to conceptualize disrupted memory, carry a history within them that cannot be translated into narrative or

---

6   Agamben, 'The Camp', 108.
7   Caruth, 'Traumatic Awakenings', 208.

cognitive patterns of understanding, they 'become themselves the symptom of a history that they cannot entirely possess. [...] the dreams, hallucinations and thoughts are absolutely literal, unassimilable to associative chains of meaning'.[8] If the double figure Max as Itzig is interpreted as Itzig who is haunted by survivor guilt, the traumatic experience of the loss of his family possesses him in a way that is 'unassimilable to associative chains of meaning'. The loss always hits him in the form of 'repeated flashbacks, nightmares'—and many of the chapters following Max/Itzig's emigration can be read in terms of these repetitive patterns, marked by images of grotesque physical distortion: examples are his mutilated and obese wife and his stillborn baby, as well as the various traumatized characters visiting his barber shop in Tel Aviv.

One of the clearest signs of a personality split that betrays a repetitive pattern of traumatic experience can be found in Book Four, a series of letters and imagined dialogues between the 'old Itzig', who is apparently dead, and the 'new Itzig', who is supposedly the mass murderer Max Schulz after his transformation and 'conversion'. The new Itzig addresses the dead one:

Schade, dass Du den jüdischen Schwarzhändler nie kennengelernt hast! Itzig Finkelstein in Berlin. Itzig Finkelstein ... der mit dem schwarzen Mercedes. Das war ne Type sag ich Dir. Den haben sie aus dem Stürmer ausgeschnitten. (176)

It's a pity you never knew the Jewish black marketer Itzig Finkelstein. Itzig Finkelstein in Berlin. Itzig Finkelstein ... his black Mercedes ... he was quite a guy, let me tell you. Right out of the *Stürmer*. (162)

Later on he confides to one of his letters the story of his encounter with Hanna Lewisohn on the exile ship *Exitus*, her survival in the Berlin air raids, her incurable sickness and the grotesque kind of sexuality they share. She is haunted and possessed by nightmares of anthropophagism and torture. This imagined correspondence or dialogue between the two Itzigs establishes a parallelism between the Hanna episode and the experiences of the new Itzig: Hanna's story and its rendition in the letters sheds light on (and displaces) the new Itzig's traumatic disposition, which is marked by going through the same feelings again and again when confronted with certain memory triggers. The repetitive nature of these feelings is captured in the powerful image of canned food, which the new Itzig on board the *Exitus* associates with kissing

---

8   Caruth, *Trauma*, 5–6.

Hanna for the first time—an experience he also relates to his uncanny encounter with Frau Holle:

Ich betastete ihr Gesicht wie ein Blinder. Oder wie ein blinder Massenmörder. Und Hanna Lewisohn sagte nichts, hatte die Augen geschlossen, atmete heftig gegen meine Hand, auch gegen mein Gesicht … über dem ihren … im Finstern. Ihr Atem roch nach Corned beef, lieber Itzig, so wie das Corned beef bei Frau Holle … den wir hier auf der Exitus fressen fast nur Corned beef, sind Corned-beef-Fresser, weil unsere Vorratskammern bis zum Rand mit Konservenbüchsen angefüllt sind. (198–9)

I fondled her face like a blind man would fondle it. Or like a blind mass-murderer. And Hanna Lewisohn said nothing, kept her eyes closed, panting, panting against my hand, and against my face above her own, in the dark. Her breasts smelled like corned beef, dear Itzig, like the corned beef I had eaten at Frau Holle's … because here on board the Exitus we eat almost only corned beef, we are corned-beef maniacs because our provisions hoard is filled right to the top with canned food. (183)

The exile ship, filled to the brink with canned food, functions as a metaphor for the collective nature of the trauma of post-Holocaust European Jewry that frames the entire novel.

Apart from these collective historical dimensions of his story, Hilsenrath dramatizes the rift between the pre-traumatic and the post-traumatic dimension of the individual character Itzig Finkelstein. The imaginary correspondence and exchange between these two parts of Itzig's character is facilitated and interrupted by the accumulation of grotesque physical imagery that highlights the main paradox of trauma, namely the experience that 'the most direct seeing of a violent event may occur as an absolute inability to know it, that immediacy, paradoxically, may take the form of belatedness'.[9] This 'belatedness' is what marks Book Four and some of the subsequent chapters in the novel, and roots the identity of Itzig as Itzig in the trauma (and guilt) of surviving. What Itzig cannot grasp, according to this complementary reading of the novel, is the death of his entire family, which, through its perpetual 'belatedness', turns into the foundation of Itzig's post-traumatic identity.

The fragile schizoid nature of the new Itzig is spelt out towards the end of the Hanna episode:

---

9   Caruth, 'Traumatic Awakenings', 208.

> Was sagst Du, Itzig? Das hat sie gar nicht erzählt? Dieses Gespräch
> zwischen mir und Hanna Lewisohn hat nie stattgefunden? Ich
> hätte mir das alles nur ausgedacht?
> Wenn Itzig Finkelstein ein Spinner wäre … wer wäre dann der
> Spinner: ich oder du? Sei vorsichtig, Itzig! Zank nicht mit mir! Wir
> müssen uns vertragen. Wir beide! Du und ich! (202)

> What's that you're saying Itzig? She didn't tell that story at all?
> This conversation between me and Hannah Lewisohn never took
> place? It's just something I made up?
> If Itzig Finkelstein were mad … who would be the one to talk
> nonsense then? Me or you? Be careful, Itzig! Don't quarrel with
> me! We have to get on well with each other! The two of us! You
> and I! (186)

The new Itzig (on his way to Palestine) asks the old Itzig (rooted in
German culture): 'who is the madman—is it you or me?' They cannot
reach an agreement about the nature of their past experience, since
they are connected through the loss of the entire family. The ontological
status of the traumatic re-living in relation to the actual past ('statt-
gefunden' versus 'ausgedacht') cannot be determined since it is always
marked by the aforementioned 'belatedness', or, more precisely, the
omission of the traumatic reality by the 'immediacy' of its repetition
or re-living. Cathy Caruth has, with reference to Freud, characterized
the ensuing 'gap' as that which 'carries the force of the event and does
so precisely at the expense of simple knowledge and memory. The
force of this experience would appear to arise […] in the collapse of
its understanding.'[10] Itzig's personality split reflects this very 'gap';
although he re-lives his trauma over and over again, its roots remain
incomprehensible, inaccessible—a blank.

Earlier on in the novel, the narrator throws an ambiguous and
disturbing phrase at the reader by stating that he, Max Schulz, had
actually died in Poland in 1945. (91) Again, one possible interpretation
would suggest his actual physical death (rather than the 'death' of
his role or persona as prototypal 'Aryan') and Itzig's schizophrenic
adoption of Max's identity as his surrogate personality. The literary
and imaginative power of Hilsenrath's novel is rooted in the fact that
these two readings of Max/Itzig as 'Max', the shape-shifter and SS
officer, or as 'Itzig', the traumatized victim, ambiguously coexist. The
protagonist's obsession with Jewish identity and Israeli society, even
his involvement with the paramilitary underground in Israel, can be
read either as characteristic picaresque versatility (Max, playing the

---

10 Caruth, *Trauma*, 7.

role of Itzig) or as attempts to overcome survivor guilt (the old Itzig turned new Itzig).[11]

The narrative structure of Hilsenrath's novel sheds further light on the proposed dual reading of the picaresque trajectory. The second and fourth books prove most elucidating in this context. Book Two mingles the third-person narrator overlooking a picture-frame stage with elements of a third-person narrative mode limited to the protagonist's perspective (the *personale* narrator comparable to Kafka). It dramatizes the transition from the third-person narrator to a *personale* narrative position, but it does not further sketch it out; it rather oscillates between these two modes without allowing any of the narrator figures to emerge from it victoriously: the omniscient narrator is restricted by the insertion of this limited third-person voice, while the coherence of this voice is undermined by the sense that there is some manipulating author persona in the background. As a whole, these sequences bear resemblance to the modernist point-of-view technique. Here is a good example:

> Und durch die zerschossenen, ausgebombten Straßen zu humpeln, mit leerem Magen und einem Holzbein fragwürdiger Herkunft … das war für eine 59jährige Frau, die erst 49 war, bestimmt kein Vergnügen.
> Frau Holle war von den Russen vergewaltigt worden. Das war in Berlin gewesen in den ersten Maitagen des Jahres 1945.
> Genau 59mal, dachte Frau Holle jetzt wütend und versuchte schneller zu humpeln, obwohl sie genau wusste, dass die Russen nicht in Warthenau waren, sondern die Amerikaner.—59mal! (65)

> And to limp through the bombed-out, rubble-filled streets on an empty stomach and with a wooden leg of questionable origin … that was no fun for a fifty-nine-year-old woman who was only forty-nine.
> Frau Holle had been raped by the Russians. It had happened in Berlin during the first days of May 1945.
> Fifty-nine times exactly. Frau Holle tried to hop along a little more quickly, although she knew that it was not the Russians who were in Warthenau, but the Americans. Fifty-nine times! (65–6)

At the beginning of this passage, the narrator seems to be playing in a Dickensian manner with his character ('fragwürdiger Herkunft', 'bestimmt'). With 'Frau Holle war von den Russen vergewaltigt worden', however, things change. The reader will learn later on that

---

11 Cf. Lorenz, *Massenmord*, 288.

she was not raped by Russian soldiers but by Americans. The narrator absorbs Frau Holle's distortion of these facts into his own perspective and thereby destabilizes the otherwise carefully balanced narrative construction. On a micro-level, this technique shows how different narrative voices coexist, thus supporting the macro-structure of the double narrative. Book Four, as shown above, consists of letters which the new Itzig persona sends back to the old Itzig persona—a series of self-addressed letters that dramatize Itzig's inner self as a schizoid *psychomachia*. Books Two and Four frame Book Three, which relates the seemingly unequivocal central transformation from Max to Itzig, and thus call into doubt the very unequivocal nature of that transformation.

A further indicator of this narrative ambiguity is the ending, or rather the fact that Hilsenrath omitted the ending in the final authoritative German version (1977), which was published only six years after its English translation, since German publishers did not want to get their fingers burnt with rather unconventional renditions of the Holocaust. The ending of the English version is set in heaven. God condemns Max/Itzig and then finds himself condemned for being an absent, non-committal God—a *deus absconditus*:

> '[…] where were you? […]'
> And the One and Only says: 'I watched!' […]
> 'Then your guilt is greater than mine!' I say. 'If that is true … then you cannot be my judge!' […] And the One and Only climbed down from his seat of judgment and placed himself next to me at my side. (302)

In the German version, Hilsenrath also uses these leitmotifs of theodicy and an absent God, but refrains from God's final judgement on Max/Itzig, thus not allowing a final closure.[12] The ending of the English edition eclipses the ambiguity of identity, focusing on the protagonist as Max-turned-Itzig, while the German original maintains the central ambiguity throughout—the double story of perpetrator and victim.

This also reinforces the novel's high level of complexity as regards reflecting the genealogy of anti-Semitism. Sander Gilman analyses the historical backdrop to Hilsenrath's novel as follows, partly borrowing from Simmel's exploration of the stranger figure (and its strong yet covert relation to assimilated Jewry in Central Europe around 1900). 'The fantasy of the outsider', he writes,

> is not merely an artifact of marginality, for the privileged group, that group defined by the outsider as a reference for his or her

---

12   Cf. Stenberg, 'Hilsenrath und der abwesende Gott', 185–7.

own identity, wishes both to integrate the outsider (and remove the image of its own potential loss of power) and to distance him or her (and preserve the reification of its power through the presence of the powerless). Thus the liberal promise and the conservative curse exist on both sides of the abyss that divides the outsider from the world of privilege.[13]

This social logic at the heart of Central European anti-Semitism is preserved in the picaresque double narrative Hilsenrath employs. The parallel configuration Max-turned-Itzig versus old-Itzig turned-new-Itzig dramatizes Gilman's concept of a double betrayal of the Jewish attempt to assimilate into German culture and relates it to the post-Holocaust issue of survivor guilt. The logic of assimilation and identification with the 'host' culture was tantamount to the internalization of an idealized Germanic cultural sphere rather than its socio-political reality. Accepting the failure or corruption of this ideal would have meant accepting the failure and corruption of an adopted personal identity that marked the very goal of the long and troublesome road to emancipation through assimilation. Max/Itzig can be even read as a grotesque rendition of Jewish self-hatred or as a search for atonement from survivor guilt by acting out the perpetrators' fantasies of supremacy (through certain psychosomatic symptoms). Both of these interpretations would illustrate Gilman's thesis of Jewish self-hatred as a 'double-bind model of identification and projection'.[14]

These two readings of the novel—Max as a perpetrator, who changes his identity and thrives on post-war philo-Semitism, versus Itzig as a schizophrenic victim, who identifies himself with the murderers of his family—are like the two pictures inherent in an optical illusion, in which only one can be seen at any given time. The readers may only see one version at a time, but they are always aware of the presence of the other. The two versions coexist without blending, an effect that can be compared to the duck-rabbit pictures from the *Fliegende Blätter* (1892), which Ludwig Wittgenstein famously used in his *Philosophical Investigations*. This allows for a powerful rendition of the Holocaust in a narrative voice which tries to achieve a triple goal: coming to grips with a traumatic past, preserving oneself in the face of this past and, at the same time, moulding a sense of post-traumatic identity.

The Picaresque and the Grotesque

Hilsenrath conflates the pseudo-autobiography of a Holocaust

---

13 Gilman, *Jewish Self-Hatred*, 2.
14 Ibid., 392.

perpetrator with what many people in the Western hemisphere embrace as their genuine tradition of individualism, the prototypal biography of the self-made man, who is endowed with free will and ready to adjust to rapidly and radically changing circumstances. This blasphemous juxtaposition is also reflected in the incompatibility of the ghastly historical backdrop, on the one hand, and the ease with which the protagonist manoeuvres through his picaresque adventures, on the other. The casual narrative tone is pitched against the vastness of the grotesque imagery, thus reinforcing the discrepancy between the horror of a perverted world and the psychological triviality of mundane survival strategies in such a world. It undercuts the possibility of distinguishing between order and chaos, between the lives of average citizens and the crimes of the genocide, between psychology and politics—and it does so without putting them morally on a par.[15]

The grotesque raises the epistemological question to what extent humans are able to distinguish between good and evil, but it avoids relativizing these categories. As such the grotesque is not simply a monstrous exaggeration which pastes everything over with the label of nausea and world-weariness, rather it establishes a new mode of communicability between radical opposites, a new dialectical dynamism of imagery within a polarity conventionally regarded as unbridgeable. At the beginning of this potential dialectics of the grotesque stands the author's refusal to grant the reader any sense of coming to grips with the horror of the narrated topic: 'The grotesque is not concerned with fear of death but with fear of life (*Lebensangst*). The structure of the grotesque also implies that our categories of orientation in the world fail [...].'[16] The grotesque is not predominantly defined as a literary or rhetorical device, nor as a technique for undermining language by an excessive semiosis. It is rather a form of experiencing and structuring the world, neither aiming at what the world looks like once deprived of all its deceptive veils, nor providing a unifying principle for reconciling the horror of life and the instinctive ease with which humans, in the face of these horrors, manage to conduct their lives. Rather than constituting a coherent fictional world, the grotesque forms a perpetual incentive to engage in questioning the modes of representing this world—in short, it reflects the 'structure of human consciousness in operation'.[17] The readers are perpetually disappointed

---

15 On similarities between Hilsenrath and Grass in this regard see Graf, 'Erzählperspektive', 140–2.
16 Kayser, *Groteske*, 135f.
17 Pietzker, 'Groteske', 88.

in their hermeneutic anticipation, as the grotesque 'allows neither the subordination nor the synthesis of its negative terms'.[18]

All grotesque traditions are based on the fundamental principles of distortion and alienation through mingling disparate and heterogeneous elements, for example forming hybrids between the animal and human worlds or between the mechanic and the organic. The grotesque preys on conventional reality and is not perceived as something completely alien to or separate from it, despite its destructive impact upon that very reality. Its characteristic feature is the *mundus inversus* topic. This inversion, however, is not perceived by the recipients— reader or spectator—as being out of order, but is rather fully integrated into their epistemology of normality. The grotesque depicts a world of turmoil, in which the effects of turmoil are destructive, yet their causes remain opaque and part of a cohesive concept of reality. It turns the ghastly into the ridiculous, and the ridiculous into the ghastly. In this ongoing process, the reader of grotesque literature is expected not to give in to the emerging epistemological normality, but rather to decipher the grotesque imagination (and one's conscious participation in it) as a socio-historical symptom. Accordingly, I understand the grotesque as the intervention of something extraordinary in ordinary life without causing an epistemological clash or conflict.

Hilsenrath develops the full potential of the grotesque by eliciting an ambiguous suspension of disbelief in the reader that vacillates between fascination and revulsion. It is this simultaneity of critical distance and credulous curiosity in the reader's mind which qualifies Hilsenrath's work as a grotesque picaresque novel. Its imagery often revolves around archetypal female mother figures: Veronja, Frau Holle and Kriemhild. The protagonist's obsession with grotesque images of females does not seem to be related to what Freud describes as symptoms of a psychotic confusion of the conscious and the unconscious, it is closer to the pre-conscious realm of the abject. According to Julia Kristeva, humans are born out of the act of abjection of the preconscious principle of the mother, which is rooted in the unity of subject and object, of ego and mother during pregnancy. By entering the symbolic code of language, humans are able to establish object relations. Language is, if we follow Kristeva, however, always marked as the vehicle of this primordial event of abjection.[19] The return of the maternal body and its destabilization of language shows itself in the repetitive patterns of grotesque imagery, which surface in Max/Itzig's story:

---

18 Robertson, *Grotesque Interface*, 2.
19 Kristeva, *Pouvoirs de l'horreur*, 20–1. My account of Kristeva is partly based on Anne Fuchs in *Space of Anxiety*.

Und sehen Sie nicht, Herr Finkelstein … spiralförmige Bewegungen … und eine feuchte Zunge und vogelknochenartig-zerbrechliche, lange, stammbaumgeprägte, glattgezupfte Frauenbeine … und den Stiernacken des Mannes? Und alles ineinander verschlungen? Und die Beine lachen die Zunge aus und wollen dem Mann das Genick brechen! Und zartes Fleisch und Pfirsichhaut saugen ihm das Mark aus den Knochen. Und die Knochen sind die letzten einer Kette, die Jahrtausende alt ist, mit angeschlagenen und angespuckten Gliedern. (142)

And don't you see, Herr Finkelstein … movements like spirals … and a damp tongue, and long female legs stamped with their ancestry, plucked smooth, as brittle as a bird's … and the bull neck of the man? And all that wrapped in an embrace? And the legs laughing at the tongue and almost breaking the man's neck! While tenderest flesh and peachy skin squeeze the marrow from his bones. And the bones are the last of a chain thousands of years old, with limbs damaged and spat upon! (131–2)

The return of the abject mother—marked by legs that resemble a family tree and by bones that belong to 'a chain thousands of years old'—is cast in an imagery that dissolves the categories of subject and object through acts of perversion and inadvertently triggers responses of disgust. For Kristeva the memory of the abstract, preconscious maternal body is a phobic experience, since it reinstates the moment of self-abjection, especially in recurrent moments of individual language crisis. One's own being is experienced as rooted in the initiating act of loss, but this loss can only be experienced anew as disgust.

Hilsenrath's novel and its obsessive focus on the perverted maternal body can be related to Kristeva's concept of the abject in so far as it shows historical trauma as reduplicating the experience of primordial loss. The symptoms of this loss are inscribed into the language of the grotesque as a re-visitation of language by the pre-linguistic. Anne Fuchs has shown that the abject as a psychological disposition within which the trauma of birth is re-experienced can be found throughout German-Jewish literature in the twentieth century from Freud's *Der Mann Moses und die monotheistische Religion* to Hilsenrath, whose protagonists often drift through 'a space of anxiety where their alienation from the outer world is matched by a sense of self-abjection.'[20] Hilsenrath's grotesque and obsessive rendition of the abject finds a particular outlet in the imagery of the female as monster or witchlike hag, who seduces men and simultaneously threatens male identity:

---

20 Fuchs, *Space of Anxiety*, 178.

'[...] loathing and desire are only the two sides of the same libidinal economy which preserves a fragile male identity by abjecting the castrating (m)other'.[21]

An extreme form of this doubleness is embodied by Mira, the later wife of Max/Itzig in Israel, a Holocaust survivor who has lost her voice in the camp. An 'old woman', who survived a massacre with her, relates Mira's story:

> Und als wir 1945 wieder herauskamen, da war die Mira so mager wie ein Skelett: ein Knochengerippe mit Augen ... Augen, die sich manchmal bewegten.
> Und dann fing Mira zu essen an. Aß von früh bis abends. Kaute sogar im Schlaf.
> Eine Freßmaschine. Stumm. Eine stumme Freßmaschine. (262)

> And when we came out again in 1945, Myra was as thin as a skeleton: a stew of ribs with eyes ... eyes which sometimes moved.
> And then Myra began to eat. To eat from morning to night: even dreamed of food in her sleep! A mute eating machine. (246)

Max/Itzig's reaction is psychosomatic:

> Sehen Sie, Mira verkörpert irgend etwas für mich, was ich zu kennen glaube und doch nicht recht begreife. Wenn ich an sie denke, dann kriege ich Lust, zuzustoßen, zu zertrümmern, aufzufressen, mir einzuverleiben, verliere dabei guten Samen ... und nachdem ich den Samen verloren hab, da möchte ich alles wieder ausspucken, zusammenflicken, streicheln, versöhnen ... aber nicht loslassen, als müsste ich es festhalten, um es wieder zu fressen. (263)

> You see, for me Myra embodies something. I think I know what it is and yet can't be sure. Whenever I think of her the urge to destroy wells up within me, I feel an overwhelming desire to smash the world around me, to swallow it piece by piece, till it runs along my blood, swells my veins, I lose good semen, once I have lost the semen I want to spit it all out again, stick everything together again, stroke it, pat it ... but not let go, as though I had to hold on in order to take new mouthfuls. (247)

---

21 Ibid., 173. On the image of the 'ugly old woman' in aesthetic theory see Menninghaus, *Ekel*, 132–43.

The connection between virility and castration fear throughout the novel is imbricated with the grotesque imagery of the human body on the battlefields and in the camps as abject, dismembered and disjointed. The body functions as a projection screen for dissociate impulses of 'einverleiben' and 'ausspucken', incorporation and dejection. Frau Holle, in many respects the counter figure to Mira, is the epitome of indifference; she arouses her lovers with her prosthetic leg which she can take off—a metaphorical nexus of dismemberment, castration and aggression (72–5/72–4).

Hilsenrath pushes the picaresque genre and its political imaginary to its extreme by inverting the topic of Jewish assimilation to German culture into Max Schulz's mimicry of a model Jew. The grotesque undermines both Max/Itzig's mimicry of identification and the picaresque illusion of absolute shape-shifting.[22] As opposed to the fantastic, the grotesque does not represent a particular extra-ordinary situation but rather renders a specific perception of the human condition itself. The grotesque, like the fantastic, is an alien intruder, but it does not cause surprise in those affected by the intrusion. They do not oppose the grotesque in the same way as E. T. A. Hoffmann's or E. A. Poe's characters oppose the fantastic that encroaches upon their lives and worlds; they appropriate this perfectly possible reality, which the reader interprets as an uncanny vacillation between the conscious and the unconscious, perception and deception, desire and fear: '[G]rotesque art presents us not with the world as we know it to be, but with the world as we fear it might be.'[23] The evil becomes banal, since the reader realizes that it is at the heart of many deep-rooted psychological, social and political realities. The subversion of reason that the art of the grotesque evokes in the reader is based on the all-encompassing consistency of the grotesque imagination within the novel. Grotesque literature renders our world as it is, yet in a non-mimetic fashion: it evokes a perception in the reader that creates a credible degree of consistency holding together the centrifugal tendencies inherent in its imagery.

Race Trouble: Conceptual Jews and Germans

One of the recurrent grotesque features of the novel is the image of 'the Jew' as a stereotypical stock character. In his various investigations on the Holocaust, rooted in critical theory, Zygmunt Bauman introduces the related notion of the 'conceptual Jew', the stereotypical notion of 'the Jew' as an accumulation of mental images—an imagological construct that reveals more about the one who projects than the one

---

22 Cf. Gerstenberger and Pohland, 'Wichser', 80–4.
23 Fiedler, *Freaks*, 11.

who is projected. It is this depersonalized 'conceptual Jew' who, or, rather *that*, in various forms, populates the pages of Hilsenrath's novel:

The age of modernity inherited 'the Jew' already firmly separated from the Jewish men and women who inhabited its towns and villages. […] The conceptual Jew was a semantically overloaded entity, comprising and blending meanings which ought to be kept apart, and for this reason a natural adversary of any force concerned with drawing borderlines and keeping them watertight. […] The conceptual Jew performed a function of prime importance; he visualised the horrifying consequences of boundary-transgression, of not remaining fully in the fold, of any conduct short of unconditional loyalty and unambiguous choice; he was the prototype and arch-pattern of all nonconformity, heterodoxy, anomaly and aberration. […] *The conceptual Jew carried a message; alternative to this order here and now is not another order, but chaos and devastation.*[24]

Young Itzig is a kind of stock and mock exaggeration of the 'conceptual Jew' as a distorted socio-cultural image: the perpetual stranger, parasite, polygamist. This image is dramatized in one of the novel's early scenes, Itzig's circumcision, which shows the stereotypical contradictory double coding of this rite in a predominantly Christian environment—emasculation and virility:

[Hilda, the maiden:] 'Unser kleiner Itzig ist heute acht Tage alt. Deshalb wird ihm heute das Schwänzchen abgeschnitten! Das ist so bei den Juden. Immer am achten Tag nach der Geburt.'
'Das ist ja furchtbar', sagte meine Mutter. 'Da wird der Kleine ja nicht mehr pinkeln können … und später auch nicht mehr ficken.'
'Gar nicht so furchtbar', sagte die dürre Hilda. 'Das Schwänzchen wächst ja wieder nach. […] Das ist nämlich so: Da ist so ein Kerl, den nennen sie den "Mohel". Der hat ein langes Messer, das an beiden Seiten geschliffen ist. Damit schneidet er dem kleinen Juden das Schwänzchen ab. Dann murmelt er ein paar Zaubersprüche, und der abgeschnittene Schwanz wächst dann wieder nach … weder zu lang noch zu kurz … gerade die richtige Länge … dafür besonders dick und kräftig. Deshalb der Kindersegen der Juden.' (10)

[Hilda, the maiden:] 'Little Itzig is eight days old today. And so

---

he's having his willy cut off. That's always what happens with Jews. Always on the eighth day after birth.'

'But that's horrible', said my mother. 'The poor little kid will never be able to have a proper piss again—and later won't be able to fuck.'

'Oh it's not so horrible', said Scraggy Hilda. 'His dick will grow again. [...] This is what happens: there's a fellow called the "mohel". He has a long knife with two sharp edges. He cuts the little Jewish boy's willy off then mumbles a few magic words and then the cock he's cut off starts to grow back again ... till it's neither too long nor too short ... and is exactly the right length ... but on the other hand especially thick and strong. That's why Jews are blessed with so many children.' (10)

Circumcision has often been charged with contradictory anxieties about castration (disempowerment) and fertility (uncontrollable power) in the history of Jewish–Christian coexistence (or lack thereof).[25] Hilsenrath moulds these contradictory collective fantasies into a grotesque imagery that runs like a satirical leitmotif through his entire novel.

This kind of satirical combination of comical form and serious content bears resemblance to Jean Paul's theory of humour. He differs from both the English tradition of literary humour in the eighteenth century and the German early Romantics in so far as he did not integrate his concept of humour into a wider discourse on individual authenticity. Whereas his predecessors regard humour as the voice of an intuitive and pristine self prior to human socialization, Jean Paul sees it as a means of coming to terms with the tension between the transcendental process of human self-awareness and the roles imposed on humans by social and cultural institutions. In his writings, *humour* features as a rhetorical and imaginative device that dramatizes this ambiguity between the transcendental constitution of the individual and ascribed social roles as a form of higher, sublated consciousness.[26] The *comic*, by contrast, merely mimics reality and thereby reduplicates its main structures, however much it distorts and blurs its features; it thus provokes a feeling of epistemological inadequacy in humans, as well as a sense of proximity to the world of phenomena as symptoms of the causalities that shape human life.[27] The tendency of the comic to create 'an identity between an opposing and excluded agent with the excluding

---

25 Cf. Gilman, *Difference and Pathology*, 48–54, 66–72, 152.
26 Cf. Jean Paul, *Vorschule der Ästhetik*, § 32 ('Humoristische Totalität').
27 Preisendanz, 'Humor als Rolle', 432.

agent'[28] is transcended by humour as the formal self-reflection which prevents the comic from turning into a purely mechanical rhetorical device. In this sense, humour brings together suppressed collective and individual anxieties and refracts them through the lenses of grotesque stylization and comical juxtaposition.

Jean Paul's notion of humour as 'the inverse sublime' (*das umgekehrte Erhabene*) is one of the first modern concepts of the grotesque. It revolves around the idea that humorous 'contempt' for life enables humans to overcome the 'mechanical determinism' of their reliance on sensual impressions. This 'contempt' triggers humorous laughter in ever more rapid changes of perspectives:

> Humor, as the inverse sublime, annihilates not the individual but the finite by contrasting it with the idea. It knows no individual foolishness, no fools, but only folly and a mad world; unlike the common joker, delivering sideswipes, it does not single out a particular folly; rather it hauls down the great, but—unlike parody—in order to put it next to the small, and raises the small, but—unlike irony—in order to put it next to great and thus to annihilate both, because in the face of infinity all is equal and nothing.[29]

Humorous contempt for life, accordingly, amounts to relativizing the comic itself. The re-evaluation of values in the notion of the comic is called into doubt by subjecting it to the humorous exercise of an infinite regress. For Jean Paul, the encounter between the fragmentary *real* and the holistic *ideal* leads to mutual deconstruction and thereby illuminates their mutual dependency. This exposes the comic as unsustainable on its own; it needs humour as a constant questioning of its effects in order to perpetuate its function as an 'inverse sublime', as a deconstruction of conventionalized forms of perception: 'The comical quality of horror is complemented by the horrible quality of the comical.'[30]

---

28 Ritter, *Subjektivität*, 78.

29 See Jean Paul, *A Reader*, 250; *Vorschule der Asthetik*, § 32: 'Der Humor, als das umgekehrte Erhabene, vernichtet nicht das Einzelne, sondern das Endliche durch den Kontrast mit der Idee. Es gibt für ihn keine einzelne Torheit, keine Toren, sondern nur Torheit und eine tolle Welt; er hebt—ungleich dem gemeinen Spaßmacher mit seinen Seitenhieben—keine einzelne Narrheit heraus, sondern er erniedrigt das Große, aber—ungleich der Parodie—um ihm das Kleine, und erhöhet das Kleine, aber—ungleich der Ironie—um ihm das Große an die Seite zu setzen und so beide zu vernichten, weil vor der Unendlichkeit alles gleich ist und nichts.'

30 Preisendanz, 'Geschichtserfahrung', 164.

Humour is a device to conceive imaginatively of the incommensurability of human experience and ideals and thus transcends an ethical dilemma: the impossibility of adequately expressing suffering and the simultaneous need to remember those who suffered. In Hilsenrath's novel, the new Itzig tells his story in his letters to the old Itzig and, at the same time, tries to enter into a dialogue with him: 'Kannst Du mich hören, Itzig? Und kannst Du mich sehen? Komm! Spiel mit mir! Wo bin ich? Wo hab ich mich versteckt?' ['Can you hear me, Itzig? And can you see me? Come! Play with me! Where am I? Look for me!'] (173/158) 'Play with me!'—that also epitomizes the picaresque communication between Itzig/Max and his conversation partners, be they living (Hanna), abstract (the collective memory) or dead (the old Itzig). This ambiguous dialogue situation manifests, as sketched out in the previous chapter, the potential of grotesque humour to create a language of remembrance: the mass murderer Max remembers his victims, according to the first (conventional) reading of the novel, or, alternatively, the émigré, ridden by survivor guilt, remembers his former self. The constant shift between an intuitive response of disgust to the grotesque imagery and its humorous reflection in the communication situation between text and reader sustains the novel's creative dynamism. This play with the reader's voyeurism and intellectual curiosity also pre-empts the contradictory obsession of postmodern relativism with 'super-icons' like Auschwitz.[31]

The following example illustrates this double strategy of infinite semiosis of the grotesque and its containment by the satirical meta-narrator, who elicits an uncomfortable poise between repulsion and reader identification:

> Mein Stiefvater sah es nicht gern, wenn ich mit Itzig Finkelstein, dem Sohn seines Rivalen Chaim Finkelstein, spielte.
> Ich spielte aber gern mit Itzig Finkelstein. Ich zeigte dem Itzig, wie man Rattenfallen aufstellt, wie man lange, schwarze Lakritzstangen in die Weich- und Hinterteile der betäubten Ratten einführt, zeigte ihm den Unterschied zwischen stumpfen und spitzen Nadeln, erklärte ihm, dass ein Regenwurm auch ohne Kopf in sozusagen zerhacktem Zustand weiter beweglich blieb, was bedeutet, dass der Wurm oder seinesgleichen das Würmerdasein nicht aufgeben will und letzten Endes die Hand überlebt, die ihn zerschneidet. [...] (22)

> My stepfather was not pleased when he saw me playing with Itzig

---

31   See Stenberg, 'Memories of the Holocaust', 284–9, and Goetschel, 'Sprachlosigkeit von Bildern', 135–41.

Finkelstein, son of the barber Chaim Finkelstein, his competitor. But I liked playing with Itzig. I showed Itzig how to set up rat traps, how to push long, sharp sticks into the backsides of drugged rats, explained to him that worms, even without their heads, still keep moving, which I interpreted to mean that the worm and its kind don't want to give up their worm-like existence and in the end survive the hand that cuts them up. (22–3)

This reads like a metaphorical foreshadowing of the ghastly brutality of the novel, a retrospective voice of sarcasm that relates the itinerary of Max/Itzig to the historical backdrop of the Holocaust. This is quite obviously not Max/Itzig's picaresque voice of an *apologia*, of self-awareness, self-justification or repentance, which sets the tone for the last few chapters of the novel. It is rather the voice of a somewhat detached meta-narrator, extra-diegetic arranger or indirect commen-tator, who introduces a counterbalance to the grotesque imagery. A different kind of blending of voices can be observed just a page later:

Im Hause Finkelstein wurde jiddisch gesprochen, denn das war die Muttersprache des Herrn Friseur Chaim Finkelstein und seiner Frau Sara Finkelstein. Jiddisch ist eine Art Mittelhochdeutsch, eine Sprache, die dem deutschen Wesen verwandter ist als unser Hochdeutsch, das ja im Grunde nur—wie mir der Herr Friseur Chaim Finkelstein erklärte—'ein verhunztes, zersetztes, hochge-stochenes Jiddisch ist'. (23)

At the house of the Finkelstein family, Yiddish was the language since that was the mother tongue of the barber Chaim Finkelstein and his wife Sarah Finkelstein. Yiddish is a kind of Middle High German, a language which has more affinity with the German character than our own High German, which is basically only, as the barber Chaim Finkelstein said to me once, 'a butchered, distorted, affected Yiddish'. (23–4)

In this case, a naïve adolescent tone is prevalent and permeates one of the main satirical techniques of the whole novel, the inversion of colonizer and colonized, perpetrator and victim, Aryan and Jew, and of the cultural stereotypes of physiognomy and physique—blonde, blue-eyed, tall (the 'conceptual Aryan') versus dark, dark-eyed, short (the 'conceptual Jew'). The inversion of the contemporary notion of the Yiddish language as a degenerate pidgin version of standard German is shared by both the naive persona of Max and the retrospective persona of Max-turned-Itzig. These two voices are blended here with the ironic voice of a meta-narrator (impersonated by the father Chaim

Finkelstein), whose presence is apparent in the clause that highlights the kinship of Yiddish with previous stages of the German language ('Mittelhochdeutsch').[32] This satirical meta-narrator also makes his appearance at the beginning of the novel, anticipating the figural ambiguity of the novel by sending both Max and Itzig on an imaginary journey to Israel: 'Wir sprachen oft von Jerusalem, Itzig und ich. Einmal sagte ich zu meinem Freund: "Weißt du … wenn wir erwachsen sind … dann fahren wir mal rüber. Das gucken wir uns an."' ['Often we spoke of Jerusalem, Itzig and I. One day I said to my friend, "Do you know … when we are grown up … then one day we'll take a trip across there. We'll take a look at it together."'] (23/24)

This narrative triangle between narrated and narrating personae and meta-narrator is further elaborated in an aside that also forms part of the novel's exposition:

Ich weiß, was Sie sagen: 'Max Schulz spinnt! Ein Alptraum! Nichts weiter!'
Aber warum behaupten Sie das? Hat der liebe Gott nicht die Unschuld erfunden, damit sie zertreten wird … hier auf Erden? Und werden die Schwachen und Wehrlosen nicht von den Starken überrumpelt, niedergeknüppelt, vergewaltigt, verhöhnt, in den Arsch gefickt? Zu gewissen Zeiten sogar einfach beseitigt? Ist es nicht so? Und wenn es so ist … warum behaupten Sie dann, dass Max Schulz spinnt? (19)

I know what you're saying, 'Max Schulz is going off his rocker! A nightmare! Nothing but a nightmare!'
But why do you insist on that? Is it not true that God invented innocence in order to have it trampled in the mud … here on earth? And is it not true that the weak and defenceless are always trodden upon by the strong, clubbed to the ground, raped, despised, buggered? And at times in certain periods simply done away with? Is that not so? And if it is so … why is it that you maintain that Max Schulz is going off his rocker? (19)

Hilsenrath plays with the perspective of the young innocent Max and his childlike and seemingly plausible view of human society. This passage offers a submerged voice demonstrating the uncanny innocence of the grotesque. The sentence 'Zu gewissen Zeiten sogar einfach beseitigt?' resonates with the notion of innocence in this passage, but it also shows how common language is infiltrated by the jargon of the Third Reich. Words like 'beseitigen' (to remove), for

---

32   Cf. Gilman, *Jewish Self-Hatred*, 107–14.

example, stand euphemistically for something else—in this case for extermination. This linguistic splinter inverts the naive perspective without superseding it. These two voices and their satirical companion orchestrate the art of the grotesque in Hilsenrath's novel.

By eliciting reactions that are torn between feeling sympathy or contempt for the protagonist, between fear of or complicity with the day-to-day-life shrewdness of Max/Itzig, between tentative models of explanation and total dismissal of any form of interpretation, the novel manages to create an implied reader who cannot come to grips with the past, who does not pretend to be able to achieve any form of *Vergangenheitsbewältigung*, but takes on the burden of constantly being aware of the potentially abysmal character of human nature and its attempts to turn flesh and blood humans into 'conceptual' humans.

Conclusion

Grotesque imagery—as long as it is embedded in a complex narrative superstructure such as the picaresque pseudo-autobiography—allows us to speak about the unspeakable. Paul Celan calls this the literary perspective 'from the unburiable', as in his poem 'Denk Dir':

> [...]
> Denk dir:
> das kam auf mich zu,
> namenwach, handwach
> für immer,
> vom Unbestattbaren her.
>
> Think of it:
> This came towards me,
> name-awake, hand-awake
> for ever,
> from the unburiable.[33]

By means of an ingenious combination of picaresque narrative structure and grotesque imagery, Hilsenrath accomplishes a form of commemoration from the perspective of the 'unburiable' and restores some of the dignity of those who cannot be buried. Both Celan's hermetic poetry and Hilsenrath's cruel picaresque prove to be 'namenwach'—awake in the face of the unburied and unburiable names. Hilsenrath defies both a purely analytical and a sentimental-autobiographical approach to the topic of genocide. He wants to *tell* a story and, in so doing, *shows* the complicity of language with structures of power. *Der Nazi*

---

33 'Denk Dir' from the collection *Fadensonnen*, Celan, *Poems*, 268–9.

und der Friseur is not predominantly a satire of anti-Semitism or fascist ideology, it is more importantly a satire about the futility of 'making sense' of them and a moral tale about the imperative to keep on trying to understand their mechanisms. Framed by the imagery of mirrors and shot through with the central metaphors of gaze and blindness, Hilsenrath's picaresque tale keeps the readers always 'blind' and one step behind the narrator, but also 'namenwach' and one step ahead of deluding themselves.

Picaresque Topoi III
Third Agents: The Inclusion of the Excluded

Both the emergence of the classic pícaro and the revival of his modern avatar are closely related to paradigmatic changes in the topicality of individuality within their respective social contexts. In the Middle Ages and the early Renaissance, individuality was predominantly represented (and maybe communicated) in terms of qualities that transcend the limits of the individual, for example beauty or virtue. One of the aims of medieval romances, for example, is the embellishment of an ideal history with accessories that resemble reality; the individual is rendered as a concrete example of the workings of history and functions as the human verification of a divine history of redemption. The double adventure cycle, which was prominent in the French, Provençal and German traditions of the heroic epic, provided the secularized duplication of the exegetic analogy between the Hebrew Scriptures and the New Testament (typology), and can be regarded as a precursor of literary modes of conceptualizing the individual and his or her relationship to God, nature and history. The protagonists in these traditions infringe on social codes and are temporarily evicted from society. They have to go through two cycles of adventures in the wilderness and on the fringes of society before they are admitted into society again and, after the second cycle, adopt the role of a social model and leader, often based on biblical typology.[1] This framework allows for the temporary and provisional literary exploration of individuality outside the conventional topicality, at least during the episodic adventures that typically dramatize moments of social crisis.[2]

---

1   The epics by Chrétien de Troyes and Hartmann von Aue are prominent examples for this double cycle. Wolfram von Eschenbach's *Parzival* forms the climax of this tradition.

2   Cf. Blamires, *Characterization and Individuality*, 152–74; 208–17.

This kind of individuality was a religious concept that maintained that humans are indivisibly rooted in a divine principle. The eighteenth century and its turn to introspection and the idea of human perfectibility brought about a lasting change, the results of which have shaped modern self-perception. This notion of perfectibility came with an enhanced trust in organization and administration as the governing principle of all life—be it in the form of spiritual self-control, economic self-reliance or social bureaucracy. This arguably led to new modes of and a new emphasis on self-reflexivity in the form of self-love, self-determination and self-interest. These terms demarcate the rise of the concept of individuality as subjectivity that underpins the idea of a self-reflective individual who potentially encompasses in her mind the entire object world, an idea prominently articulated in German Idealism, especially by Fichte and Schelling.[3]

As a result of this new calibration of individuality as subjectivity, moral considerations are projected onto a temporal dimension of future perfectibility rather than directly onto a particular individual in the present. They become subject to an internalized debate about adequate behaviour in specific situations rather than to public negotiations. The notion of perfectibility abandons fixed concepts of social conduct and replaces them with the idea of introspective and pragmatic self-organization. Christian movements such as Pietism in Germany and Evangelicalism in the English-speaking world during the second half of the eighteenth century created social subsystems of inclusion that epitomized the predicament of modern individuality: excluded from society, individuality forms the precondition for the establishment of modern meritocratic society. The modality of self-organization as the new guiding principle of life forces the individual to organize a private sphere first before re-entering society. Individuality thus becomes the prime social value.

Returning to some of Luhmann's ideas discussed above, the systemic genealogy of the modern individual as subject can be summarized as follows. The original extra-societal constitution of the individual through its self-reflexivity is the condition for her inclusion in the social system. It is this original exclusion which facilitates the re-entry of 'individuality' into society as the moral value, that is to say, the potential for self-perfection.[4] The differentiation between role and person in a stratum-based society was guided by an undisputed concept of social hierarchy. A conflict between role and person was either imposture or pretence—it always amounted to an infringement of social and religious laws. In a functionally differentiated society, based on the

---

3   See Frank, *Philosophical Foundations*, 39–54 and 97–112.
4   Cf. Luhmann, 'Individuum, Individualität, Individualismus', 162.

emerging principle of meritocracy, by contrast, we are faced with a different situation. It is no longer pedigree and social rank that define the code of behaviour and structure of personality, but rather the array of different roles offered by society. Humans in a meritocratic society are faced with various sets of role models, into which they can insert themselves by virtue of a certain social and professional conduct and affiliation. Societal role and extrasocietal individuality add value to one another and allow for new mixed concepts of identity. By pretending to be the product of an individual choice, role playing as a principle of social conduct adopts the character of authenticity and is communicated as an inherent part of a person's identity. Because different and even conflicting roles are available at the same time, the concept of individuality as a free agent between these available roles functions as a prominent social value.

Meritocracy fosters a kind of social behaviour that emphasizes difference (between the social position of a person and her individuality) rather than congruence (as in the medieval notion of the *homo duplex* discussed in the introduction). The picaresque go-between, as dramatized in modern literary imagination, spells out the paradox of social inclusion and exclusion in the development of modern individuality. He presents himself as an imposter who is set up to be marginalized but cannot be replaced since otherwise the hidden constitution and power tectonics of society would become visible. He is included by being excluded.

As a double agent between shape-shifter and underdog, between self-assertion and ostracism, the modern pícaro provides an ideal literary mode for reflecting on the complex relation between the mechanisms of inclusion and exclusion in modern societies. The understanding of this interrelation is the key to adequately comprehending picaresque renditions of the Holocaust, which seem to create a counter-intuitive contrast with the ludic disposition of the genre. My reading of Hilsenrath's novel has shown that these two personae cannot be separated from one another in the modern picaresque.

Giorgio Agamben's philosophy is also concerned with the socio-political configuration of excluded inclusion. In his investigation of the theory and practice of the 'state of exception' and how it evolved from classical antiquity to the present, he situates modernity within a political history that started with Hobbes and his definition of sovereignty as the power which establishes peace. Modernity, accordingly, is seen as the rationalistic turn towards reinforcement of power structures through the creation of a perpetual state of civil war, which allows the sovereign power to step in and act as pacifying agent, in order to confirm its own efficiency and legitimacy. Agamben asserts that, after Hobbes, the state of exception

> tends to be included within the juridical order and to appear as a true and proper 'state' of the law. The principle according to which necessity defines a unique situation in which the law loses its *vis obligandi* [...] is reversed, becoming the principle according to which necessity constitutes, so to speak, the ultimate ground and very source of law.[5]

That is to say, the state of exception creates a situation of indecision between abstract law and social reality. According to Agamben, it is this zone of indecision which sovereign power, as it is conceived of by Hobbes, enacts in order to perpetuate itself. The act of suspending law allows the sovereign power to define itself anew, even if the law does, in fact, change in the course of this operation. In order to establish this zone in which the enforcement of law is suspended while its character as sovereign legality is regenerated, the sovereign power—and this marks its genocidal potential for Agamben—makes a fundamental distinction between human life as part of the body politic (the citizen), on the one hand, and human life as a biological rather than a social category ('bare life'), on the other. The latter is bereft of all rights and reduced to what Agamben calls *homo sacer*, a legal term used in ancient Rome to describe the double ostracism of losing both the civil rights and the right to be sacrificed in a religious ritual.[6] William Rasch summarizes Agamben's argument as follows: 'the sovereign decision, exception, or ban—the sovereign self-exemption in other words— places the sovereign [...] Both within and without the space or system that the sovereign decision demarcates. [...] this ambiguous zone of inclusion and exclusion in which the sovereign finds himself is also occupied by the sovereign's logical or structural analog, the [...] *homo sacer*.'[7] The act of sovereign intervention depends on the existence of a *homo sacer*: as much as the sovereign power tries to eliminate the ostracized (for example, as 'parasites' of the body politic), so does it depend on the existence of this element in society in order to exercise its perpetual self-legitimization.[8] Agamben regards this post-Hobbesian paradigm of power as one of the foundations of modernity, ultimately leading to the Nazi concentration camp, 'not as a historical fact and an anomaly belonging to the past [...], but in some way as a hidden matrix

---

5   Agamben, *State of Exception*, 26. For a critique of these key terms see Fitzpatrick, 'Bare Sovereignty'; LaCapra offers a balanced account in 'Approaching Limit Events', esp. 161–2.
6   Cf. Agamben, *Homo Sacer*, 73–4.
7   Rasch, 'From Sovereign Ban to Banning Sovereignty', 100.
8   For a critique of this move in Agamben's argument see Schütz, 'The Fading Memory of *Homo non Sacer*'.

and *nomos* of the political space in which we are still living'.[9] He thus challenges the Western political consensus that assumes a fundamental incommensurability between liberalism and totalitarianism.[10]

Koselleck analyses the roots of this development: 'Hobbes's man is fractured, split into private and public halves: his actions are totally subject to the law of the land while his mind remains free, "in secret free". From here on the individual is free to migrate into his state of mind without being responsible for it.'[11] Humans, according to Hobbes, are free and individual only 'in secret'; otherwise they are subject to the sovereign and the power he exerts in a perpetual state of exception. He neutralizes the relevance of divine legitimization of morality for the realm of politics which is defined exclusively by the aforementioned sovereign act of putting an end to (civil) war.[12] Only through an act of division does the human become indivisible; only through the act of subjection to the sovereign power that established peace does the individual gain rights as a citizen, according to Agamben's *'nomos'*. For him, this has shaped Western societies ever since: 'In the system of the nation-state, the so-called sacred and inalienable rights of man show themselves to lack every protection and reality at the moment in which they can no longer take the form of rights belonging to citizens of a state.'[13]

The picaresque narrative provides a structure within which the nature of modern totalitarianism and the predicament of the *homo sacer*—both in Agamben's specific post-Hobbesian sense and in its broader sense of human disenfranchisement and reduction to 'bare life'—can be articulated and reflected. Its characteristic narrative double structure facilitates the rendition of victimhood and psychological self-assertion at the same time. The narrative act of memory is both an *apologia* that asserts the individual and a testimony that testifies to its perpetual irretrievability, as in Hilsenrath's picaresque experiment. This act of narrative witnessing can be related to the testimony of 'the jews'—a term Jean-François Lyotard, similar to Bauman, uses to define an imaginary constituent of profound political implications in European history—a parameter for suppressed Jewry and 'all those who, wherever they are, seek to remember and to bear witness to something that is constitutively forgotten, not only in each individual

---

9   Agamben, 'The Camp', 106, see also 113–14.
10   See, for example, Agamben, *State of Exception*, §1.10. For a critique, see, for example, LaCapra, 'Approaching Limit Events', 137–40.
11   Koselleck, *Critique and Crisis*, 37 (*Kritik und Krise*, 29).
12   Cf. Hobbes, *Leviathan*, part II, 'Of Common-Wealth'. See also Sorell, *Hobbes*, 123–6. For a competing interpretation see Martinich, *The Two Gods of Leviathan*, 74–99.
13   Agamben, *Homo Sacer*, 126.

mind, but in the very thought of the West. And it [the concept "the jews", spelt with a minuscule to distinguish it from the actual ethnic or religious group] refers to all those who assume this anamnesis and this witnessing as an obligation, a responsibility, or a debt, not only toward thought, but toward justice.'[14] 'The jews' in Lyotard's ruminations represent the witnesses of exclusion as one of the foundational acts in Western societies—a foundational act that bases individual and collective identity on excluding others, and thus on the inclusion of the excluded witness. For this mechanism, which is so crucial in Agamben's thinking, Lyotard chooses the contestable metaphorical term 'the jews'.

The pícaro both plays with roles and is tied to a role, the role of the third agent between autonomy and heteronomy, between shape-shifter and underdog. He is an agent who demonstrates that the modern individual is defined by his or her very divisibility, that he or she is the product of foundational processes of inclusive exclusion. It is only through the interference of a third figure that society emerges and can differentiate itself and thereby recreate the condition of its existence. A third agent is both the presupposition for social inclusion and the excluded by-product of its creation (and the witness of that very *ur*scene of society). He is the agent reduced to 'bare life' (in Agamben's interpretation of modernity), yet, at the same time, he presents himself as successfully switching from the scapegoat to the beneficiary of those powers that define sovereignty in a given society. This narrative flexibility of the picaresque, which is epitomized by the protagonist of the next chapter, Oskar Matzerath, also questions Agamben's concept by exhibiting various forms of self-empowerment that cannot be subsumed under his genealogy of the modern *zoon politikon*.

Many of the modern picaresque characters belong to what Bauman terms the group of 'undecidables'[15] between exclusion and inclusion, as it is epitomized by Simmel's stranger figure.[16] The stranger, as he defines him, is a crucial part of modern society, someone who has settled down but still inherits the legacy of nomadism between cultures, the 'relaxed attitude of arriving and departing'. He combines the forces of intimate understanding and objective distance and inserts himself into society 'not [...] as the wanderer who comes today and goes tomorrow, but rather as the person who comes today and stays tomorrow'.[17] This position, Simmel argues, becomes ever more

---

14 Lyotard, *Political Writings*, 141.
15 Bauman, *Modernity and Ambivalence*, 55. In *Postmodernity and its Discontents*, 72, Bauman uses the term 'parvenu' without referring to its Simmelian origins.
16 Cf. 'Exkurs über den Fremden', see also Schutz, 'The Stranger'.
17 Simmel, 'The Stranger', 37; 'Exkurs über den Fremden', 764.

prominent in money economies in general and modern capitalism in particular; it is marked by the double perspective of exterritoriality and mutuality. The stranger is both outside the political territory he inhabits and, at the same time, in perpetual mutual exchange with its social, economic and cultural code.

I would like to relate this perspective to the systemic position of the pícaro as half-outsider discussed above with reference to Guillén's analysis. The stranger finds himself in a position of intimate objective knowledge about the host society; at the same time the intimacy of his knowledge is, more often than not, attacked as the stigma of hyper-acculturation rather than as a sign of successful assimilation; assimilation is, historically speaking, frequently perceived as dissimulation.[18] The greater the assimilatory efforts of the stranger, the more emphatically will his or her social environment insist on the features which mark him or her as different. Simmel reads the history of European Jewry, which forms the historical backdrop of his argument, as the history of the stranger between assimilation and dissimulation and its inherent cultural strengths and devastating problems.

Because Simmel's strangers are not fully part of their environment, they are potentially always on the move, but choose to stay and make social claims. The presence of strangers in modern societies demonstrates two issues. It exposes a blind spot in the rationalistic underpinnings of modern social design, namely its dependence on the presence of a scapegoat figure, whose marginalization serves the justification and legal confirmation of the given sovereign power, as Agamben has argued.[19] This potential scapegoat figure is the suppressed witness of the violence and arbitrariness of cultural foundation acts and their rootedness in exclusion mechanisms. The presence of the stranger makes apparent the precarious human condition in a highly differentiated society and economy that is poised between perpetual assimilation and dissimulation. In other words, Simmel's stranger epitomizes the modern picaresque paradox: the assimilation into a social framework which consists predominantly of multiple processes of dissimulation.

The strangers are part of the common daily routine within the host society, but they are also potentially sidetracking the system, and it is this quality, according to Simmel, that defines how they are perceived by others. The stranger's dual position—between an external observer of and a fully initiated participant in society—is seen as a potential menace. Bauman interprets this indeterminate character as 'potency':

---

18 Cf. Robertson, 'Jewish Question', 345–78.

19 Agamben, 'The Camp', 114, see also *Homo Sacer*, 91–103. See also Girard, *Scapegoat*, esp. chapter 2, and *Violence and the Sacred*, chapter 4.

'Undecidables brutally expose the artifice, the fragility, the sham of the most vital of separations. They bring the outside into the inside, and poison the comfort of order with suspicion of chaos.'[20] Strangers, in Simmel's and Bauman's sense, are inadvertently caught up in a dilemma of loyalty, which does not allow them to settle down:

> The stranger's unredeemable sin is, therefore, the incompatibility between his presence and other presences [...]. The stranger is [...] the bane of modernity [...]—an entity ineradicably *ambivalent*, sitting astride an embattled barricade [...], blurring a boundary line vital to the construction of a particular social order or a particular life-world.[21]

Like Simmel's stranger, the modern picaresque hero both suffers from and deliberately creates a zone of 'incompatibility' between his social position of indecision and his environment. His position as half-outsider endows him with intimate knowledge about the host society, which also makes him potentially dangerous. His intellectual nomadism is potentially both his birth certificate, providing him with a tentative sense of belonging, and his death sentence, resulting from the intolerance towards ambivalence inherent in modern societies, as Bauman has argued.

The final close reading of this study is concerned with a character who is a 'half-outsider' (by virtue of his mixed ethnic origin) as well as an insider (as a member of a *volksdeutsche* family in Nazi Germany) and an outsider (as a 'dwarf' who is subject to Nazi euthanasia legislation): Oskar Matzerath, a pícaro who straddles the boundaries between inclusion and exclusion, who suffers from the position of inclusive exclusion of the stranger and yet inflicts the very precariousness of that situation on others wherever and whenever he is given a chance—a destroyer of shams and conventions, a debunking moralist who does not hesitate to conform with the most immoral intolerance towards 'ambivalence', in Bauman's terms both one of the 'undecidables' and a perpetrator.

---

20 Bauman, *Ambivalence*, 56.
21 Bauman, *Ambivalence*, 60–1.

6.   The Eternal Recurrence of the Picaresque Body: Günter Grass's *Die Blechtrommel*

The Patchwork of Identity

Throughout this study the modern picaresque has been related in different ways to repetitive and cyclical patterns, with regard to the protagonist, his plotting of individual and collective histories. These three levels produce a diegetic template for a nuanced exploration of the interstices between identity and alterity, teleology and repetition. In my final close reading I shall tie together the major features already discussed by examining the connections between the repetitive and cyclical concepts of body and history in the most complex modern picaresque novel, Günter Grass's *Die Blechtrommel* (1959), whose narrative structure and imaginative power exerted influence far beyond the German-speaking world and inspired authors such as John Irving, Salman Rushdie and Jeffrey Eugenides.

'Ich gehöre zu den hellhörigen Säuglingen, deren geistige Entwicklung schon bei der Geburt abgeschlossen ist und sich fortan nur noch bestätigen muss.' ['I was one of those clairaudient infants whose mental development is complete at birth and thereafter simply confirmed.'] (52/35)—so Oskar Matzerath, the child-dwarf narrator-protagonist, boldly claims at the beginning of his story. His statement summarizes a quintessential feature of the picaresque, namely a static psychology spelt out in dynamic yet repetitive itineraries. Earlier in my argument I used Kafka's *Der Verschollene* to illustrate this repetitive dynamic as one of the two principal default positions of the modern German picaresque. The result is a centrifugal movement of self-projection into external agencies which are subsequently re-imagined as one unified individual agency. These centrifugal trajectories always return to the place from where they originated as figments of imagination. This place marks the point of narcissistic self-projection onto the totality of life. In Oskar's case this place is his bed in the asylum, which is associated with his mother's womb. After all, he aims to return to the umbilical cord (229/164).

Grass—contrary to his own claim—makes systematic use of the picaresque format.[1] I shall argue that the novel's structure is closer to the picaresque template than to Bakhtin's concept of the carnivalesque body, one of the critics' favourite tools for pigeonholing *Die Blechtrommel*.[2] My analysis of the human body and history in Grass offers an alternative interpretation which acknowledges the philosophical subtexts of absurdity and life-affirmation in the novel and their structural integration into the picaresque framework.

Die Blechtrommel dramatizes the loss of home and its omnipresence in memory. Pre-war Danzig is recreated in the *apologia* of Oskar, inmate of a mental asylum, who finishes his autobiography on the eve of his thirtieth birthday. He enacts a form of Sartrean *néantisation du réel*, a willed absence of the represented object (Danzig), as the source of its imaginability. Only in the seclusion of the asylum does he summon the courage to face the past. His wish to render the past irretrievable by narrating it (and the futility of this attempt) form the structural vertebra of the novel. Oskar evokes the past in order to exorcize it, he renders it present in order to ascribe it to the realm of absence. Grass pushes the traditional template of the picaresque to its extreme: he presents us with a hero whose physical presence and narrative self-enactment testify to a reality inextricably intertwined with guilt and who nevertheless engages in a powerful attempt to rewrite himself in a history beyond guilt.

Oskar's rewriting of his story and history is captured in the initial staging of the narrative situation:

Zugegeben: ich bin Insasse einer Heil- und Pflegeanstalt, mein Pfleger beobachtet mich, lässt mich kaum aus dem Auge; denn in der Tür ist ein Guckloch, und meines Pflegers Auge ist von jenem Braun, welches mich, den Blauäugigen, nicht durchschauen kann. (9)

Granted: I'm an inmate in a mental institution; my keeper watches me, scarcely lets me out of sight, for there's a peephole in the door, and my keeper's eye is the shade of brown that can't see through blue-eyed types like me. (3)

This initial double-perspective which is mirrored on various levels throughout the novel, most prominently in the occasional shift of

---

1   Loschütz, *Grass in der Kritik*, 212. See also Mews, *Grass and His Critics*, 22–8.
2   Cf. Minden, 'A Post-Realistic Aesthetic'.

the narrator from 'I' to 'he', is most prominently reinforced by the constitutive double perspective of the picaresque between narrator and narrated personae, who together create an *apologia* that consists of both memory and testimony. *Die Blechtrommel* takes us from 1899 to 1954 through the eyes (or the prenatal memory) of two main narrative voices: Oskar as child-dwarf, who, at the age of three, decides to stop growing (or so he claims), and as the thirty-year-old inmate of an asylum.[3] He thus combines the subversive gaze of a child, who continues to develop mentally within an infant's body and social role, with the retrospective gaze of a lunatic, who compulsively reinvents his past. In the final vision of the Black Cook the process of writing, which takes about two years (1952–4), and the narrated plot eventually converge.

Starting with the conception of his mother (a narrative move that outsmarts *Tristram Shandy*'s parody of the *ab ovo* motif), Oskar's *apologia* neither amounts to the confessional *apologia* prevalent in the baroque picaresque, such as in Grimmelshausen,[4] nor does it strike the balance Lazarillo aims at, the simultaneous expression of social determinism and individual merit. By contrast, Oskar presents his narrative identity as a polyphony of aesthetic acts that defies any notion of physical or mental development. Since Oskar presents himself always already one step ahead of any possible new personal experience, his narrative life is a series of events which are designed to confirm his instinctive and intuitive knowledge about the world. His escape from the world (reminiscent of the baroque *Weltflucht*) into the asylum is analogous to his obsession with the world (*Weltsucht*), for it is only through using the world as a cornucopia of stimuli that he can imagine himself as the non-begotten creator of himself. In this regard, his trajectory follows the one of *Simplicissimus*, yet without the baroque novel's final twist of the surprise discovery that the poor farmer's boy (Simplicius Simplicissimus) is, in fact, of aristocratic pedigree (Melchior Sternfels von Fuchsheim).

Oskar experiences daily life in Danzig before and after its *Anschluss* to Nazi Germany with the eyes of a child. He is both complicit and detached. By virtue of the double structure of the picaresque *apologia*, Grass explores the notions of omniscient historical knowledge and conscious oblivion or ignorance: Oskar often describes himself as being

---

3   Some of these motifs are borrowed from Christian Reuter's *Schelmuffskys warhafftige curiöse und sehr gefährliche Reisebeschreibung zu Wasser und Lande* (1696/7).

4   See chapters 22–24 of Book V and chapters 9–12 of the 'Continuatio' in *Simplicius Simplicissimus*; see Breuer, 'Grimmelshausens simplicianische Schriften'; Schweitzer, 'Grimmelshausen and the Picaresque Novel', 158–9.

endowed with the power to conjure up the past through his drumming, while in other passages drumming reflects the self-absorption of an asocial attitude.

Like many picaresque novels, *Die Blechtrommel* interlaces a high degree of verisimilitude and metareflexivity.[5] This combination can be related to the discussion of the grotesque in the chapter on Hilsenrath: the self-reflexive narrator incites both a willing suspension of disbelief in the reader and simultaneously conjures a plausible reality rooted in those very grotesque disparities. This position is reflected in chapters such as 'Das Fotoalbum', where Oskar talks about one of his great hobby horses, cutting and pasting photographs:

> Nicht nur dem eigenen Abbild widerfuhren diese Montagen: Klepp lieh sich Details bei mir aus, ich erbat mir Charakteristisches von ihm: Es gelang uns neue, und wie wir hofften, glücklichere Geschöpfe zu erschaffen. Dann und wann verschenkten wir ein Foto. (60)

> Nor did we keep our montages separate; Klepp borrowed details from me, I took traits from him: we were creating new, and we hoped happier, creatures. Now and then we gave a photo away. (41)

Oskar does not develop new photographs in an acid bath, he simply juxtaposes existing ones. He yokes together incompatible elements and playfully illustrates the concept of montage as opposed to an organic notion of development (or *Bildung*), thereby imagining himself as both creator and creature. The ludic and aggressive manipulation of himself and his environment cuts both ways: he presents himself simultaneously as God-like *prima causa* and as subject to the arbitrariness of a fragmented world. Oskar dissolves this distinction in the serial nature of his patchwork humans and metaphorically conflates procreation (or creativity) and mechanical reproduction in the imageries of sexuality and geometry. Arranging the 'Triumvirat' of Mama, Matzerath and Bronski as a love triangle, Oskar yokes together absurd images of sexual arousal and the cycle of life in an extended geometrical metaphor:

> Eine Zeitlang war ich dumm genug, mit einem Schulzirkel, den Bruno mir kaufen musste, mit Lineal und Dreieck die Konstellation dieses Triumvirats—denn Mama ersetzte vollwertig einen Mann—ausmessen zu wollen. Halsneigungswinkel, ein Dreieck mit ungleichen Schenkeln, es kam zu Parallelverschiebungen,

---

5   Cf. Hall, 'Danzig Quartet', 73–5.

zur gewaltsam herbeigeführten Deckungsgleichheit, zu Zirkelschlägen, die sich bedeutungsvoll außerhalb, also im Grünzeug der Kletterbohnen trafen und einen Punkt ergaben, weil ich einen Punkt suchte, punktgläubig, punktsüchtig, Anhaltspunkt, Ausgangspunkt, wenn nicht sogar den Standpunkt erstrebte. (64)

For a time I was silly enough to try to plot the constellation formed by this triumvirate—for Mama gave the full value of a man—with a school compass Bruno had to buy for me, and a ruler and triangle. The angle of inclination of the neck, a triangle of unequal sides, led to divergent parallels, to forced congruencies, to circles of the compass that closed significantly outside the triangle, that is, in the greenery of the pole beans, and produced a central point, because I was seeking a point, believed in the point, was addicted to the point, longed for a reference point, a departure point, perhaps even a viewpoint. (44)

'Punkt' and 'Dreieck' as symbols for female sexuality are mapped onto the geometrical topography of 'Anhaltspunkt', 'Ausgangspunkt' and 'Standpunkt', suggesting chosen rather than given vantage points. Images of creation and procreation (mother) are blurred with Oskar's eroticism of hermeneutics, his narrative attempts to make sense of his story and history. Poiesis and mimesis, creation and imitation, are blended in this far-fetched metaphor.[6]

Oskar's inner polyphony resonates with the polymorphous character of history. History in *Die Blechtrommel* is the product of a double process of mediation. It is both dependent on linguistic, visual or acoustic records and on the various points of 'reference', 'departure' and 'view' the human mind adopts in the course of processing (and mediating) these records as part of individual identity constructions. In Oskar's case the act of remembering is linked to characteristic misalliances of history with everyday culture. History is reduced to a structural device for ordering the plot, for example in the case of the destruction of the synagogue in the chapter 'Glaube Hoffnung Liebe' ('Faith Hope Love'): the incident is not linked to the Nazi pogroms, but rather idiosyncratically seen as a challenge for the local fire brigade. Historical incidents are perceived in their trivial effects on the monomaniac narrator and his willed naivety. The rise of the Nazi economy, for example, is viewed in terms of the increased availability of sherbet, which the

---

6   Rickels, 'Zwischen Schelmen- und Bildungsroman', 113, points out that Oskar eavesdropping on triangular relationships is a reference to the arch-pícaro Hermes, who is associated with the number 4.

adolescent Oskar uses to arouse girls, in the chapter 'Brausepulver' ('Fizz Powder'). This 'alienation between subjectivity and an autonomous objectivity, between poetic imagination and reified empiricism' is dramatized as a play between manifest and suppressed levels of the given historical situation and constitutes the humorous strain of the novel.[7] An example can be found in this passage, which refers to a propaganda rally for the *Anschluss* of Danzig (a city that was part of the neutral corridor established and administered by the League of Nations after World War One):

> Sie werden sagen, musste es unbedingt die Maiwiese sein? Glauben Sie mir bitte, dass an Sonntagen im Hafen nichts los war, daß ich mich zu Waldspaziergängen nicht entschließen konnte, daß mir das Innere der Herz-Jesu-Kirche damals noch nichts sagte. Zwar gab es noch die Pfadfinder des Herrn Greff, aber jener verklemmten Erotik zog ich, es sei hier zugegeben, den Rummel auf der Maiwiese vor; auch wenn sie mich jetzt einen Mitläufer heißen. (147)

> You may well ask why of all places it had to be the Maiwiese. Believe me, there was nothing going on at the waterfront on Sundays, I had no intention of hiking through the woods, and the interior of the Church of the Sacred Heart as yet meant nothing to me. True, there were Herr Greff's Boy Scouts, but at the risk of being called a fellow traveler I have to admit I preferred the commotion on the Maiwiese to that repressed eroticism. (104)

The mundane questions about how to spend a Sunday afternoon contrast with the historical gravity of the situation, while the reference to political conformism ('Mitläufer') betrays an acute awareness of the implications a post-war reader might associate with this particular historical context. Oskar presents himself as the naive observer and simultaneously as the stage director of this naive persona. In doing so, he breaks up what Hans Blumenberg, with reference to the creation of fictional worlds in general, has called 'the immunization of consciousness through consistence'.[8]

The photo album is Oskar's 'Schatz' ['treasure'] and 'Familiengrab' ['family grave'] (56/38). It both pleases and frightens him. For him the exercise of cutting and pasting is closely linked to re-imagining his family and his search for an unattainable identity. At the very core of his identity lies the uncertainty about his father—a motif

---

7   Preisendanz, *Humor*, 350; see also 'Humor als Rolle', 429.
8   Blumenberg, 'Wirklichkeitsbegriff', 9.

reminiscent of *Guzmán de Alfarache* and many other picaresque tales. Did his mother conceive him from her German husband Alfred Matzerath or from her Polish cousin and lover Jan Bronski? Oskar's dovetailing of the imagery of geometry, sexual obsession and quest for identity intermeshes physicality and history. History is imprinted onto bodies. Oskar is the child of a Kashubian mother and a German or Polish father. Kaszuby is the homeland of an old Slavic tribe which settled in what is now Northern Poland between the Oder and the Vistula rivers during the so-called Migration of the Peoples. Especially since the rule of the Teutonic Order along the Baltic coast, this territory became heavily Germanized, leaving lasting marks on the language. The love triangle Alfred–Agnes–Jan is a metaphorical rendition of an inner-European form of colonialism.[9] The rifts and ruptures of a historical body politic are mapped onto individual human bodies.

The Scarred Body

The most prominent scene dealing with history shaping and disfiguring bodies is the 'Niobe' chapter. Herbert Truczinski, one of Oskar's friends, used to work in a bar for sailors at the waterfront. Once or twice a month, Herbert would come home in an ambulance, stabbed in the back by a sailor. As soon as his massive back was healed again, Oskar would be allowed to inspect the scars. He compares them to the sexual organs of the women he claims to have known. Oskar reflects on the regressive motivation behind this game and, in one of the frequent subtle narrative moves, distances himself from it by switching from the first to the third person narrator: 'Sie werden es erraten haben: Oskars Ziel ist die Rückkehr zur Nabelschnur; allein deshalb der ganze Aufwand und das Verweilen bei Herbert Truczinskis Narben.' ['I'm sure you've guessed by now: Oskar's goal is a return to the umbilical cord; that's the sole purpose of all this effort, why I've lingered over Herbert Truczinski's scars.'] (229/164) The dichotomy death/violence versus birth/fertility is cast into the grotesque imagery of Oskar's attempt to spell out the language of procreation and regression on Herbert's scarred back. Eventually Herbert obtains a position at the Maritime Museum as a guard of the collection's pride, a figurehead from a Florentine galleon dating from 1473, the carving of a naked woman known as Niobe. The historical model for this figurehead was put on trial for witchcraft after the completion of the sculpture, and the sculptor's hands were cut off. Over the centuries, every single one of the sculpture's owners suffered some great misfortune and Danzig's

---

9   Cf. Grass, 'Auf deutsch, auf polnisch'.

citizens begin to blame much of their misfortune as a community on the continuing presence of the sculpture among them. One day Oskar wants to visit Herbert and finds him hanging dead from Niobe's front; he had plunged a safety axe into her wooden body and driven the other end into himself—a grotesque tableau of sexual union.

The Niobe myth replaces the myth of Mnemosyne and the nine Muses, in particular Clio, the Muse of history. The shift from Clio to Niobe signals a shift from active memory to passive memory, from reflection to endurance, from agency to victimhood. First and foremost, it is a move from divine knowledge, embodied by Clio, to human fallibility. In the Greek myth, Niobe, the wife of the King of Thebes, brags about her seven children in order to humiliate the goddess Leto, who has only two children, Apollo and Artemis. In revenge for Niobe's insult, Leto kills all of her seven children. Petrified by pain, Niobe turns into a weeping rock. Throughout art history, she is depicted as an example of both human hubris and mourning.

The coalescence of the mythological Niobe with witchcraft in the perception of Danzig citizens underlines the seductive character of the past and the impossibility of foregoing its persistent presence. As he often does when agitated, Oskar again switches to the third person singular, when he conjures Herbert in his imagination:

> Auch jetzt, in der Anstalt, da er [Oskar] sich diesen Versuch einer Liebe zwischen Holz und Fleisch zurückruft, muss er mit Fäusten arbeiten, um noch einmal Herbert Truczinskis Rücken wulstig, farbig, das harte und empfindliche, alles vorbedeutende, alles vorwegnehmende, alles an Härte und Empfindlichkeit über-bietende Narbenlabyrinth zu durchirren. Einem Blinden gleich liest er die Schrift dieses Rückens. (252)

> Even now, in the institution, as he recalls this attempt at love between wood and flesh, he must work with his fists to wander once more through the labyrinth of scars on Herbert Trucinski's back, puffy, multicolored, hard and sensitive, foretelling all, anticipating all, surpassing all in hardness and sensitivity. Like a blind man he reads the script of that back. (180)

The conflation between mind and matter, life and death, individual body and body politic in the very act of blind reading envisages both individuality and history as circular entities.

These grotesque conflations bear an evident relation to Bakhtin's categories of the carnivalesque, although Grass inverts Bakhtin's assessment of the carnivalesque as a liberating force that challenges dogmatic social institutions and cultural practices.[10] The difference between Bakhtin and Grass becomes evident once we compare their concepts of the body. While Bakhtin praises the rendition of the body in the carnivalesque tradition as life-enhancing, Grass is more interested in the disintegration of the body into a grotesque cycle, most notably in the metaphor of the merry-go-round ('Desinfektionsmittel', 'Disinfectant') and the inversion of the Pauline doctrine ('Glaube Hoffnung Liebe').[11] Oskar's desire to return to his mother's womb is also his desire to opt out of the cycle of meaningless life. Grass's depiction of Oskar as messianic dwarf is very different from Bakhtin's carnival:

> Carnival's hell represents the earth which swallows up and gives birth, it is often transformed into a cornucopia; the monster, death, becomes pregnant. Various deformities, such as protruding bellies, enormous noses, or humps, are symptoms of pregnancy or of procreative power. Victory over fear is not its abstract elimination; it is a simultaneous uncrowning and renewal, a gay transformation. Hell has burst and has poured forth abundance.[12]

Rather than endorsing Bakhtin's praise of abundance and 'gay transformation', Grass highlights the fact that modern man can no longer rely on the regenerative powers of nature and the body. What serves as an emblem for procreation and creativity in Bakhtin, is turned into an emblem of sterility, a form of creativity which has lost touch both with nature as creation (Aristotle's *natura naturata*) and with nature as a creative, demiurgic force (*natura naturans*).

While Oskar does exercise Bakhtin's subversive qualities of the carnivalesque body to a certain extent, his subversion only *performs* a form of subversion which is always already contained by a social rationale. Bakhtin thought that the unofficial world of popular culture was one of the tributaries of the revolution of human consciousness during the European Renaissance,[13] whereas Grass shows both the individual and society tied up in vicious cycles. Oskar's protest is not subversive but rather an aggression which has to be explained within

---

10 Cf. Dunn, *Spanish Picaresque*, 306.
11 Cf. Reddick, *Danzig Trilogy*, 14–22.
12 Bakhtin, *Rabelais and His World*, 91.
13 This concept in itself has attracted criticism from historians who regard Bakhtin's carnival as a choreographed event designed to contain potential rebellions against established power structures, see for example Ruiz, *Spanish Society*, 132–40.

the logic of his own solipsistic portmanteau identity. His narrated persona marks Oskar as the picaresque half-outsider, whose 'combination of super-cleverness and apparent retardedness means that he can watch the most intimate goings-on of his family circle without being either involved, or suspected as a Peeping Tom'.[14] Oskar as his own narrator, however, comments on this self-enactment as an endless cycle. On that level, the novel is not—as a reading inspired by Bakhtin would suggest—a liberation of the individual, but its self-encapsulation in a quintessentially absurd situation, as explored by Albert Camus:

> [...] in a universe suddenly divested of illusions and lights, man feels an alien, a stranger. His exile is without remedy since he is deprived of the memory of a lost home or the hope of a promised land. This divorce between man and his life, the actor and his setting, is properly the feeling of absurdity.[15]

Grass's novel dramatizes this 'divorce between man and his life' and differs from other modern picaresque fiction. It is not so much concerned with a re-appropriation of life through either Bakhtin's celebration of the organic functions of the body or Nietzsche's aesthetic fashioning of the body. This becomes evident in the gruesome recurring images of eating and being eaten, most notoriously in the chapter 'Karfreitagskost' ('Good Friday Fare') and the eel scene, which conflates the imagery of death and resurrection by describing eels feasting on a dead horse's head.[16] This morbid metaphor for procreation and marital guilt receives its final twist when Agnes eats herself to death on fish—suppression of guilt as suicide, a veritable exile 'without remedy'. The absurd nature of this cycle is underscored by the speculation that her father Koljaiczek may have been devoured by eels when he drowned while trying to escape the police—assuming he did not manage to make it to America as Joe Colchic. (36/23, 194/138) The image of history as an eternal recurrence is further elaborated in the less gruesome image of the carousel (541–2/392–3)—the absurd enters the world as a nursery rhyme.[17]

While Grass does make use of a vitalistic notion of the grotesque

---

14 Reddick, *Danzig Trilogy*, 61.
15 Camus, *Myth of Sisyphus*, 13; *Essais*, 101: '[...] dans un univers soudain privé d'illusions et de lumières, l'homme se sent un étranger. Cet exil est sans recours puisqu'il est privé des souvenirs d'une patrie perdue ou de l'espoir d'une terre promise. Ce divorce entre l'homme et sa vie, l'acteur et son décor, c'est proprement le sentiment de l'absurdité.'
16 Rickels, 'Zwischen Schelmen- und Bildungsroman', 126.
17 See chapter 2 in Reddick, *Danzig Trilogy*.

(which shows a certain affinity to Bakhtin's regenerative model of culture[18]), he is more concerned with its relation to the cycle of the absurd and less with the regenerative cycle of life.[19] The myth of Sisyphus is also the myth of the picaresque: the shape-shifter in the underdog considers himself happy. Grass's affinity to the theatre of the absurd, a tradition to which he contributed several plays (most notably *Die Bösen Köche*), is reflected in the extensive use of elements of pure theatre in the novel: abstract scenic effects, clowning and fooling and verbal nonsense. The following episode, just before Bronski is lethally wounded, displays some of the characteristic features of pure theatre, namely the dissociation of physical impulses and objects from human consciousness: 'da griff Maschinengewehrfeuer ins Kinderzimmer, vor dem Portal detonierten Panzerabwehrgranaten [...]. Da lag Oskar, und Jan Bronski, mein süßer blauäugiger Onkel, hob nicht einmal die Nase [...]' ['machine-gun fire entered the nursery and antitank shells exploded at the main entrance [...]. There lay Oskar, and Jan Bronski, my sweet blue-eyed uncle, didn't even lift his nose [...]'] (299/215). The historical event of the German siege of the Polish post office of Danzig/Gdańsk and the tragic fate of Oskar's uncle are pitched against an array of objects, independent agents with lives of their own. Oskar's obsession with drums is one of them; it saves him miraculously and ultimately leads to the death of his uncle.

Stasis and Repetition

Grass combines two cycles of absurdity, that of the modern individual, which he translates into Oskar's simulation of naivety, and that of history, which he transposes into a cosmos without eschatology. The bed in a mental hospital is as close as the modern Sisyphus gets to redemption: Oskar is not only a conflation of the Nietzschean principles of Apollo and Dionysus, in the form of Eduard from Goethe's *Die Wahlverwandtschaften* and Rasputin, as frequently pointed out. (111–14/78–81)[20] He also encompasses the two main agencies of the novel—petit bourgeois self-assertion and artistic self-apotheosis— by imagining himself as both Zarathustra and dwarf, Messiah and philistine. His very name (Old English 'Osgar') means 'God's spear' or 'God's angel', suggesting a messianic quality, which is, however,

---

18 This applies in particular to the four categories Bakhtin analyses in *Problems of Dostoevsky's Poetics*: 'familiarization' (decontextualizing cultural elements), 'eccentricity' (observing society from the margins), 'misalliance' (mixing the incongruous), 'profanation' (debasing the sacred). Fischer discusses their applicability to Grass in *Inszenierte Naivität*, 155–7, 170; see also Lachmann, *Intertextualität*, 236–8.

19 See Frizen, 'Literatur des Absurden', 180–9.

20 Cf. Fischer, *Inszenierte Naivität*, 127.

inverted by the fact that he retreats into an asylum at the very age when the gospels report the beginning of the public life of Jesus as a preacher and healer.

Not only the dichotomy Apollo versus Dionysus but also Nietzsche's late writings, from *Also sprach Zarathustra* onwards, run through *Die Blechtrommel*—as imaginative correlative and satirical target. The Nietzschean subtext works on three levels. First, life and history in *Die Blechtrommel* are enacted through Oskar's body—a *discours* of nervous sensations as opposed to the *histoire* into which this is plotted by the retrospective narrator. Identity, fleeting as it may be, is presented as being rooted in physical impulses.

Second, the ensuing notion of individuality as a divisible entity is based on a concept of the human will akin to Nietzsche's concept of the will to power, that is to say, the affirmation of the illusionary character of identity. In order to maintain this *fiction* of identity, however, Nietzsche has to introduce the idea of re-willing the originally un-willed. He thus endorses a fictitious cohesion of identity as a psychological survival stratagem and champions art and aesthetic self-fashioning as a vital human evolutionary drive.[21] Only by accepting the aesthetic enactment of the self as an identity which one can re-will in eternity, does life, according to Nietzsche, constitute itself as a self-appropriating will to power.[22] This nexus combines the figural archetypes who emerge again and again in the modern picaresque: the shape-shifter, the child, the savior—all of which converge in Oskar.

Third, *Die Blechtrommel* dovetails the Nietzschean concept of life as an aesthetic project and the meta-reflexivity of its narrative structure. In one of his *Nachgelassene Fragmente* from 1885 Nietzsche notes:

Der Mensch als eine Vielheit von 'Willen zur Macht': jeder mit einer Vielheit von Ausdrucksmitteln und Formen. Die einzelnen angeblichen 'Leidenschaften' (z.B. der Mensch ist grausam) sind nur fiktive Einheiten, insofern das, was von den verschiedenen Grundtrieben her als gleichartig ins Bewusstsein tritt, synthetisch zu einem 'Wesen' oder 'Vermögen', zu einer Leidenschaft *zusammengedichtet* wird. Ebenso also, wie die 'Seele' selber ein Ausdruck für alle Phänomene des Bewusstseins ist: den wir aber als Ursache aller dieser Phänomene auslegen (*das 'Selbstbewusstsein' ist fiktiv!*).

Man is a multiplicity of 'wills to power': each one with a multiplicity of means of expression and forms. The individual *supposed* 'passions'

---

21 Cf. Nehamas, *Life as Literature*, 153–63; Reginster, *Affirmation of Life*, 202–5, 219–22.
22 Cf. Nietzsche, *Zarathustra*, II, § 12.

(e.g., man is cruel) are merely *fictitious unities*: that which enters consciousness from the different fundamental drives as *of the same kind* becomes, through a synthesizing fiction, a 'being' or 'faculty'—a passion. Just as the 'soul' itself is an *expression* of all the phenomena of consciousness which, however, we *interpret as the cause of these phenomena* ('self-consciousness' is a fiction!).[23]

Nietzsche's analysis of the misunderstanding of an effect (for example, 'the soul') for a cause (conflicting 'wills to power' rooted in neural impulses) does not only constitute the quintessence of his critique of modern culture, it is also at the core of his critique of the modern concept of the individual as subject. The synthesis of being ('Wesen'), faculty ('Vermögen') and passion ('Leidenschaft') is for Nietzsche the product of diverse impulses, each of which follows the will to power.[24] The belief in the 'fictitious unity' of these impulses is part of the human faculty of self-deceit (commonly understood as self-knowledge) as survival strategy. In Nietzsche, the bottom line is always the interpretation of physical sensations, primarily the acoustic and olfactory senses (both of which are, indeed, magically developed in Oskar).[25] He connects the cohesion of the body with that of the self, and intertwines identity with the *history* of the body-sense-mind nexus. Pierre Klossowski underscores this aspect: 'The dread of physical dissolution requires a retrospective vision of its own cohesion. Thus, because the *self*, as a product of the body, attributes this body to itself as its own, and is *unable* to create another, the self too has its own *irreversible* history.'[26] This irreversibility is experienced as individual accomplishment, as

Ideal des übermüthigsten lebendigsten und weltbejahendsten Menschen, der sich nicht nur mit dem, was war und ist, abgefunden und vertragen gelernt hat, sondern es, so wie es war und ist, wieder haben will, in alle Ewigkeit hinaus, unersättlich da capo rufend, nicht nur zu sich, sondern zum ganzen Stücke und Schauspiele, [...]—Wie? Und dies wäre nicht—circulus vitiosus deus?

ideal of the most high-spirited, vital, world-affirming individual, who has learned not just to accept and go along with what was and what is, but who wants it again *just as it was and is* through

<hr>

23 Nietzsche, *Nachgelassene Fragmente 1885–1887*, 25; *Late Notebooks*, 60 (1 [58]).
24 Hamacher, 'Disgregation of the Will', 119–22.
25 Cf. Rickels, 'Zwischen Schelmen- und Bildungsroman', 114; Blondel, *Body and Culture*, 200–38.
26 Klossowski, *Nietzsche*, 23.

all eternity, insatiably shouting *da capo* not just to himself but to the whole play and performance, [...]—What? And that wouldn't be—*circulus vitiosus deus?*[27]

Nietzsche here describes the formation of the self through an assumed yet deceptive coherence of unstructured neural impulses, as a performative 'da capo' of life-affirmation and its psychosomatics.

This triad of language, will and *physis* is also at stake in *Die Blechtrommel*. Oskar reduces language as a system of symbols to the code of drumming, moving away from the discursive and referential to the rhythmic and poetic function of human expression, from cognitive to mantic or magical functions, conjuring the recurrence 'through all eternity' of the grotesque body—his own, his parents', his ethnic body—as a 'circulus vitiosus deus'. This aesthetic performance is integrated into the wider context of regression, infancy and naivety which governs *Die Blechtrommel* on both its diegetic and metaphorical levels. Through his drumming and glass-shattering scream, Oskar is able to defend his self-fashioning as 'innocent' through his 'histrionic renunciation of interpretation and causality'.[28] History is thus never translated into a meaningful plot but remains a vicious circle. Oskar's Nietzschean ideal of the 'weltbejahendsten [...] Menschen' tilts into the (decadent, to speak with Nietzsche) forms of escapism.

The central metaphors for creativity in its productive (drumming) and destructive (screaming) forms and their implicit Nietzschean overtones of aestheticization converge with the Nietzschean notion of will, which Grass enacts as the original sin, the fall:

Da hatte ich also mit einem einzigen, zwar nicht harmlosen, aber doch von mir wohldosierten Sturz nicht nur den für die Erwachsenen so wichtigen Grund des ausbleibenden Wachstums geliefert, sondern als Zugabe und ohne es eigentlich zu wollen den guten harmlosen Matzerath zu einem schuldigen Matzerath gemacht. (74)

So with a single fall, by no means harmless, but self-administered in a carefully measured dose, I managed to provide the cause grown-ups needed for my failure to grow—repeatedly confirmed by the doctors—and, as an added bonus, to unintentionally transform a decent and harmless Matzerath into a guilty Matzerath. (52–3)

---

27   Nietzsche, *Jenseits von Gut und Böse*, 75; *Beyond Good and Evil*, 50–1 (§ 56).
28   Fischer, *Inszenierte Naivität*, 118.

This enactment of the self as will in Oskar is closely related to the novel's narrative technique: Grass's extensive use of *Dingsymbole* as seemingly objective correlatives for historical events undermines the distinction between story and history as well as the one between individual and political bodies. However, the dissolution of any objectifiable relation between signifier and signified leads to an excessive semiosis which illustrates two aspects seminal for an understanding of the novel: the chaos of the realm of *physis* and its dramatization as *poiesis* by Oskar. The excessive imagery marks reality as simulacra of reality, as a rendition of Oskar's will to deceive. Oskar's images enact and inaugurate his will as artist rather than, in fact, create objective correlatives for the reality into which he inscribes himself. He rather establishes a network of simulacra (*Trugbilder*), designed, as Nietzsche remarks in a seminal passage, 'einer bestimmten Art von Unwahrheit zum Siege und zur Dauer zu verhelfen, ein zusammenhängendes Ganze [*sic*] von Fälschungen als Basis für die Erhaltung einer bestimmten Art des Lebendigen zu nehmen'. ['its real task is to help a certain kind of untruth to victory and permanence, to take a connected whole of falsifications as the basis for preserving a certain kind of living things'.][29]

This active agency is counterbalanced by the alienation inherent in Oskar's semiosis. While he envisages reality as an extension of his will (in what can be read as a parody of Nietzsche), his motivation for action is often shown as rooted in the world of objects rather than in the organizing individual as subject. An example is the continuation of the scene quoted above, which will lead to Bronski's death. After a bombshell hit the Polish post office, Oskar is the only one who remains unscathed—he rescues his drum and then reluctantly offers his help to Bronski:

> Mir aber, der ich mich, wie es zu einem Dreijährigen passte, während des Granateinschlags im Schutzengelwinkel des Kinderzimmers befunden hatte, mir fiel das Blech zu, die Trommel zu—und sie hatte nur wenige Sprünge im Lack und gar kein einziges Loch, Oskars neue Blechtrommel.
> Als ich von meinem frischgewonnenen, sozusagen hastenichtgesehn direkt vor die Füße gerollten Besitz aufblickte, sah ich mich gezwungen, Jan Bronski zu helfen. (302)

> But finding myself, as befits a three-year-old, in the guardian-angel corner of the nursery right under the window when the shell struck, the drum, the drum made of tin fell to me—no holes at all and scarcely a crack, Oskar's new tin drum.

---

29 Nietzsche, *Nachgelassene Fragmente 1884–1885*, 699; *Late Notebooks*, 50 (43 [1]).

When I looked up from my newly won prize, which had rolled to
my feet in the blink of an eye, I saw I'd have to help Jan Bronski.
(217)

Michael Minden describes this plot-driving agency of objects and
matter as follows: 'It is the drum, not the drummer, from which the
ramified narrative springs.'[30] As always in the modern picaresque,
active and passive agencies condition one another. *Die Blechtrommel*
reduplicates and parodies this duality in the powerful image of the
Schwarze Köchin, a maternal figure of folksong and fairy-tale origin
(and an inversion of the Black Madonna of Częstochowa, strongly
associated with Polish liberation and nationalism), who allows Oskar
to make his last powerful affirmation of will ('Ja—Ja—Ja!'), rephrasing
Zarathustra's vision of time as eternal recurrence, as a gate between
two eternities—the past and the future:

> Fragt Oskar nicht, wer sie ist! Er hat keine Worte mehr. Dann was
> mir früher im Rücken saß, dann meinen Buckel küsste, kommt
> mir nun und fortan entgegen:
>> Schwarz war die Köchin hinter mir immer schon.
>> Dass sie mir nun auch entgegenkommt, Schwarz.
>> Wort, Mantel wenden ließ, Schwarz.
>> Mit schwarzer Währung zahlt, Schwarz.
>> Während die Kinder, wenn singen, nicht mehr singen:
>> Ist die Schwarze Köchin da? Ja—Ja—Ja! (779)

> Don't ask Oskar who she is. He's run out of words. For what was
> once behind my back, then kissed my hump, is now and forever
> coming toward me:
>> Black was the Cook always somewhere behind me.
>> And now she comes toward me at last all in black.
>> Her words and her garment all twisted and black.
>> And the debts she pays are all paid in black.
>> And children who sang: Is the Black Cook coming?
>> No longer need ask, they'd better start running.
>> Better start running, the Black Cook's coming!
>> Ha! Ha! Ha! (563)

Oskar's relation to maternal figures runs counter to the teleology of
Christian redemption. He moves from his grandmother Anna Bronski
on the Kashubian potato fields in the East to the mythological Terrible
Mother who awaits him in the Western metropolis of Paris. In this

---

30 Minden, 'Post-Realist Aesthetic', 154; see also Just, *Darstellung und Appell*, 119.

sense, *Die Blechtrommel* certainly zooms in on historical events 'from the perspective of [Nietzsche's concept of] eternal recurrence', as Laurence Rickels observes, without going into any detail.[31]

The witchlike Terrible Mother is a mythological figure who appears in many picaresque novels. She forms an imaginative correlative for schizophrenia, both in a psychiatric sense, as employed by C. G. Jung, and in a philosophical sense, as proposed by Deleuze and Guattari. Jung reads the Terrible Mother in mythology, fairy-tales and folk tales as a reflection of the psychological conflict between a desire to return to the realm of maternal security and a fear of precisely this desire and the threat it poses to individual identity. This double coding of the maternal principle as the goal of deepest desire and the source of profound fears is, according to Jung, closely related to schizophrenia.[32] Oskar's movement from East to West, from innocence to sin, from Anna to the Black Cook, is turned into a cyclical structure at the end of the novel, when the embrace of the Terrible Mother coincides with his arrest and subsequent transfer to the asylum (with its white bed as a surrogate womb). This circularity is reflected in the perpetual reversal of certain leitmotif dichotomies: he is both of Slavic and Germanic descent, Rasputin and Goethe. He also enacts himself as both a messianic figure and a dwarf. This latter dichotomy deserves closer analysis, since it highlights memory and the act of writing as something physical that cannot transcend itself.

Grass's earliest lyrical experiment with the figure of Oskar, dating from 1952, imagines him as a stylite and 'Zwerg, der die Röcke der alten Weiber zählt'.[33] It foreshadows Oskar as an 'umgepolter Säulenheiliger', an inverse pillar saint, who changes with ease from his 'supporting leg' to his 'playing leg' (*Stand- und Spielbein*).[34] The duplication stylite/dwarf can be related to the chapter 'Vom Gesicht und Räthsel' ('Of the Vision and the Riddle') in *Zarathustra*, in which Nietzsche conceives of the human being as composed of both the self-transcending mental powers of Zarathustra, linked to asceticism and solitude, and the chthonic nature of the dwarf on Zarathustra's shoulder.[35] Yet, Grass undermines this dichotomy. In Oskar these two figures—the self-transcending shape-shifting narrator and the threatened underdog—merge in multiple ways.

The dwarf activates a mythological subtext that deals with the mutual dependence of creation and destruction and features prominently in

---

31 Rickels, 'Zwischen Schelmen- und Bildungsroman', 114.

32 Jung, *Symbole der Wandlung*, 400.

33 Grass, 'Der Säulenheilige', 240.

34 Neuhaus, *Die Blechtrommel*, 61.

35 Nietzsche, *Zarathustra*, III, §2.

Die Blechtrommel: 'Oskar has much in common with the dwarf figures of mythology, the Tom Thumbs, dactyls and Cabiri, who all possess a phallic aspect. They are personifications of creative forces, of the *libido*.'[36] The central metaphor for this creative power is drumming, which is related to rhythm and fire, the latter through the (Polish) white and red design on the drum and its role as a central *Dingsymbol* during the German army's attack on the Polish post office. This motif nexus hints at the divine child Hermes, the inventor of fire (destruction) and the lyre (drum)—and the seminal mythological point of reference in the modern picaresque. It also refers to its very bifurcation in Oskar's grandparents, the Earth Mother Anna and the arsonist Koljaiczek, whose procreative powers and adaptive skills are reminiscent of the mythological trickster figure. Conception and fire, food and death are further developed in the figures of Alfred Matzerath who 'Gefühle in Suppen zu wandeln verstand' ['could convert his emotions into soup'] (47/31), and Agnes, who dies of food because she wants to abort her second child. All this creates a 'grotesque vision of life as the eternal cycle of the flesh that feeds and is fed upon'.[37]

In the overdetermination of Oskar as both dwarf and Messiah, Grass pens a parody of Zarathustra's affirmation of life through will. Nietzsche's intuition of the eternal recurrence is the affirmation of the total economy and creative unity of life as will to power. Maudemarie Clarke regards this act of affirmation as a psychological confidence game that aims at tricking oneself into imagining 'eternal recurrence in an uncritical and preanalytical manner, suspending all doubts concerning its [...] conceivability.'[38] The resulting 'innocence of becoming',[39] as opposed to the petrifaction of time in the past, is, however, deconstructed in Grass's narrative operations as untenable for any form of historical enquiry, as I will elaborate in the following section.

Underdog and *Übermensch*

Nietzsche's eternal recurrence of the same as an attempt to reconnect the human with the sources of life, to retranslate 'the *"conscious"* semiotic* into the *semiotic of the impulses*',[40] writes an anamnesis of modernity, whose alleged therapeutic merits Grass calls into doubt (whether or not with direct reference to Nietzsche). Towards the end of

---

36 Roberts, 'Psychology and Mythology', 47.
37 Ibid., 52; see also the entry 'Zwerg' in Hoffmann-Krayer and Bächtold-Stäubli, *Handwörterbuch des deutschen Aberglaubens*.
38 Clarke, *Nietzsche*, 270.
39 Stambaugh, *Eternal Return*, 12.
40 Klossowski, *Nietzsche*, 39.

the novel, Oskar receives and begins to venerate the ring finger of the murdered nurse Dorothea (742/537). Just before Oskar returns to the metaphorical womb of the asylum, the story of his mother's complicated marriage and the associated phallic imagery of the eels comes full circle—an extended metaphor of guilt. Guilt is the one thing which can neither be willed nor re-willed and therefore cannot be overcome or transposed into a 'semiotic of the impulses'. Grass connects drumming and writing: by writing down and drumming out his story Oskar seeks to hijack an idiom outside guilt and thus attain amnesia. His revenge on the world, his drumming and writing, will, however, never afford him the desired amnesia, since his aestheticism is always underpinned by guilt and does not allow him to move from his artistic self-fashioning to life-affirmation. Nietzsche presents both as equiprimordial; Grass undercuts this philosophy in Oskar's picaresque narrative which does not manage to overcome guilt but rather shows how his self-invention is part of his guilt complex, and vice versa.

Oskar finds himself in a network of guilt which precedes and underpins the exertion of will as a survival strategy. Towards the end of the novel, which converges with the final stage of his autobiographical writing,

> Oskar fürchtete sich vor dem Tag, da der Maler jenen Gegenstand bringen würde, welcher allein bestimmt war, von mir gehalten zu werden. Als er dann schließlich die Trommel brachte, schrie ich: 'Nein!'
> Raskolnikoff: 'Nimm die Trommel, Oskar, ich habe dich erkannt!'
> Ich zitternd: 'Nie wieder. Das ist vorbei!'
> Er, düster: 'Nichts ist vorbei, alles kommt wieder, Schuld, Sühne, abermals Schuld!'
> Ich, mit letzter Kraft: 'Oskar hat gebüßt, erlasst ihm die Trommel, alles will ich halten, nur das Blech nicht!' (621)

> Oskar dreaded the day when the painter would bring the object that alone of all objects was made to be held by me. When he finally brought the drum, I cried out, 'No!'
> Raskolnikov: 'Take the drum, Oskar, I know who you are.'
> I, trembling: 'Never again. All that has ended.'
> He, darkly: 'Nothing ends, all returns, guilt, atonement, guilt again.'
> I, with my last strength: 'Oskar has repented, spare him the drum, I'll hold anything, but not the drum.' (452)

Oskar's art as *apologia* will not serve his ultimate purpose of transcending, annihilating or sublating time. His drumming, which serves as a self-reflexive metaphor for his autobiographical self-fashioning, is haunting him in this intertextual play on the Rodion Raskolnikov in Dostoevsky's *Crime and Punishment*. Oskar's artistry as a drummer, which is dramatized throughout the novel as potential self-redemption, a self-invention *ex nihilo*, is here tied in with the 'nothing ends' of concrete historical guilt. Oskar's Zarathustrian attempt to re-will the non-willed past as a picaresque *apologia* is the attempt of a buffoon and imposter. The qualities of the tempter and experimenter, which Nietzsche regards as part of Zarathustra's transcending of the vicious circle, are here mapped onto his counterpart, the dwarf without Zarathustra.[41]

Die Blechtrommel is underpinned by a dense network of references to the European dwarf-tale tradition: the Grimm Brothers' Tom Thumb (*Däumling*), Charles Perrault's *le petit poucet* and Wilhelm Hauff's *Kunstmärchen* 'Der Zwerg Nase' and 'Die Geschichte vom kleinen Muck'.[42] While the Nietzschean context suggests a conflation with the *Übermensch* figure and thereby a parody of Zarathustra, the dwarf tradition grafts a further double code onto Oskar: it combines the ludic trickster, who celebrates the functions of the individual body, with the *homo sacer* ostracized from the Nazi body politic. Grass's employment of the picaresque template exploits the potential of this conjunction to the full.

Oskar is overdetermined by a set of conflicting references. His (allegedly self-inflicted) handicap makes him a potential victim of the Nazi euthanasia programme. He accuses his mother of having played with the idea of giving him up: 'Einen Gnom hat sie in mir gesehen. Abgetan hätte sie den Gnom, wenn sie nur gekonnt hätte.' ['She saw me as a midget. She would have done away with me if she could.'] (219/156) Oskar also barely escapes becoming a victim of eugenic 'cleansing' at the hands of the only maternal figure left towards the end of the war, Maria, with whom Oskar claims to have fathered a child named Kurt (474–5/343–4): 'Oskar embodies both the madness of the persecuted and that of the persecutors. […], he fulfils one of the central functions of the trickster, who is a figure on the threshold uniting all dichotomies.'[43]

---

41   Cf. Nietzsche, *Zarathustra*, II, §12; §§20–1.

42   The *Däumling* story, which is played as a *mise en abîme* in 'Die Tribüne', is about the eponymous hero's recurrence after a journey through the world and animals' organs—a rite of passage from the mother to the father, cf. Arnds, *Eugenics*, chapter 3. Oskar's attachment to his mother, however, symbolized through the maternal gift of the drum, turns his story into the eternal recurrence of the female principle as opposed to the '*Bildungsroman*' of Grimm's *Däumling*. Oskar's return to the mother is symbolized by the wedding ring finger of the nurse, whom he allegedly murdered. The drum, which he receives at the age of three, and the ring finger, which he receives aged thirty, establish the cyclical structure of the novel.

43   Arnds, *Eugenics*, 120.

Oskar is also overdetermined by Adolf Hitler, who, in his early political career, fashioned himself as 'der Trommler' and never ceased to regard himself as an artist.[44] The nexus dwarf—Hermes—trickster can be read in the context of the Jungian interpretation of Hitler as the demonic reincarnation of the ejected and suppressed trickster in Western cultures, as Peter Arnds has shown.[45] Oskar's humpback, developed after his 'father's' funeral, accordingly turns into an ambiguous metaphor, representing both his personal responsibility for Matzerath's death, collective German guilt, and his own vulnerability to Nazi social engineering. One possible reading is that Oskar escapes persecution because he disguises his physical deformation in the body of a child and then desperately tries to be perceived as a conformist member of society—as an entertainer in the front theatre.

Due to the picaresque narrative framework, the reader of *Die Blechtrommel* can never be sure how or whether these figural overdeterminations of the *character* Oskar are rooted in the *narrator* Oskar. Is his deformation diegetic reality or an extradiegetic perception of the grotesque effects of Oskar's guilt? Is his narrative a Zarathustrian enactment of 're-willing the non-willed' as a parody of many Germans' desire to re-invent themselves as the opposite of willing perpetrators? This would then reflect, in particular, the position of intellectuals who opted for an apolitical stance between 1933 and 1945, in the so-called inner emigration (as portrayed by Thomas Mann in *Doktor Faustus*). Is all this simply a form of excessive semiosis displayed in order to enact naivety and thus establish a basis for literary credibility?—Each of these possible readings is legitimate, but none of them fully encompasses the power of Grass's figural, stylistic and structural composition.[46]

Conclusion

Oskar reveals the culture of (self)deceit permeating German petit bourgeois society on the eve of World War Two and, at the same time, uses this satirical de-masking to enact his own naivety, as a

---

44 See Tyrell, *Vom 'Trommler' zum 'Führer'*, 170–4, and Kershaw, 'Ideologe und Propagandist', 266. See also Ryan, *Uncompleted Past*, 60–1, for a discussion of the Mephistophelian subtext of the Oskar figure.

45 Arnds, *Eugenics*, 103.

46 Reddick's attempt to distinguish a 'brainbox' from a 'tears' persona in *Die Blechtrommel* fails to convince. He claims that the detached picaresque-satirical perspective ('brainbox') is supplemented by a second persona that 'suffer[s] the reality', while I am trying to show that both the detached perspective and the guilt-ridden involved perspective are part of the same picaresque narrative template that blurs the boundaries between shape-shifter and underdog. See Reddick, *Danzig Trilogy*, 58–86.

simulacrum of the independent role he desires for himself. The novel both deconstructs this naivety as a narrative strategy and simultaneously relies on its operability. The following passage demonstrates how Oskar has given up his initial attempts to enact the naivety of his belief in returning to his grandmother's womb by imagining himself as the apotheosis of his grandfather Koljaiczek. While we do not know whether he ends up drowning or as the rich American Uncle Joe Colchic (39/25), he certainly is the *urpícaro* of the novel (and arguably of modern German picaresque fiction in general)—the eternal trickster combining sexual prowess and an arsonist's unquenchable desire for destruction:

> Erst im Inneren meiner Großmutter Koljaiczek oder, wie ich es scherzhaft nannte, im großmütterlichen Butterfass wäre es meinen damaligen Theorien nach zu einem wahren Familienleben gekommen. Selbst heute, da ich Gottvater, den eingeborenen Sohn und, was noch wichtiger ist, den Geist höchstpersönlich mit einem einzigen Daumensprung erreiche und gar überspringe, da ich der Nachfolge Christi, wie all meinen anderen Berufen, mit Unlust verpflichtet bin, male ich mir, dem nichts unerreichbarer geworden ist als der Eingang zu meiner Großmutter, die schönsten Familienszenen im Kreis meiner Vorfahren aus. (459)

> According to my theories at the time, it was only inside my grandmother Koljaiczek, or, as I put it in jest, in the grandmotherly butter tub, that true family life was possible. Today, when God the Father, his only begotten Son, and most important of all, the Holy Spirit himself are such a short hop away that I could jump right over them—for in addition to all my other callings, I am reluctantly committed to the Imitation of Christ—and though nothing is farther from me now than the entrance to my grandmother, I still picture the most beautiful of family scenes in the circle of my forebears. (331)

It is this (hidden) paternal figure of Koljaiczek whom Oskar tries to overcome in his self-inauguration as Father, Son and Holy Spirit. His father trouble is also his (Slavic-Germanic) race trouble. And it is the comic effect of this semantic surplus which allows Oskar to convey himself as naive and lunatic, as self-experimenter and victim, whose talk of 'Unlust' testifies to its opposite, a physical ludic delight in language.

Drumming out his life story as a picaresque tale of self-begetting, and self-mastery, Oskar combines the two default situations of the modern picaresque, narcissism and repetition, in a unique reflection on the complexities of historical guilt. His exuberance in inventing multiple identities for himself is driven by his wish to stay speechless (*infans* in Latin); his excessive semiosis revolves around his longing for a mother who perpetually turns into the monster of guilt: 'Ist die Schwarze Köchin da? Jajaja! Du bist schuld und du bist schuld und du am allermeisten.'—'Better start running, the Black cook's coming! You're to blame, and you're to blame, and you are most of all. Better start running … ' (778/563)

The modern picaresque has not only enriched the imagination of many readers, it has also added several exclamation marks and a profoundly absurd twist to Nietzsche's denigration of Western philosophy discussed above: 'das "Selbstbewusstsein" ist fiktiv!' ['"self-consciousness" is a fiction!'] It is both a kind of fiction about the complexities of human self-consciousness and a self-reflexive dramatization of the fictitiousness of human life in all its power and cruelty. The pícaro enacts his various personae, ranging from self-assertive shape-shifter to ostracized underdog, as a survival trick in an absurd world, as life-enhancing and life-destroying forms of self-deceit. He is Nietzsche's sleepwalker, quoted as motto of this study—the dreamer who wants to stay asleep and forego reality, in order to be able to master it, to re-will it in eternity. He is subject to the same suspension of disbelief which Camus' Sisyphus has to exercise in order to be able to regard himself as happy.[47] The philosophical myth of the twentieth century may be *le mythe de Sisyphe*, but its fairy tale is the picaresque— the story of an orphan born out of his own will and unable to regain this will other than in a narrative act.

---

47 The most obvious allegorical rendition of the Sisyphus myth in the novel is the moth flying against the light during Oskar's birth and its metaphorical relation to drumming. It illustrates the baroque topos that the beginning of life is the beginning of dying and marks Oskar's attempted *regressio ad uterum* as a version of Camus' Sisyphus, see Neuhaus, 'Zaubertrommel', 68.

Conclusion: Drumming (Out) Life Stories

'I am. But I do not have myself'—this is how Ernst Bloch begins his reflections in *Spuren* (*Traces*).[1] The modern pícaro articulates the opposite. It is true that the narrative acts of 'boxing in' one's life story, as dramatized in Brecht's "Samson-Körner", and 'drumming it out', as in Grass's *Blechtrommel*, exhibit an unprecedented degree of (literary) individual freedom. The modern pícaro takes the liberty to freely partake in a large number of social circles and thus keeps on boxing in his life with different codes of social conduct, following Guzmán's 'libre albedrío' and Lazarillo's motto 'válete por ti'—help yourself, take good care of yourself.[2] The pícaro is how we can think about the individual in modernity without thinking in predominantly negative terms.

Yet, the narrative structure within which the pícaro drums out the fleeting affiliations with his environment also betrays multiple structures of suppression and guilt that underpin the narrative confidence game of picaresque self-possession. 'Boxing in' and 'drumming out' are the traces of the modern German pícaro, who witnesses the most powerful explosion of modernity and its deepest crises. He is hammering home one message incessantly: I have to have myself, otherwise I am not; or, to phrase it in tune with the pícaro's rhetoric: as long as I *have* myself, I can pretend that I *am*.

At the secret core of Alfred Döblin's *Berlin Alexanderplatz* is the story of the pícaro Stefan Zannowich. After Franz Biberkopf's release from the Tegel prison, he chances upon two sympathetically disposed fellow humans, who take him to a Rabbi's home: Nachum (which means comforter) and Eliser (which means God's help). They tell him the story of Stefan Zannowich, suggesting that there is a lesson

---

1   Bloch, *Spuren*, frontispiece.
2   *Lazarillo de Tormes*, 59.

for Biberkopf to learn from it. With this story, these altruistic mentors want to convey the idea that an individual can only survive with the help of others—a lesson Biberkopf does not comprehend until the (highly allegorical) ending of the novel.[3] The Zannowich episode offers the image of a pícaro whose playful attitude towards the world has a liberating effect on his environment and fellow humans. Nachum and Eliser, the two Jewish outsiders, offer Franz, the Christian underdog recently released from jail, the ethics of a ludic pícaro:

> [...] wodurch ist der Zannowich weitergekommen, der junge wie der alte? Ihr meint, sie haben ein Gehirn gehabt, sie sind klug gewesen. Sind noch andere klug gewesen und waren mit achtzick Jahren nicht so weit wie Stefan mit zwanzick. Aber die Hauptsache am Menschen sind seine Augen und seine Füße. Man muß die Welt sehen können und zu ihr hingehen.

> [...] how did Zannovich get that far, both the young and the old man? You think because they had brains, they were clever. Other people were clever, too, and hadn't got as far at eighty as Stefan was at twenty. But the main things about a man are his eyes and his feet. He should be able to see the world and go after it.[4]

But then Stefan Zannowich gets carried away with his con games: he is dabbling in European politics and lobbying for warfare in order to make more money. In Döblin's narrative vignette, the picaresque story is not an *apologia*, but a didactic story, a Brecht-like *Lehrstück* about the comfort and divine nature of a playful attitude towards one's own self and life, which ultimately would help de-escalate aggression among humans. Franz Biberkopf does not follow this path, he opts for the path which Zannowich and many modern pícaros eventually follow—a path that will, sooner or later, confront them with guilt. Many of them make use of their ludic potential, but they lose themselves in strategies of self-defence and are ultimately thrown back onto their meritocratic concept of selfhood and its inherent calculating (and capitalist) rationale. Nachum's and Eliser's ideal of a picaresque ludic overcoming of the predicaments of modern individuality will ultimately prove ineffective for all these protagonists. Their shape-shifting is always underpinned by the logic of possession—be it in the form of autonomy (possessing, or 'having' oneself) or of heteronomy (possessing, or exerting power over others).

Modern picaresque fiction is aporetic. It poses an insoluble paradox which is concerned with the disorientation of the human being in the

---

3   Cf. Mahlendorf, 'Schelm und Verbrecher', 98–9.
4   Döblin, *Berlin Alexanderplatz*, 18/19.

world. It dramatizes the reduction of humans to the resources of their senses and instincts while simultaneously celebrating human imagination. And it renders these two aspects mutually dependent. It is a genre about manipulating our cognitive capacities and revelling in the sensual pleasures of the world—and about realizing that the gaze into the world is always a gaze into the human self. In that sense the picaresque is 'transcendental': it explores the conditions of the possibility of human knowledge. At the same time, however, it is a parody of this very exploration. The picaresque is firmly rooted in the irony of Nietzsche's aperçu that pokes fun at any transcendental logic and highlights the psychology of projection: 'Wahrlich, wir haben ein Bild vom Menschen—das machten wir aus uns. Und nun wenden wir's auf uns selber an,—uns zu verstehen!' ['Truly, we have an image/idea of man—this we created using ourselves as models. And now we are applying it to ourselves,—in order to comprehend ourselves.']⁵

The *Bildungsroman* measures out the limitations of human experience or agency and translates it into a dialectical movement of progression. The picaresque, by contrast, presents humans as defined by their sensual impulses and the imaginative transposition of these impulses (the drumming of their narrative). Imagination as a transgression of the human sensual boundaries relies on a suspension of disbelief and on a deliberately staged self-deceit which ignores human epistemological limits. While the formative theatre experience in the *Bildungsroman* leads to individual transformation and self-awareness, the modern pícaro never leaves the theatre (much as Oskar hurls his glass-shattering shriek against the municipal theatre). He turns the world (and himself) into a stage and imagines himself as the stage director (of himself).

What is more, modern picaresque fiction is narcissistic. It continues a romantic heritage which seeks immediacy of self-awareness in the perpetual ironic debunking of abstract individuality and its life forms. In treating life *in toto* as appearance, the ironic pícaro is able to enact himself as prime agent and total medium. His ironic mastery of performative authenticity is a perpetual comment on the derivative nature of human identity. This psychology of projection in the modern picaresque is also one of its prime high modernist features. It dramatizes, as Stanley Cavell notes, 'the beginning of the moment in which each of the arts becomes its own subject as if its immediate artistic task is to establish its own existence. The new difficulty which comes to light in the modernist situation is that of maintaining one's belief in one's own enterprise [...].'⁶ The modern picaresque is part of the modernist narcissistic task of creating 'its own existence'; and its

---

5   Nietzsche, *Nachgelassene Fragmente 1882–1884*, 408 (12 [40]), trans. B. M.
6   Cavell, *Must We Mean What We Say*, xxii.

protagonist-narrator is engaged in that very project of 'maintaining one's belief in one's own enterprise'. They combine elements of disenfranchisement and self-empowerment as the two quintessential human experiences of modernity. This duality reflects modern trends of accelerated social mobility, industrialization, democratization, on the one hand, and concurrent tendencies to tackle heightened degrees of complexity and differentiation through systemic mechanisms of exclusion, on the other. The ostracized modern pícaro—the stranger, the pariah, the *homo sacer*—has to implement his art of trickery as a survival strategy and uses narrative self-reflexivity as a means of holding his ground between social subsystems. Picaresque self-reflexivity is a double-edged sword, it either refines the pícaro's confidence game or it leads to self-inhibition. The narrator uses his own nakedness and its enactment as part of his confidence trickery with the (implied) reader; in doing so, he dramatizes a kind of authenticity which gains its credibility through deliberate satirical self-mockery. Through this communicative trick the readers find themselves trapped in a kind of meta-identification: while they dissociate themselves from the diegetic confidence schemes, they are convinced by the narrator's playful meta-fictional (and often satirical) performance of selfhood.

This double strategy is rooted in the narrative template of the Spanish picaresque. The classic pícaro writes an *apologia* about a life marked by his underprivileged origins and subsequent criminal career. Modern picaresque fiction is apologetic. Its heroes reinvent themselves as naive young pícaros who are forced to make ends meet in a cruel society, but they simultaneously retain their persona as the mature retrospective narrator. This double narration, whose narrator is both predator and prey, was of special interest for writers in the twentieth century, since it reveals an ambiguity that is very much at the core of the experience of modernity. As a result, the modern picaresque self-empowerment always runs the risk of collapsing into a form of self-deceit which cannot be cashed as semantic and literary surplus value. The danger of being marginalized is countered by the picaresque excess of semiosis as a restitution of ambivalence. This restitution through engendering semantic surplus value is the reflex of a capitalist logic, which I described as the political unconscious of the modern picaresque. Centrifugal forces in the picaresque character and rhetoric are part of an economy which is based on disseminating desire without ever being able to fully gratify it. The ensuing sense of debt or guilt has no fixed addressee, hence the shifting *destinataire* of the modern picaresque—between the (implied) reader, on the one hand, and society or a specific social institution (church, court, prison, asylum), on the other.

In his essay on the adventure, Simmel conceives of modern man as a gambler of the self, someone who turns the repetitive nature of existence into a systemic nexus which he *performs* rather than *finds* in life. It is in moments of taking risks, of gambling, that human beings are thrown back upon demiurgic instincts which would otherwise remain undetectable:

> The adventure is the exclave of life, the 'torn-off' whose beginning and end have no connection with the somehow unified stream of existence. And yet, as if hurdling this stream, it connects with the most recondite instincts and some ultimate intention of life as a whole—and this distinguishes it from the merely accidental episode, from that which only externally 'happens' to us.[7]

It is the lack of connection with existence and the denial of this connection in adventure which reinstates an experiential immediacy and demiurgic creativity untenable in the classic picaresque polarity between *Weltsucht* and *Weltflucht*. This adventurism of life is, however, the hidden point of reference of the modern picaresque existence.

At the same time, the modern pícaro replaces the Aristotelian presupposition that something cannot be one and another thing at the same time (*tertium non datur*) by the logic of the *tertium datur*. He is neither one (the embodiment of the individual as autonomous subject) nor another (the emdodiment of a particular imagined community), but enacts himself as a third agent between the two. This third agency, however, is an agency without foundation. Its lack of foundation has to be patched up in the performative quality of role-plays, confidence games and narrative tricks. The modern pícaro is the copy of an original that never existed. As such, he poses a great danger to anyone who claims to *be* that original, to participate, in particular, in the foundation myth of the rational, autonomous modern individual, since he embodies the individual as divisible multiplicity—'das Subjekt als Vielheit'.[8] Modern picaresque fiction is simulacral.

The pícaro is by definition a reactive character, although he always claims to be ahead of the game and turns whatever situation he finds himself in to his advantage. Thus, whenever the role of the underdog, victim, scapegoat or *homo sacer* is imposed upon him, he projects the idea of self-determination; whenever he finds himself in the position

---

7   Simmel, 'The Adventure', 228; 'Das Abenteuer', 178: 'Das Abenteuer ist die Exklave des Lebenszusammenhanges, das Abgerissene, dessen Beginn und Ende keinen Anschluss an die irgendwie einheitliche Strömung der Existenz haben—während es dennoch, wie über diese Strömung hinweg und ihrer Vermittlung unbedürftig, mit den geheimsten Instinkten und mit einer letzten Absicht des Lebens überhaupt zusammenhängt und sich dadurch von der bloß zufälligen Episode, dem, was uns bloß äußerlich 'passiert', unterscheidet.'

8   Nietzsche, *Nachgelassene Fragmente 1884–1885*, 650; *Late Notebooks*, 46 (40[42]).

of the confidence man, shape-shifter or *homo ludens*, he will sooner or later find himself enmeshed in inflicted and self-incurred dependencies. In both cases, the picaresque narrator captures in one literary discourse the conditions of individuality in modernity. Boxed into the 'monastery of modernity', as Elias Canetti, referring to Robert Walser, called the lunatic asylum, the pícaro drums out his scorn about and his dedication to the world (and observes himself doing so).[9] His is a story about the very human desire for freedom, impossible or unattainable as it may seem, or, as the abbess of Canetti's monastery, Fräulein Benjamenta, puts it: freedom is 'etwas Winterliches, Nicht-lange-zu-Ertragendes' ['something very wintry, and cannot be borne for long'].[10] As Sisyphus, the pícaro considers himself happy, as pícaro, Sisyphus considers himself free.

---

9   Canetti, *Über die Dichter*, 94.
10   Walser, *Jakob von Gunten*, 101/84.

Bibliography

Primary Literature

Alemán, Mateo (1987): *Guzmán de Alfarache*. Ed. José María Micó. Madrid: Cátedra. [1602]

Anon. (1987): *Lazarillo de Tormes*. Ed. Francisco Rico. Madrid: Cátedra. [1554]

—— (2000): *The Life of Lazarillo de Tormes*. Trans. David Rowland. Warminster: Aris & Phillips. [1586]

—— (2005): *The Life of Lazarillo de Tormes. His Fortunes and Adversities*. Trans. W. S. Merwin. New York Review Books.

Brecht, Bertolt (1983): 'Life Story of the Boxer Samson-Körner'. In *Collected Stories*. Ed. John Willett and Ralph Manheim. New York: Arcade Publishing, 207–24.

—— (1997): 'Der Lebenslauf des Boxers Samson-Körner. Erzählt von ihm selbst, aufgeschrieben von Bert Brecht'. In *Große kommentierte Berliner und Frankfurter Ausgabe*, vol. 19. Ed. Werner Hecht *et al.* Frankfurt/Main: Suhrkamp, 216–35. [1926]

Celan, Paul (2002): *Poems. A Bilingual German/English Edition*. Trans. Michael Hamburger. New York: Persea.

Döblin, Alfred (1990): *Berlin Alexanderplatz. Die Geschichte vom Franz Biberkopf*. Munich: Deutscher Taschenbuch Verlag. [1929]

—— (2003): *Berlin Alexanderplatz. The Story of Franz Biberkopf*. Trans. Eugene Jolas. New York: Continuum.

Fielding, Henry (1967): *The History of the Adventures of Joseph Andrews*. Oxford: Clarendon. [1742]

Fries, Fritz Rudolf (1966): *Der Weg nach Oobliadooh*. Frankfurt/Main: Suhrkamp.

—— (1995): *Don Quixote flieht die Frauen oder die apokryphen Abenteuer des Ritters von der traurigen Gestalt*. Berlin: Katzengraben-Presse.

Goethe, Johann Wolfgang (1981): *Werke. Hamburger Ausgabe*, vol. 7: *Wilhelm Meisters Lehrjahre*. Ed. Erich Trunz. Munich: Beck.

—— (2002) *Werke. Hamburger Ausgabe*, vol. 9: *Autobiographische Schriften I*. Ed. Erich Trunz. Munich: Beck.

—— ([12]2003): *Werke. Hamburger Ausgabe*, vol. 10: *Autobiographische Schriften II*. Ed. Erich Trunz. Munich: Beck.

—— ([14]2008): *Werke. Hamburger Ausgabe*, vol. 12: *Schriften zur Kunst. Schriften zur Literatur. Maximen und Reflexionen*. Ed. Erich Trunz and H.-J. Schrimpf. Munich: Beck.

Grass, Günter (1987): 'Der Säulenheilige'. In *Werkausgabe*, vol. 1. Ed. Volker Neuhaus. Neuwied: Luchterhand, 240.

—— (2002): *Die Blechtrommel*. Munich: Deutscher Taschenbuchverlag. [1959]

—— (2009): *The Tin Drum*. Trans. Breon Mitchell. Boston: Houghton Mifflin Harcourt.

Grimmelshausen, Hans Jakob Christoffel von (2005): *Simplicissimus Teutsch*. Frankfurt/Main: Deutscher Klassiker Verlag. [1668/9]

Hilsenrath, Edgar (1971): *The Nazi and the Barber*. New York: Doubleday.

—— (1990): *Der Nazi und der Friseur*. Munich: Piper. [1977]

Joyce, James (1992): *Ulysses*. Harmondsworth: Penguin. [1922]

Kafka, Franz (1946): *Amerika*. Ed. Max Brod. New York: Schocken. [1927]

—— (1965): *The Diaries of Franz Kafka 1914–1923*. Ed. Max Brod, trans. Martin Greenberg. New York: Schocken.

—— (1983): 'The Truth about Sancho Panza'. In *The Complete Stories*. Ed. Nahum N. Glatzer. New York: Schocken, 430.

—— (1994): *Der Verschollene*. In *Gesammelte Werke* 2. Ed. Hans-Gerd Koch. Frankfurt/Main: Fischer. [1912/14]

—— (1994): *Tagebücher 1914–1923*. In *Gesammelte Werke* 11. Ed. Hans-Gerd Koch. Frankfurt/Main: Fischer.

—— (1994): 'Die Wahrheit über Sancho Pansa'. In *Gesammelte Werke* 6: *Beim Bau der chinesischen Mauer*. Ed. Hans-Gerd Koch. Frankfurt/Main: Fischer, 167. [1917]

Llull, Ramon (1906): *Doctrina pueril*. In *Obres doctrinalis del illuminate Doctor Mestre Ramon Llull*. Ciutat de Mallorca: Comissió Editora Llulliana.

Mann, Thomas (1955): *Confessions of Felix Krull, Confidence Man. Memoirs Part I*. Trans. Denver Lindley. London: Secker & Warburg.

—— (1963): *Briefe 1933–1947*. Ed. Erika Mann. Frankfurt/Main: Fischer.

—— (1965): *Briefe 1948–1955 und Nachlese*. Ed. Erika Mann. Frankfurt/Main: Fischer.

—— (1974): *Gesammelte Werke*, vol. 13: *Nachträge*. Frankfurt/Main: Fischer.

—— (2000): *Bekenntnisse des Hochstaplers Felix Krull*. Frankfurt/Main: Fischer. [1954]

Melville, Herman (2005): *The Confidence-Man. His Masquerade*. Ed. by Hershel Parker and Mark Niemeyer. New York: Norton. [1857]

Novalis (1987): *Werke*, vol. 2: *Das philosophisch-theoretische Werk*. Ed. H.-J. Mähl. Munich: Hanser.

Ovid (1984): *Metamorphoses*. Ed. F. J. Miller. Cambridge/MA: Harvard University Press.

Sterne, Laurence (1980): *The Life and Opinions of Tristram Shandy, Gent*. Ed. Howard Anderson. New York: Norton. [1760–7]

Valbuena Prat, Ángel (ed.) (1956): *La novela picaresca española*. Madrid: Aguilar.

Walser, Robert (1975): *Briefe*. Ed. Jörg Schäfer and Robert Mächler. Geneva: Kossodo.

—— (1985): *Jakob von Gunten. Ein Tagebuch*. Zurich: Suhrkamp. [1909]

—— (1985): 'Tobold (II)'. In *Sämtliche Werke* V. Ed. Jochen Greven. Zurich: Suhrkamp, 224–58. [1917]

—— (1995): *Institute Benjamenta*. Trans. Christopher Middleton. London: Serpent's Tail. [1969]

Specialist Literature

The Spanish Picaresque and its Historical and Intellectual Context

Alcalá, Ángel (1995): *Judíos, sefarditas, conversos. La expulsión de 1492 y sus consecuencias*. Valladolid: Ámbito.

Barrio Olano, José Ignacio (1998): *La novela picaresca y el método maquiavélico.* Madrid: Editorial Pliegos.

Bataillon, Marcel (1931): *Le roman picaresque.* Paris: La Renaissance du livre.

Beinart, Haim (1992): 'The Great Conversion and the *Converso* Problem'. In Beinart Heim (ed.): *The Sephardi Legacy*, vol. 1. Jerusalem: Magnes Press, 346–82.

—— (2002): *The Expulsion of the Jews from Spain.* Oxford: Littman.

Brownlee, Marina S. and Hans Ulrich Gumbrecht (eds) (1995): *Cultural Authority in Golden Age Spain.* Baltimore: The Johns Hopkins University Press.

Castro, Américo (1949): *Aspectos del vivir hispánico. Espiritualismo, mesianismo, actitud personal en los siglos XIV al XVI.* Santiago de Chile: Cruz del Sur.

—— (1960): *Hacia Cervantes.* Madrid: Taurus.

—— (²1962): *La realidad histórica de España.* Mexico: Editorial Perrúa.

—— (1977): *An Idea of History. Selected Essays of Américo Castro.* Ed. and trans. Stephen Gilman and Edmund L. King. Columbus: The Ohio State University Press.

Chevalier, Maxime (1976): *Lectura y lectores en la España de los Siglos XVI y XVII.* Madrid: Ediciones Turner.

Criado de Val, Manuel (ed.) (1979): *La Picaresca. Origenes, textos y estructuras.* Madrid: Fundación Universitária Española.

Cruz, Ann J. (1999): *Discourses of Poverty. Social Reform and the Picaresque in Early Modern Spain.* Toronto University Press.

—— (2007): 'The *pícaro* Meets *Don Quixote*: the Spanish Picaresque and the Origins of the Modern Novel'. In Jenny Mander (ed.): *Remapping the Rise of the European Novel.* Oxford: Voltaire Foundation, 127–37.

Darst, David H. (1998): *Converting Fiction: Counter-Reformational Closure in the Secular Literature of Golden Age Spain.* Chapel Hill: University of North Carolina Press.

Dunn, Peter N. (1979): *The Spanish Picaresque Novel.* Boston: Twayne.

—— (1993): *Spanish Picaresque Fiction. A New Literary History.* Ithaca: Cornell University Press.

Gumbrecht, Hans Ulrich (1990): Eine *Geschichte der spanischen Literatur.* 2 vols. Frankfurt/Main: Suhrkamp.

—— (1995): 'Cosmological Time and the Impossibility of Closure. A Structural Element in Spanish Golden Age Narratives'. In Marina S. Brownlee and Hans Ulrich Gumbrecht (eds): *Cultural Authority in Golden Age Spain.* Baltimore: The Johns Hopkins University Press, 304–21.

Hanrahan, Thomas (1967): *La mujer en la novela picaresca española.* 2 vols. Madrid: Ediciones José Porrua Turanzas.

Harvey, L. P. (2005): *Muslims in Spain 1500–1614.* University of Chicago Press.

Herrero, Javier (1979): 'Renaissance Poverty and Lazarillo's Family: The Birth of the Picaresque Genre'. *PMLA* 94, 876–9.

Herrero García, Miguel (1937): 'Nueva interpretatión de la novela picaresca'. *Revista de Filología Española* 24, 343–62.

Hoffmeister, Gerhart (1987): 'Das spanische Modell: Alemáns *Guzmán de Alfarache* und die albertinische Bearbeitung'. In Gerhart Hoffmeister (ed.): *Der deutsche Schelmenroman im europäischen Kontext. Rezeption, Interpretation, Bibliographie.* Amsterdam: Rodopi, 29–48.

Hoogstraten, Rudolf van (1986): *Estructura mítica de la picaresca.* Madrid: Espiral Hispano-Americana.

Israel, Jonathan I. (1997): *European Jewry in the Age of Mercantilism 1550–1750.* Oxford: Littman.

Jauss, Hans Robert (1957): 'Ursprung und Bedeutung der Ich-Form im *Lazarillo de Tormes*'. *Romanistisches Jahrbuch* 8, 290–311.

Maiorino, Giancarlo (ed.) (1996): *The Picaresque: Tradition and Displacement*. Minneapolis: University of Minnesota Press.

—— (2003): *At the Margins of the Renaissance. Lazarillo de Tormes and the Picaresque Art of Survival*. University Park: Pennsylvania State University Press.

Maravall, J. Antonio (1976): 'La aspiración social de medro en la novela picaresca'. *Cuadernos Hispanoamericanos* 312, 590–625.

—— (1986): *La literatura picaresca desde la historia social (Siglos XVI y XVII)*. Madrid: Taurus.

Márquez Villanueva, Francisco (2006): *De la España judeoconversa—doce estudios*. Barcelona: Ediciones Bellaterra.

Navarro Durán, Rosa (2003): *Alfonso de Valdés, Autor del* Lazarillo de Tormes. Madrid: Editorial Gredos.

Netanyahu, Benzion ([3]1999): *The Marranos of Spain. From the Late 14th to the Early 16th Century. According to Contemporary Hebrew Sources*. Ithaca: Cornell University Press. [1966]

Parker, Alexander A. (1967): *Literature and the Delinquent. The Picaresque Novel in Spain and Europe 1599–1753*. Edinburgh University Press.

Pérez Venzalá, Valentín (2004): 'El Lazarillo sigue siendo anónimo. En respuesta a su atribución a Alfonso de Valdés'. *Espéculo* 27 (2004), www.ucm.es/info/especulo/numero27/lazaril.html

Resina, Joan Ramon (2006): 'The Short, Happy Life of the Novel in Spain'. In Franco Moretti (ed.): *The Novel*, vol. 1. Princeton University Press, 291–312.

Rico, Francisco (1984): *The Spanish Picaresque Novel and the Point of View*. Cambridge University Press.

—— (1997): 'Introducción'. In *Lazarillo de Tormes*. Madrid: Cátedra, 13–127.

—— (2006): 'Lazarillo de Tormes'. In Franco Moretti (ed.): *The Novel*, vol. 2. Princeton University Press, 146–51.

Roth, Norman (2002): *Conversos, Inquisition, and the Expulsion of the Jews from Spain*. Madison: The University of Wisconsin Press.

Ruiz, Teofilo (2001): *Spanish Society, 1400–1600*. Harlow: Longman.

Sieber, Harry (1977): *The Picaresque*. London: Methuen.

—— (1995): 'Literary Continuity, Social Order, and the Invention of the Picaresque'. In Marina S. Brownlee and Hans Ulrich Gumbrecht (eds): *Cultural Authority in Golden Age Spain*. Baltimore: Johns Hopkins University Press, 143–64.

Stallaert, Christiane (2006): *Ni una gota de sangre impura. La España inquisitorial y la Alemania nazi cara a cara*. Barcelona: Galaxia Gutenberg.

Tierno Galván, Enrique (1972): *Sobre la novela picaresca y otros escritos*. Madrid: Editorial Tecnos.

Whitbourn, Christine J. (1974): "Moral Ambiguity in the Spanish Picaresque Tradition". In Christine J. Whitbourn (ed.): *Knaves and Swindlers. Essays on the Picaresque Novel in Europe*. Oxford University Press, 1–24.

Yovel, Yirmiyahu (2003): 'The Birth of the Picaro from the Death of Shame'. *Social Research* 70/4, 1297–1326.

—— (2009): *The Other Within. The Marranos. Split Identity and Emerging Modernity*. Princeton University Press.

Franz Kafka

Adorno, Theodor W. (1977): 'Aufzeichnungen zu Kafka'. In *Gesammelte Schriften*, vol. 10.1. Frankfurt/Main: Suhrkamp, 254–87.

Anderson, Mark M. (ed.) (1989): *Reading Kafka. Prague, Politics and the* Fin de Siècle. New York: Schocken.

—— (1992): *Kafka's Clothes. Ornament and Aestheticism in the Habsburg* Fin de Siècle. Oxford: Clarendon.

Baioni, Giuliano (1994): *Kafka: Literatur und Judentum*. Stuttgart: Metzler.

Beißner, Friedrich (1983): *Der Erzähler Franz Kafka*. Frankfurt/Main: Suhrkamp.

Benjamin, Walter (1977): "Franz Kafka. Zur zehnten Wiederkehr seines Todestags". In *Gesammelte Schriften*, vol. II.2. Ed. Rolf Tiedemann and Hermann Schweppenhäuser. Frankfurt/Main: Suhrkamp, 438-65.

—— (1999): 'Franz Kafka. On the Tenth Anniversary of His Death'. In *Selected Writings*, vol. 2: 1927–1934. Ed. Michael W. Jennings, Howard Eiland, and Gary Smith. Cambridge/MA: Harvard University Press, 795–818.

Binder, Hartmut (1976): *Kafka-Kommentar. Zu den Romanen, Rezensionen, Aphorismen und zum Brief an den Vater*. Munich: Winkler.

—— (ed.) (1979): *Kafka-Handbuch*, vol. 2. Stuttgart: Kröner.

—— (1983): *Kafka. Der Schaffensprozeß*. Frankfurt/Main: Suhrkamp.

Born, Jürgen (1990): *Kafkas Bibliothek. Ein beschreibendes Verzeichnis*. Frankfurt/ Main: Fischer.

Brod, Max (1946): 'Nachwort zur ersten Ausgabe'. In Franz Kafka: *Amerika. Ein Roman*. New York: Schocken, 311–14.

Corngold, Stanley (1988): *Franz Kafka. The Necessity of Form*. Ithaca: Cornell University Press.

—— (2004): *Lambent Traces. Franz Kafka*. Princeton University Press.

Duttlinger, Carolin (2006): 'Visions of the New World: Photography in Kafka's *Der Verschollene*'. *German Life and Letters* 59/3, 423–45.

—— (2007): *Kafka and Photography*. Oxford University Press.

Fuchs, Anne (1997): 'A Suitcase, Passport and a Photograph: The Iconography of Abjection in Kafka's *Der Verschollene*'. In Jeff Morrison and Florian Krobb (eds): *Text into Image: Image into Text*. Amsterdam: Rodopi, 192–201.

—— (2002): 'A Psychoanalytic Reading of *The Man who Disappeared*'. In Julian Preece (ed.): *The Cambridge Companion to Kafka*. Cambridge University Press, 25–41.

Glišović, Dušan (1991): 'Kafkas "denationalisierte" Imagologie. Das "Eigene" als "Fremde" am Beispiel Karl Roßmanns'. In Yoshinori Shichiji (ed.): *Internationaler Germanisten-Kongreß in Tokyo. Sektion I: Theorie der Alterität*. Munich: Iudicium, 184–92.

Goebel, Rolf J. (2002): 'Kafka and Postcolonial Critique: *Der Verschollene*, "In der Strafkolonie", "Beim Bau der chinesischen Mauer" '. In James Rolleston (ed.): *A Companion to the Works of Franz Kafka*. Rochester/NY: Camden House, 187–212.

Hellbich, Wolfgang (1997): 'Different, But Not Out of This World: German Images of the United States between Two Wars, 1871–1914'. In David E. Barclay and Elisabeth Glaser-Schmidt (eds): *Transatlantic Images and Perceptions: Germany and America since 1776*. Cambridge University Press, 109–29.

Heimböckel, Dieter (2003): ' "Amerika im Kopf". Franz Kafkas Roman *Der Verschollene* und der Amerika-Diskurs seiner Zeit'. *Deutsche Vierteljahrsschrift für Literaturwissenschaft und Geistesgeschichte* 77/1, 130–47.

Hiebel, Hans H. (1986): 'Parabelform und Rechtsthematik in Franz Kafkas Romanfragment *Der Verschollene*'. In Theo Elm and Hans H. Hiebel (eds): *Die Parabel. Parabolische Formen in der deutschen Dichtung des 20. Jahrhunderts*. Frankfurt/Main: Suhrkamp, 219–54.

Holitscher, Arthur (1912): *Amerika. Heute und Morgen. Reiseerlebnisse*. Berlin: Fischer.

Ivanovic, Christine (2006): 'Amerika, Kafkas verstoßener Sohn. Deterritorialisierung und "topographic turn"'. In Jochen Vogt and Alexander Stephan (eds): *Das Amerika der Autoren. Von Kafka bis 09/11*. Munich: Fink, 45–66.

Jahn, Wolfgang (1965): *Kafkas Roman Der Verschollene ('Amerika')*. Stuttgart: Metzler.

Keller, Thomas (1997): 'Verkehrte Akkulturation: Vom realen zum imaginären Amerika'. In Philippe Wellnitz (ed.): *Franz Kafka, Der Verschollene: Le disparu/ l'Amérique. Écritures d'un nouveau monde?* Strasbourg: Presses universitaires, 211–32.

Kittler, Wolf (2008): 'Dead Beat Father. Zu Kafkas Roman *Der Verschollene*'. In Friedrich Balke, Joseph Vogl and Benno Wagner (eds): *Für Alle und Keinen. Lektüre, Schrift und Leben bei Nietzsche und Kafka*. Zurich: Diaphanes, 161–75.

Kobs, Jörgen (1970): *Kafka: Untersuchungen zu Bewusstsein und Sprache seiner Gestalten*. Ed. Ursula Brech. Bad Homburg: Athenäum.

Kremer, Detlef (1994). 'Verschollen. Gegenwärtig. Franz Kafkas Roman *Der Verschollene*'. *text & kritik* VII (Sonderband), 238–53.

Kurz, Gerhard (1980): *Traum-Schrecken. Kafkas literarische Existenzanalyse*. Stuttgart: Metzler.

Loose, Gerhard (1968): *Franz Kafka und Amerika*. Frankfurt/Main: Vittorio Klostermann.

Metz, Joseph (2004): 'Zion in the West: Cultural Zionism, Diasporic Doubles, and the Direction of Jewish Literary Identity'. *Deutsche Vierteljahrsschrift für Literaturwissenschaft und Geistesgeschichte* 78/4, 646–71.

Neumann, Gerhard (1985): 'Der Wanderer und der Verschollene. Zum Problem der Identität in Goethes *Wilhelm Meister* und in Kafkas *Amerika*-Roman'. In J. P. Stern and J. J. White (eds): *Paths and Labyrinths. Nine Papers from a Kafka-Symposium*. London: Institute of Germanic Studies, 43–65.

Nicolai, Ralf R. (1981): *Kafkas Amerika-Roman Der Verschollene. Motive und Gestalten*. Würzburg: Königshausen & Neumann.

—— (1987): 'Zwischen Ursprung und Utopie: Die thematische Einheit in Kafkas fiktionalen Texten'. In Karl Erich Grözinger (ed.): *Franz Kafka und das Judentum*. Frankfurt/Main: Athenäum, 161–77.

Northey, Anthony (1991): *Kafka's Relatives. Their Lives and His Writing*. New Haven: Yale University Press.

Politzer, Heinz (1965): *Franz Kafka, der Künstler*. Frankfurt/Main: Fischer.

Robertson, Ritchie (1985): *Kafka. Judaism, Politics, and Literature*. Oxford: Clarendon.

—— (1985): '"Antizionismus, Zionismus": Kafkas Responses to Jewish Nationalism'. In J. P. Stern and J. J. White (eds): *Paths and Labyrinths: Nine Papers from a Kafka Symposium*. London: Institute of Germanic Studies, 25–42.

Schillemeit, Jost (1985): 'Das unterbrochene Schreiben. Zur Entstehung von Kafkas Roman *Der Verschollene*'. In Barbara Elling (ed.): *Kafka-Studien*. New York: Lang, 137–52.

—— (2004): 'Karl Roßmann und das Theater. Zur Genese eines Motivs in Kafkas Roman *Der Verschollene*'. In *Kafka-Studien*. Ed. Rosemarie Schillemeit. Göttingen: Wallstein, 272–8.

Seferens, Horst (1992): 'Das "Wunder der Integration": Zur Funktion des "großen Theaters von Oklahama' in Kafkas Romanfragment *Der Verschollene*.' *Zeitschrift für deutsche Philologie* 111, 577–93.

Sokel, Walter (1964): *Franz Kafka—Tragik und Ironie. Zur Struktur seiner Kunst*. Munich: Langen/Müller.

—— (1975): 'Zwischen Drohung und Errettung. Zur Funktion Amerikas in Kafkas Roman *Der Verschollene*'. In Sigrid Bauschinger, Horst Denkler, Wilfried Malsch (eds): *Amerika in der deutschen Literatur*. Stuttgart: Reclam, 246–71.

Soukup, František (1912): *Amerika: řada obrazů amerického života*. Prag: Arbeiter-Zentralbücherei.

Spector, Scott (2000): *Prague Territories. National Conflict and Cultural Innovation in Franz Kafka's* Fin de Siècle. Berkeley: University of California Press.

Spilka, Mark (1963): *Dickens and Kafka. A Mutual Interpretation*. Bloomington: Indiana University Press.

Stach, Reiner (1989): 'Kafka's Egoless Woman: Otto Weininger's *Sex and Character*'. In Mark Anderson (ed.): *Reading Kafka. Prague, Politics, and the* Fin de Siècle. New York: Schocken, 149–69.

Sussman, Henry (1982): *Franz Kafka. Geometrician of Metaphor*. Baltimore: Johns Hopkins University Press.

Theisohn, Philipp (2003): 'Erde/Papier. Kafka, Literatur und Landnahme'. In Bernhard Greiner (ed.): *Placeless Topographies. Jewish Perspectives on the Literature of Exile*. Tübingen: Max Niemeyer, 61–87.

Tucholsky, Kurt (1975): 'Auf dem Nachttisch'. *Gesammelte Werke*, vol. 7. Reinbek: Rowohlt, 43–9. [1929]

Vogl, Joseph (1990): *Ort der Gewalt. Kafkas literarische Ethik*. Munich: Fink.

Wirkner, Alfred (1976): *Kafka und die Außenwelt*. Stuttgart: Klett.

Wolff, Kurt (1966): *Briefwechsel eines Verlegers. 1911–1963*. Ed. Bernhard Zeller and Ellen Otten. Frankfurt/Main: Scheffler.

Zilcosky, John (2003): *Kafka's Travels: Exotism, Colonialism and the Traffic of Writing*. New York: Palgrave Macmillan.

Robert Walser

Antonowicz, Kaja (1995): 'Der Mann mit der eisernen Maske—Rollen und Masken in der Kurzprosa von Robert Walser'. *Colloquia Germanica* 28/1, 55–71.

Benjamin, Walter (1977): 'Robert Walser'. In *Illuminationen. Ausgewählte Schriften 1*. Frankfurt/Main: Suhrkamp, 349–52.

—— (1999): 'Robert Walser'. In *Selected Writings*, vol. 2: 1927–1934. Ed. Michael W. Jennings, Howard Eiland, and Gary Smith. Cambridge/MA: Harvard University Press, 257–61.

Bloemen, Henri (1990): 'Durch die "inneren Gemächer" geführt. Zur Lektüre von Robert Walsers *Jakob von Gunten*'. In L. Lambrechts and J. Hové (eds): *Bild-Sprache. Texte zwischen Dichten und Denken*. Leuven University Press, 51–66.

Borchmeyer, Dieter (1980): *Dienst und Herrschaft. Ein Versuch über Robert Walser*. Tübingen: Niemeyer.

—— (ed.) (1999): *Robert Walser und die moderne Poetik*. Frankfurt/Main: Suhrkamp.

Engel, Manfred (1986): 'Außenwelt und Innenwelt: Subjektivitätsentwurf und moderne Romanpoetik in Robert Walsers *Jakob von Gunten* und Franz Kafkas *Der Verschollene*'. *Jahrbuch der deutschen Schillergesellschaft* 30, 533–70.

Evans, Tamara (1989): *Robert Walsers Moderne*. Bern: Francke.

Fuchs, Annette (1993): *Dramaturgie des Narrentums. Das Komische in der Prosa Robert Walsers*. Munich: Fink.

Geulen, Eva (1999): 'Autorität und Kontingenz der Tradition bei Robert Walser'. In Jürgen Fohrmann, Ingrid Karsten and Eva Neuland (eds): *Autorität der/in Sprache, Literatur, Neuen Medien*. Bielefeld: Aisthesis, 805–18.

Gößling, Andreas (1992): *Abendstern und Zauberstab. Studien und Interpretationen zu Robert Walsers* Der Gehülfe *und* Jakob von Gunten. Würzburg: Königshausen & Neumann.

Grenz, Dagmar (1974): *Die Romane Robert Walsers. Weltbezug und Wirklichkeitsdarstellung*. Munich: Fink.

Greven, Jochen (1978): 'Figuren des Widerspruchs: Zeit- und Kulturkritik im Werk Robert Walsers'. In Katharine Kerr (ed.): *Über Robert Walser*, vol. 2. Frankfurt/Main: Suhrkamp, 164–93.

—— (2009): *Existenz, Welt und reines Sein im Werk Robert Walsers. Versuch zur Bestimmung von Grundstrukturen*. Munich: Fink. [1960]

Hiebel, Hans H. (1991): 'Robert Walsers *Jakob von Gunten*. Die Zerstörung der Signifikanz im modernen Roman.' In Klaus-Michael Hinz and Thomas Horst (eds): *Robert Walser*. Frankfurt/Main: Suhrkamp, 240–75.

Kerr, Katharina (ed.) (1978): *Über Robert Walser*. 2 vols. Frankfurt/Main: Suhrkamp.

Lemmel, Monika (1999): 'Robert Walsers Poetik der Intertextualität'. In Dieter Borchmeyer (ed.): *Robert Walser und die moderne Poetik*. Frankfurt/Main: Suhrkamp, 83–101.

Liebrand, Claudia (1999): 'Jakob von Guntens Maskeraden: Spielkonfigurationen in Robert Walsers Tagebuchroman'. *Colloquia Germanica* 32/4, 345–62.

Magris, Claudio (1991): 'In den unteren Regionen: Robert Walser'. In Klaus-Michael Hinz and Thomas Horst (eds): *Robert Walser*. Frankfurt/Main: Suhrkamp, 343–57.

Naguib, Nagi (1970): *Robert Walser. Entwurf einer Bewußtseinsstruktur*. Munich: Fink.

Peeters, Wim (2004): ' "Wenn kein Gebot, kein Soll herrschte in der Welt, ich würde sterben": Jakob von Gunten als Glossator'. In Rüdiger Campe and Michael Niehaus (eds): *Gesetz. Ironie. Festschrift für Manfred Schneider*. Heidelberg: Synchron, 179–96.

Pleister, Michael (1992): '*Jakob von Gunten*: Utopie oder Resignation? Studie zu Robert Walsers Tagebuch-Roman'. *Sprachkunst* 23/1, 87–103.

Tobias, Rochelle (2006): 'The Double Fiction in Robert Walser's *Jakob von Gunten*'. *German Quarterly* 79/3, 293–307.

Utz, Peter (1984): 'Der Schwerkraft spotten. Spuren von Motiv und Metapher des Tanzes im Werk Robert Walsers'. *Jahrbuch der deutschen Schillergesellschaft* 28, 384–406.

—— (1998): *Tanz auf den Rändern. Robert Walsers 'Jetztzeitstil'*. Frankfurt/Main: Suhrkamp.

—— (2000): 'Robert Walsers *Jakob von Gunten*. Eine "Null"-Stelle der deutschen Literatur'. *Deutsche Vierteljahrsschrift für Literaturwissenschaft und Geistesgeschichte* 74/3, 488–512.

Walser, Martin (1981): *Selbstbewußtsein und Ironie. Frankfurter Vorlesungen*. Frankfurt/Main: Suhrkamp.

Thomas Mann

Appel, Sabine (1995): *Naivität und Lebenskunst. Die Idee der Synthese von Leben und Geist in Thomas Manns Hochstapler-Memoiren*. Frankfurt/Main: Lang.

Beddow, Michael (1975): 'Thomas Mann's *Bekenntnisse des Hochstaplers Felix Krull* and the Traditions of the Picaresque Novel and the Bildungsroman'. Unpublished doctoral thesis, University of Cambridge.

—— (1980): 'Fiction and Meaning in Thomas Mann's *Felix Krull*'. *Journal of European Studies* 10, 77–92.

Cha, Kyung-Ho (2007): 'Karnevaleskes Tier-Werden. Das Ende des Menschen in Thomas Manns *Bekenntnisse des Hochstaplers Felix Krull*'. *Zeitschrift für deutsche Philologie* 126, 221–50.

Dotzler, Bernhard J. (1991): *Der Hochstapler: Thomas Mann und die Simulakren der Literatur*. Munich: Fink.

Härle, Gerhard (1992): *'Heimsuchung und süßes Gift.' Erotik und Poetik bei Thomas Mann*. Frankfurt/Main: Fischer.

Heller, Erich (1958): *The Ironic German. A Study of Thomas Mann*. Boston: Little, Brown & Co.

Hollmann, Werner (1952): 'Thomas Mann's Felix Krull and Lazarillo'. *Modern Language Notes* 66, 445–51.

Jacobs, Jürgen (1994): 'Der Liftboy als Psychopompos? Zur Deutung von Thomas Manns *Felix Krull*'. *Euphorion* 88/2, 236–42.

Kablitz, Andreas (2009): '*Bekenntnisse des Hochstaplers Felix Krull*: Der *unreliable narrator* und die Struktur der Fiktion'. *Comparatio* 1, 113–44.

Koopmann, Helmut (³2001): *Thomas-Mann-Handbuch*. Stuttgart: Kröner.

Lubich, Frederick A. (2002): '*The Confessions of Felix Krull, Confidence Man*'. In Ritchie Robertson (ed.): *The Cambridge Companion to Thomas Mann*. Cambridge University Press, 199–212.

Nelson, Donald (1971): *Portrait of the Artist as Hermes. A Study of Myth and Psychology in Thomas Mann's* Felix Krull. Chapel Hill: University of North Carolina Press.

Porombka, Stephan (2001): *Felix Krulls Erben. Die Geschichte der Hochstapelei im 20. Jahrhundert*. Berlin: Bostelmann & Siebenhaar.

Renner, Rolf Günter (1985): *Lebens-Werk. Zum inneren Zusammenhang der Texte von Thomas Mann*. Munich: Fink.

Rosenmeyer, Thomas G. (1988): 'Das Kuckuckskapitel'. *Deutsche Vierteljahrsschrift für Literaturwissenschaft und Geistesgeschichte* 62/3, 540–8.

Schonfield, Ernest (2008): *Art and Its Uses in Thomas Mann's* Felix Krull. London: Maney.

Schulz, Kerstin (2000): *Identitätsfindung und Rollenspiel in Thomas Manns Romanen* Joseph und seine Brüder *und* Bekenntnisse des Hochstaplers Felix Krull. Frankfurt/Main: Lang.

Sebastian, Thomas (1985–6): 'Felix Krull: Pikareske Parodie des Bildungsromans'. In Gerhart Hoffmeister (ed.): *Der moderne deutsche Schelmenroman. Interpretationen*. Amsterdam: Rodopi, 133–44.

Seidlin, Oskar (1951): 'Picaresque Elements in Thomas Mann's Work'. *Modern Language Quarterly* 12, 183–200.

Sprecher, Thomas (1985): *Felix Krull und Goethe: Thomas Manns Bekenntnisse als Parodie auf Dichtung und Wahrheit*. Bern: Lang.

—— (2006): "Das grobe Muster. Georges Manolescu und Felix Krull". *Thomas Mann Jahrbuch* 19, 175–200.

Spuler, Richard (1983): ' "Im Gleichnis leben zu dürfen": Notions of Freedom in Thomas Mann's *Felix Krull'*. *Archiv für das Studium der Neueren Sprachen und Literaturen* 220/2, 343–50.

Wimmer, Ruprecht (1990): 'Der Herr Facis et (non) Dicis. Thomas Manns Übernahmen aus Grimmelshausen'. *Thomas Mann Jahrbuch* 3, 14–49.

Wysling, Hans (1974): *Dokumente und Untersuchungen. Beiträge zur Thomas-Mann-Forschung.* (Thomas-Mann-Studien III) Bern: Francke.

—— (1982): *Narzissmus und illusionäre Existenzform.* (Thomas-Mann-Studien V) Bern: Francke.

Zöller, Günter (1999): 'Schopenhauer on the Self'. In Christopher Janaway (ed.): *The Cambridge Companion to Schopenhauer.* Cambridge University Press, 18–43.

Edgar Hilsenrath

Arnds, Peter (2002): 'On the Awful German Fairy Tale: Breaking Taboos in Representations of Nazi Euthanasia and the Holocaust in Günter Grass' *Die Blechtrommel,* Edgar Hilsenrath's *Der Nazi und der Friseur* and Anselm Kiefer's Visual Art'. *German Quarterly* 75/4, 422–39.

Dopheide, Dietrich (2000): *Das Groteske und der schwarze Humor in den Romanen Edgar Hilsenraths.* Berlin: Weissensee.

Feinberg, Anat (1999): 'Die Splitter auf dem Boden. Deutschsprachige jüdische Autoren und der Holocaust'. *text & kritik* 144, 48–58.

Fuchs, Anne (2000): 'Edgar Hilsenrath's Poetics of Insignificance and the Tradition of Humour in German-Jewish Ghetto Writing'. In Anne Fuchs and Florian Krobb (eds): *Ghetto Writing. Traditional and Eastern Jewry in German-Jewish Literature from Heine to Hilsenrath.* Rochester/NY: Camden House, 180–94.

Gerstenberger, Katharina and Vera Pohland (1993): 'Der Wichser. Edgar Hilsenrath—Schreiben über den Holocaust, Identität und Sexualität'. *Der Deutschunterricht* 3, 74–91.

Gilman, Sander L. (1988): 'Jüdische Literaten und deutsche Literatur. Antisemitismus und die verborgene Sprache der Juden am Beispiel von Jurek Becker und Edgar Hilsenrath'. *Deutsche Philologie* 107/2, 269–94.

Graf, Andreas (1996): 'Mörderisches Ich. Zur Pathologie der Erzählperspektive in Edgar Hilsenraths Roman *Der Nazi und der Friseur'.* In Thomas Kraft (ed.): *Edgar Hilsenrath. Das Unsichtbare erzählen.* Munich: Piper, 135–49.

Laermann, Klaus (1993): ' "Nach Auschwitz ein Gedicht zu schreiben, ist barbarisch": Überlegungen zu einem Darstellungsverbot'. In Manuel Köppen (ed.): *Kunst und Literatur nach Auschwitz.* Berlin: Erich Schmidt, 11–15.

Lawson, Robert (2007): 'Carnivalism in Postwar Austrian- and German-Jewish Literature—Edgar Hilsenrath, Irene Dische, and Doron Rabinovici'. *Seminar* 43/1, 37–48.

Steinlein, Rüdiger (1993): 'Das Furchtbarste lächerlich? Komik und Lachen in Texten der deutschen Holocaust-Literatur'. In Manuel Köppen (ed.): *Kunst und Literatur nach Auschwitz.* Berlin: Erich Schmidt, 97–106.

Stenberg, Peter (1982): 'Memories of the Holocaust. Edgar Hilsenrath and the Fiction of Genocide'. *Deutsche Vierteljahrsschrift für Literatur und Geistesgeschichte* 56/2, 277–89.

—— (1996): ' "Ich habe Dich einen kleinen Augenblick verlassen." Edgar Hilsenrath und der abwesende Gott'. In Thomas Kraft (ed.): *Edgar Hilsenrath. Das Unsichtbare erzählen.* Munich: Piper, 178–201.

Günter Grass

Arker, Dieter (1989): *Nichts ist vorbei, alles kommt wieder. Untersuchungen zu Günter Grass'* Die Blechtrommel. Heidelberg: Winter.

Arnds, Peter (2004): *Representation, Subversion, and Eugenics in Günter Grass's* The Tin Drum. Rochester/NY: Camden House.

Böschenstein, Bernhard (1971): 'Günter Grass als Nachfolger Jean Pauls und Döblins'. *Jahrbuch der Jean-Paul-Gesellschaft* 6, 86–101.

Durzak, Manfred (1985): 'Es war einmal. Zur Märchen-Struktur des Erzählens bei Günter Grass'. In Manfred Durzak (ed.): *Zu Günter Grass. Geschichte auf dem preußischen Prüfstand*. Stuttgart: Metzler, 166–77.

Fischer, André (1992): *Inszenierte Naivität. Zur ästhetischen Simulation von Geschichte bei Günter Grass, Albert Drach und Walter Kempowski*. Munich: Fink.

Frizen, Werner (1986): '*Die Blechtrommel*—ein schwarzer Roman: Grass und die Literatur des Absurden'. *Arcadia* 21/2, 166–89.

Grass, Günter (1980): 'Über meinen Lehrer Döblin'. In *Aufsätze zur Literatur*. Darmstadt: Luchterhand, 67–91.

—— (2001): 'Auf deutsch, auf polnisch macht die Ostsee blubb, pifff, pschsch …'. *Frankfurter Allgemeine Zeitung* 161 (14 July), 47.

Hall, Katharina (2008): 'Günter Grass's "Danzig Quintet" '. In Stuart Taberner (ed.): *The Cambridge Companion to Günter Grass*. Cambridge University Press, 67–80.

Haug, Wolfgang Fritz (1985): *Die Faschisierung des bürgerlichen Subjekts, die Ideologie der gesunden Normalität und die Ausrottungspolitik im deutschen Faschismus*. Berlin: Argument.

Just, Georg (1972): *Darstellung und Appell in der* Blechtrommel. *Darstellungsästhetik versus Wirkungsästhetik*. Frankfurt/Main: Athenäum.

Loschütz, Gert (1968): *Von Buch zu Buch. Günter Grass in der Kritik. Eine Dokumentation*. Neuwied: Luchterhand.

Mews, Siegfried (2008): *Günter Grass and His Critics. From* The Tin Drum *to* Crabwalk. Rochester/NY: Camden House.

Minden, Michael (1993): 'A Post-Realist Aesthetic. Günter Grass, *Die Blechtrommel*'. In David Midgley (ed.): *The German Novel in the Twentieth Century. Beyond Realism*. Edinburgh University Press, 149–63.

Neuhaus, Volker (1982): *Günter Grass. Die Blechtrommel*. Munich: Oldenbourg.

—— (2001): 'Die Zaubertrommel'. In Eckhart Heftrich *et al.* (eds): *Thomas Mann Jahrbuch* 14. Frankfurt/Main: Vittorio Klostermann, 63–8.

Plard, Henri (1984): 'Une source du chapitre "Niobe" dans *Die Blechtrommel* de Grass'. *Études Germaniques* 39, 284–7.

Reddick, John (1975): *The 'Danzig Trilogy' of Günter Grass: a Study of the* Tin Drum, Cat and Mouse *and* Dog Years. London: Secker & Warburg.

Rickels, Laurence A. (1986): '*Die Blechtrommel* zwischen Schelmen- und Bildungsroman'. In Gerhart Hoffmeister (ed.): *Der moderne deutsche Schelmenroman. Interpretationen*. Amsterdam: Rodopi, 109–32.

Roberts, David (1973): 'Aspects of Psychology and Mythology in *Die Blechtrommel*'. In Manfred Jurgensen: *Grass. Kritik—Thesen—Analysen*. Bern: Francke, 45–73.

Sosnoski, M. K. (1971): 'Oskar's Hungry Witch'. *Modern Fiction Studies* 17/3, 1–77.

General Literature

Adorno, Theodor W. (1958): 'Standort des Erzählens im modernen Roman'. In *Noten zur Literatur I*. Ed. Rolf Tiedemann. Frankfurt/Main: Suhrkamp, 61–72.

—— (1974): 'Der Essay als Form'. In *Gesammelte Werke*, vol. 1. Frankfurt/Main: Suhrkamp, 9–34.

Adorno, Theodor W. and Max Horkheimer (1972): *Dialectic of Enlightenment*. Trans. John Cumming. London: Allen Tate.

—— (1997): *Dialektik der Aufklärung: Philosophische Fragmente*. Frankfurt/Main: Fischer. [1944]

Agamben, Giorgio (1997): 'The Camp as the *Nomos* of the Modern'. In Hent de Vries and Samuel Weber (eds): *Violence, Identity, and Self-Determination*. Stanford University Press, 106–18.

—— (1998): *Homo Sacer. Sovereign Power and Bare Life*. Stanford University Press.

—— (2002): *Remnants of Auschwitz. The Witness and the Archive*. New York: Zone.

—— (2005): *State of Exception*. The University of Chicago Press.

Alter, Robert (1964): *Rogue's Progress: Studies in the Picaresque Novel*. Cambridge/MA: Harvard University Press.

Anderson, Linda (2001): *Autobiography*. London: Routledge.

Apte, Mahadev K. (1985): *Humor and Laughter: An Anthropological Approach*. Ithaca: Cornell University Press.

Arendt, Dieter (1974): *Der Schelm als Widerspruch und Selbstkritik des Bürgertums. Vorarbeiten zu einer literatursoziologischen Analyse der Schelmenliteratur*. Stuttgart: Klett.

Arendt, Hannah (1978): *The Jew as Pariah: Jewish Identity and Politics in the Modern Age*. Ed. Ron H. Feldman. New York: Grove.

Backhaus, Jürgen G. and Hans-Joachim Stadermann (eds) (2000). *Georg Simmels Philosophie des Geldes*. Marburg: Metropolis.

Bakhtin, Mikhail (1981): *The Dialogic Imagination: Four Essays by M.M.Bakhtin*. Ed. Caryl Emerson and Michael Holquist. Austin. University of Texas Press.

—— (1984): *Rabelais and His World*. Bloomington: Indiana University Press.

—— (1984): *Problems of Dostoevsky's Poetics*. Ed. Caryl Emerson. Minneapolis: University of Minnesota Press.

—— (1986): 'The *Bildungsroman* and its Significance in the History of Realism (Toward a Historical Typology of the Novel)'. In *Speech Genre and Other Late Essays*. Ed. Caryl Emerson and Michael Holquist. Austin: University of Texas Press, 10–59.

Bathrick, David and Andreas Huyssen: *Modernity and the Text. Revisions of German Modernism*. New York: Columbia University Press 1989.

Baudelaire, Charles (1964): 'The Painter of Modern Life'. In *The Painter of Modern Life and Other Essays*. Ed. and trans. Jonathan Mayne. London: Phaidon, 1–40. [1863]

—— (1968): *Œuvres complètes*. 2 vols. Paris: Seuil.

Bauman, Zygmunt (1989): *Modernity and the Holocaust*. Cambridge: Polity.

—— (1991): *Modernity and Ambivalence*. Cambridge: Polity.

—— (1998): 'Allosemitism: Premodern, Modern, Postmodern'. In Bryan Cheyette and Laura Marcus (eds): *Modernity, Culture and 'the Jew'*. Stanford University Press, 143–56.

—— (1997): *Postmodernity and its Discontents*. New York University Press.

Baumeister, Roy (1987): 'How the Self Became a Problem: A Psychological Review of Historical Research'. *Journal of Personality and Social Psychology* 52, 163–76.

Bauer, Matthias (1993): *Im Fuchsbau der Geschichten. Anatomie des Schelmenromans*. Stuttgart: Metzler.

—— (1994): *Der Schelmenroman*. Stuttgart: Metzler.

Beermann, Wilhelm (1993): 'Luhmanns Autopoiesisbegriff—"Order from Noise?"'
In Hans R. Fischer: *Autopoiesis*. Heidelberg: Auer.

Bell, Daniel (1979): *The Cultural Contradictions of Capitalism*. London: Heinemann.

Benjamin, Walter (1999): 'Critique of Violence'. In *Selected Writings*, vol. 1:
1913–1926. Ed. Marcus Bullock and Michael Jennings, trans. Edmund Jephcott.
Cambridge/MA: Harvard University Press, 236–52.

—— (1999): 'Zur Kritik der Gewalt'. In *Gesammelte Schriften*, vol. II.1. Ed. Rolf
Tiedemann and Hermann Schweppenhäuser. Frankfurt/Main: Suhrkamp,
179–204. [1921]

—— (1974): *Charles Baudelaire. Ein Lyriker im Zeitalter des Hochkapitalismus*.
In *Gesammelte Schriften*, vol. I.2. Ed. Rolf Tiedemann and Hermann
Schweppenhäuser. Frankfurt/Main: Suhrkamp, 509–690.

—— (1974): *Gesammelte Schriften*, vol. I.3: *Anmerkungen der Herausgeber*. Ed. Rolf
Tiedemann and Hermann Schweppenhäuser. Frankfurt/Main: Suhrkamp.

Berman, Marshall (1982): *All That Is Solid Melts Into Air: The Experience of
Modernity*. New York: Simon and Schuster.

Blackburn, Alexander (1980): *The Myth of the Picaro. Continuity and Transformation
of the Picaresque Novel 1554–1954*. Chapel Hill: University of North Carolina
Press.

Blamires, David (1966): *Characterization and Individuality in Wolfram's* Parzival.
Cambridge University Press.

Bloch, Ernst (1969): *Spuren*. Frankfurt/Main: Suhrkamp.

Blondel, Eric (1991): *Nietzsche: The Body and Culture. Philosophy as a Philological
Genealogy*. London: Athlone.

Blumenberg, Hans (1969): 'Wirklichkeitsbegriff und Möglichkeitsbegriff des
Romans'. In Hans Robert Jauss (ed.): *Nachahmung und Illusion*. Munich: Fink,
9–27.

Breuer, Dieter (1984): 'Grimmelshausens simplicianische Frömmigkeit. Zum
Augustinismus des 17. Jahrhunderts'. In Dieter Breuer (ed.): *Frömmigkeit in der
frühen Neuzeit. Studien zur religiösen Literatur des 17. Jahrhunderts in Deutschland*.
Amsterdam: Rodopi, 213–52.

Brooks, Peter (1984): *Reading for the Plot: Design and Intention in Narrative*. New
York: Vintage.

Brown, Norman O. (1959): *Life Against Death. The Psychoanalytic Meaning of History*.
London: Routledge.

Brunner, Otto *et al.* (1972–97): *Geschichtliche Grundbegriffe. Historisches Lexikon zur
politisch-sozialen Sprache in Deutschland*. 8 vols. Stuttgart: Klett.

Buchanan, Ian and John Marks (eds) (2000): *Deleuze and Literature*. Edinburgh
University Press.

Calinescu, Matei (1987): *Five Faces of Modernity*. Durham: Duke University Press.

Camus, Albert (1965): *Essais*. Ed. Roger Quilliot and Louis Faucon. Paris:
Gallimard. [1942]

—— (2000): *The Myth of Sisyphus*. Trans. Justin O'Brien. Harmondsworth:
Penguin.

Canetti, Elias (2004): *Über die Dichter*. Munich: Carl Hanser.

Caruth, Cathy (1995): *Trauma. Explorations in Memory*. Baltimore: Johns Hopkins
University Press.

—— (1997): 'Traumatic Awakenings'. In Hent de Vries and Samuel Weber (eds):
Violence, Identity, and Self-Determination. Stanford University Press, 208–22.

Cavell, Stanley (1969): *Must We Mean What We Say?* New York: Scribner.

Chandler, Frank W. (1958): *The Literature of Roguery*. 2 vols. New York: Franklin. [1907]

—— (1961): *Romances of Roguery. An Episode in the History of the Novel*. 2 vols. New York: MacMillan. [1899]

Clarke, Maudemarie (1990): *Nietzsche on Truth and Philosophy*. Cambridge University Press.

Close, Anthony J. (2003): 'The Legacy of *Don Quijote* and the Picaresque Novel'. In Harriet Turner and Adelaida López de Martínez (eds): *The Spanish Novel. From 1600 to the Present*. Cambridge University Press, 15–30.

Cohn, Dorrit (1999): *The Distinction of Fiction*. Baltimore: The John Hopkins University Press.

Daghistany, Ann (1977): 'The Picara Nature'. *Women's Studies* 5, 51–60.

Dahme, Heinz-Jürgen and Ottheim Ramstedt (eds) (1984): *Georg Simmel und die Moderne: Neue Interpretationen und Materialien*. Frankfurt/Main: Suhrkamp.

Dahrendorf, Ralf (1958): 'Homo Sociologicus. Ein Versuch zur Geschichte, Bedeutung und Kritik der Kategorie der sozialen Rolle'. *Kölner Zeitschrift für Soziologie und Sozialpsychologie* 10/2, 188–208; 10/3, 345–50.

Danow, David K. (1995): *The Spirit of Carnival. Magical Realism and the Grotesque*. Lexington: University of Kentucky Press.

Deleuze, Gilles (1983): *Nietzsche and Philosophy*. Trans. Hugh Tomlinson. London: Athlone.

—— (2004): *Difference and Repetition*. Trans. Paul Patton. London: Continuum. [1968]

Deleuze, Gilles and Félix Guattari: *Kafka: Toward a Minor Literature*. Trans. Dana Polan. Minneapolis: University of Minnesota Press.

—— (2000): *Anti-Oedipus. Capitalism and Schizophrenia*. Trans. Robert Hurley *et al*. London: Continuum. [1972]

Diederichs, Rainer (1971): *Strukturen des Schelmischen im modernen deutschen Roman*. Düsseldorf: Diederichs.

Due, Reidar (2007): *Deleuze*. Cambridge: Polity.

Eakin, Paul John (1999): *How Our Lives Become Stories*. Ithaca: Cornell University Press.

Eisenberg, Daniel (1979): 'Does the Picaresque Novel Exist?' *Kentucky Romance Quarterly* 26, 203–19.

Eisenstadt, Shmuel Noah (2003): *Comparative Civilizations and Multiple Modernities*. 2 vols. Leiden: Brill.

Erdoes, Richard and Alfonso Ortiz (1998): *American Indian Trickster Tales*. London: Penguin.

Esslin, Martin (1961): *The Theatre of the Absurd*. Harmondsworth: Penguin.

Fiedler, Leslie (1978): *Freaks: Myths and Images of the Secret Self*. New York: Simon & Schuster.

Fitzpatrick, Peter (2005): 'Bare Sovereignty. *Homo Sacer* and the Insistence of Law'. In Andrew Norris (ed.): *Politics, Metaphysics and Death. Essays on Giorgio Agamben's* Homo Sacer. Durham: Duke University Press, 49–73.

Foucault, Michel: 'Of Other Spaces'. *Diacritics* 16/1, 22–7.

—— (1990): *History of Sexuality*. 3 vols. Trans. Robert Hurley. Harmondsworth: Penguin. [1984–6]

Frank, Manfred (1982): *Der kommende Gott. Vorlesungen über die Neue Mythologie*. Frankfurt/Main: Suhrkamp.

—— (1988): 'Subjekt, Person, Individuum'. In Manfred Frank, Gérard Raulet and Willem van Reijen (eds): *Die Frage nach dem Subjekt*. Frankfurt/Main: Suhrkamp, 7–28.

—— (2004): *The Philosophical Foundations of Early German Romanticism*. Albany: State University of New York Press.

Freud, Sigmund (1949): 'On Narcissism: an Introduction'. In *Collected Papers*, vol. 5: *Papers on Applied Psycho-Analysis*. Trans. Joan Riviere. London: Hogarth Press, 30–59.

—— (1949): 'The Relation of the Poet to Day-Dreaming'. In *Collected Papers*, vol. 5: *Papers on Applied Psycho-Analysis*. Trans. Joan Riviere. London: Hogarth Press, 173–83.

—— (1989): 'Zur Einführung des Narzißmus'. In *Studienausgabe*, vol. 3: *Psychologie des Unbewußten*. Ed. Alexander Mitscherlich, Angela Richards and James Strachey. Frankfurt/Main: Fischer, 37–68. [1914]

—— (2007): 'Der Dichter und das Phantasieren'. In *Studienausgabe*, vol. 10: *Bildende Kunst und Literatur*. Ed. Alexander Mitscherlich, Angela Richards and James Strachey. Frankfurt/Main: Fischer, 169–79. [1908]

Friedländer, Saul (ed.) (1992): *Probing the Limits of Representation: Nazism and the "Final Solution"*. Cambridge/MA: Harvard University Press.

Friedman, Edward H. (1987): *The Antiheroine's Voice. Narrative Discourse and Transformations of the Picaresque*. Columbia: University of Missouri Press.

Frisby, David (1984): 'Georg Simmels Theorie der Moderne'. In Heinz-Jürgen Dahme and Ottheim Ramstedt (eds): *Georg Simmel und die Moderne: Neue Interpretationen und Materialien*. Frankfurt/Main: Suhrkamp, 9–79.

—— (1992): *Sociological Impressionism. A Reassessment of Georg Simmel's Social Theory*. London: Routledge.

—— (2002): *Georg Simmel*. London: Routledge.

Fuchs, Anne (1999): *A Space of Anxiety. Dislocation and Abjection in Modern German-Jewish Literature*. Amsterdam: Rodopi.

Gay, Peter (2001): *Weimar Culture. The Outsider as Insider*. New York: Norton. [1968]

Gay, Peter du (1999): 'Is Bauman's Bureau Weber's Bureau? A Comment'. *British Journal of Sociology* 4, 575–87.

Gebauer, Mirjam (2006): *Wendekrisen. Der Pikaro im deutschen Roman der 1990er Jahre*. Trier: Wissenschaftlicher Verlag.

Genette, Gérard (1982): *Palimpsestes: la littérature au second degrée*. Paris: Seuil.

Giddens, Anthony (1987): *Social Theory and Modern Sociology*. Cambridge: Polity.

—— (1990): *The Consequences of Modernity*. Cambridge: Polity.

—— (1991): *Modernity and Self-Identity. Self and Society in the Late Modern Age*. Stanford University Press.

Giddens, Anthony and Christopher Pierson (1999): *Conversations with Anthony Giddens. Making Sense of Modernity*. Stanford University Press.

Gillespie, Gerald (1986): 'Pikara und Schelmin'. In Gerhart Hoffmeister (ed.): *Der moderne deutsche Schelmenroman. Interpretationen*. Amsterdam: Rodopi, 151–71.

Gilman, Sander L. (1985): *Difference and Pathology. Stereotypes of Sexuality, Race and Madness*. Ithaca: Cornell University Press.

—— (1986): *Jewish Self-Hatred. Anti-Semitism and the Hidden Language of the Jews*. Baltimore: Johns Hopkins University Press.

—— (1988): *Disease and Representation. Images of Illness from Madness to AIDS*. Ithaca: Cornell University Press.

Girard, René (1986): *The Scapegoat*. Baltimore: Johns Hopkins University Press. [1982]

—— (2005): *Violence and the Sacred*. London: Continuum. [1972]

Goetschel, Willi (1997): 'Zur Sprachlosigkeit von Bildern'. In Klaus Scherpe and Manfred Köppen (eds): *Bilder des Holocaust*. Vienna: Böhlau, 131–44.

Goffman, Erving (1969): *The Presentation of Self in Everyday Life*. London: Allen Lane.

—— (1990): *Stigma. Notes on the Management of Spoiled Identity*. Harmondsworth: Penguin. [1963]

Goodchild, Philip (1996): *Deleuze and Guattari. An Introduction to the Politics of Desire*. London: Sage.

Gräf, Hans Gerhard (1901): *Goethe über seine Dichtungen*, 3 vols. Frankfurt/Main: Rütten & Loening.

Gray, Richard T. (2008): *Money Matters. Economics and the German Cultural Imagination 1770–1850*. Seattle: University of Washington Press.

Greenblatt, Stephen Jay (1980): *Renaissance Self-fashioning: From More to Shakespeare*. University of Chicago Press.

Greiner, Bernhard (2001): 'Im Umkreis von Ramses: Kafkas *Verschollener* als jüdischer Bildungsroman'. *Deutsche Vierteljahrsschrift für Literaturwissenschaft und Geistesgeschichte* 77/4, 637–58.

Guillén, Claudio (1971): *Literature as System: Essays toward the Theory of Literary History*. Princeton University Press.

—— (1987): *Anatomies of Roguery. A Comparative Study in the Origins and the Nature of Picaresque Literature*. New York: Garland.

Gullì, Bruno (2007): 'The Ontology and Politics of Exception. Reflections on the Work of Giorgio Agamben'. In Matthew Calarco and Steven DeCaroli (eds): *Giorgio Agamben. Sovereignty and Life*. Stanford University Press, 219–42.

Gumbrecht, Hans Ulrich (1978): 'Modern, Modernität, Moderne'. In Otto Brunner *et al.* (eds): *Geschichtliche Grundbegriffe*. Stuttgart: Klett-Cotta, 93–131.

—— (2006): 'The Roads of the Novel'. In Franco Moretti (ed.): *The Novel*, vol. 2. Princeton University Press, 611–46.

Gusdorf, Georges (1980): 'Conditions and Limits of Autobiography'. In James Olney (ed.): *Autobiography. Essays Theoretical and Critical*. Princeton University Press, 28–48.

Habermas, Jürgen (1981): *Theorie des kommunikativen Handelns*. 2 vols. Frankfurt/ Main: Suhrkamp.

—— (1985): *Der philosophische Diskurs der Moderne. Zwölf Vorlesungen*. Frankfurt/ Main: Suhrkamp.

—— (1986/7): *The Theory of Communicative Action*. 2 vols. Trans. Thomas McCarthy. Cambridge: Polity.

—— (1987): *The Philosophical Discourse of Modernity. Twelve Lectures*. Trans. Frederick G. Lawrence. Cambridge/MA: MIT Press.

—— (1990): *Die nachholende Revolution. Kleine politische Schriften VII*. Frankfurt/ Main: Suhrkamp.

—— (1994): *Die Moderne—ein unvollendetes Projekt. Philosophisch-politische Aufsätze*. Leipzig: Reclam.

Hamacher, Werner (1986): '"Disgregation of the Will": Nietzsche on the Individual and Individuality'. In Thomas C. Heller *et al.* (eds): *Reconstructing Individualism. Autonomy, Individuality, and the Self in Western Thought*. Stanford University Press, 106–39.

Hanssen, Beatrice (1997): 'On the Politics of Pure Means: Benjamin, Arendt, Foucault'. In Hent de Vries and Samuel Weber (eds): *Violence, Identity, and Self-Determination*. Stanford University Press, 236–52.

Harrison, Paul R. (1995): 'Niklas Luhmann and the Theory of Social Systems'. In David Roberts (ed.): *Reconstructing Theory. Gadamer, Habermas, Luhmann.* Melbourne University Press, 65–90.

Hart, Francis (1970): 'Notes for an Anatomy of Modern Autobiography'. *New Literary History* 1, 485–511.

Heidenreich, Helmut (1967): *Pikarische Welten. Schriften zum europäischen Schelmenroman.* Darmstadt: Wissenschaftliche Buchgesellschaft.

Heilman, Robert (1958): 'Variations on the Picaresque'. *Sewanee Review* 66/4, 547–77.

Henrich, Dieter (1976): 'Die Grundstruktur der modernen Philosophie'. In Hans Ebeling (ed.): *Subjektivität und Selbsterhaltung.* Frankfurt/Main: Suhrkamp, 97–143.

Hirsch, Arnold (²1957): *Bürgertum und Barock im deutschen Roman. Ein Beitrag zur Entstehungsgeschichte des bürgerlichen Weltbildes.* Ed. Herbert Singer. Cologne: Böhlau.

Hobbes, Thomas (1996): *Leviathan.* Ed. Richard Tuck. Cambridge University Press. [1651]

Hoffmann-Krayer, Eduard and Hanns Bächtold-Stäubli (eds) (2002): *Handwörterbuch des deutschen Aberglaubens.* 10 vols. Berlin: de Gruyter. [1927–42]

Hoffmeister, Gerhart (ed.) (1986): *Der moderne deutsche Schelmenroman. Interpretationen.* Amsterdam: Rodopi.

—— (ed.) (1987): *Der deutsche Schelmenroman im europäischen Kontext. Rezeption, Interpretation, Bibliographie.* Amsterdam: Rodopi.

Holland, Eugene W. (1999): *Deleuze and Guattari's Anti-Oedipus: Introduction to Schizoanalysis.* London: Routledge.

Hollingdale, R. J. (1996): 'The Hero as Outsider'. In Bernd Magnus and Kathleen M. Higgins (eds): *The Cambridge Companion to Nietzsche.* Cambridge University Press, 71–89.

Honold, Alexander (2007): 'Travestie und Transgression. Pikaro und verkehrte Welt bei Grimmelshausen'. In Christoph Ehland and Robert Fajen (eds): *Das Paradigma des Pikaresken.* Heidelberg: Universitätsverlag Winter, 201–27.

—— (2007): 'Kafkas Trickster: Zum Auftritt des Fremden in der Schrift'. In Arne Höcker and Oliver Simons (eds): *Kafkas Institutionen.* Bielefeld: transcript, 295–320.

Horace (1929): *Satires. Epistles. Art of Poetry.* Trans. H. R. Fairclough. Cambridge/MA: Harvard University Press.

Huizinga, Johan (1970): *Homo Ludens. A Study of the Play Element in Culture.* London: Temple Smith. [1944]

Hutcheon, Linda (1984): *Narcissistic Narrative: The Metafictional Paradox.* New York: Methuen.

Huyssen, Andreas (1986): *After the Great Divide: Modernism, Mass Culture, Postmodernism.* Bloomington: Indiana University Press.

Iser, Wolfgang (1978): *The Act of Reading.* Baltimore: Johns Hopkins University Press.

Jacobs, Jürgen (1983): *Der deutsche Schelmenroman. Eine Einführung.* Munich: Artemis.

—— (1986): 'Bildungsroman und Pikaroroman. Versuch einer Abgrenzung'. In Gerhart Hoffmeister (ed.): *Der modern deutsche Schelmenroman. Interpretationen.* Amsterdam: Rodopi, 9–18.

Jung, Carl Gustav (1952): *Symbole der Wandlung. Analyse des Vorspiels zu einer Schizophrenie.* Olten: Walter.

Kaler, Anne K. (1991): *The Picara: From Hera to Fantasy Heroine*. Bowling Green State University Popular Press.

Kayser, Wolfgang (1957): *Das Groteske*. Oldenburg: Stalling.

Kershaw, Ian (1992): 'Ideologe und Propagandist. Hitler im Lichte seiner Reden, Schriften und Anordnungen 1925–1928'. *Vierteljahrshefte für Zeitgeschichte* 40/2, 263–71.

Klee, Ernst (ed.) (1989): *'Euthanasie' im NS-Staat. Die 'Vernichtung unwerten Lebens'*. Frankfurt/Main: Fischer.

Kleist, Heinrich von (2010): 'Über das Marionettentheater'. In *Sämtliche Werke und Briefe*, vol. II. Ed. Roland Reuß and Peter Staengle. Munich: Hanser, 425–33. [1810]

Klossowski, Pierre (2005): *Nietzsche and the Vicious Circle*. London: Continuum. [1969]

Koopmann, Helmut (1986): 'Pikaro in der Romantik? Eine Spurensuche'. In Gerhart Hoffmeister (ed.): *Der moderne deutsche Schelmenroman. Interpretationen*. Amsterdam: Rodopi, 19–40.

Koschorke, Albrecht (1999): 'Die Grenzen des Systems und die Rhetorik der Systemtheorie'. In Albrecht Koschorke and Cornelia Vismann: *Widerstände der Systemtheorie: kulturtheoretische Analysen zum Werk von Niklas Luhmann*. Berlin: Akademie Verlag, 49–60.

Koselleck, Reinhart (1973): *Kritik und Krise. Eine Studie zur Pathogenese der bürgerlichen Welt*. Frankfurt/Main: Suhrkamp.

—— (1979): *Vergangene Zukunft. Zur Semantik geschichtlicher Zeiten*. Frankfurt/Main: Suhrkamp.

—— (1985): *Futures Past. On the Semantics of Historical Time*. Cambridge/MA: MIT Press.

—— (1988). *Critique and Crisis. The Pathogenesis of Modern Society*. Oxford: Berg.

—— (2002): 'The Eighteenth Century as the Beginning of Modernity'. In Reinhart Koselleck: *The Practice of Conceptual History. Timing History, Spacing Concepts*. Trans. T. S. Presner. Stanford University Press, 154–169.

—— (2002) 'On the Anthropological and Semantic Structure of *Bildung*'. In *The Practice of Conceptual History. Timing History, Spacing Concepts*. Trans. T. S. Presner. Stanford University Press, 170–207.

Kristeva, Julia (1980): *Pouvoirs de l'horreur. Essai sur l'abjection*. Paris: Seuil.

LaCapra, Dominick (1994): *Representing the Holocaust: History, Theory, Trauma*. Ithaca: Cornell University Press.

—— (2007): 'Approaching Limit Events. Siting Agamben.' In Matthew Calarco and Steven DeCaroli (eds): *Giorgio Agamben. Sovereignty and Life*. Stanford University Press, 126–162.

Lachmann, Renate (1990): *Gedächtnis und Literatur. Intertextualität in der russischen Moderne*. Frankfurt/Main: Suhrkamp.

Lange, Sigrid (1999): *Authentisches Medium. Faschismus und Holocaust in ästhetischen Darstellungen der Gegenwart*. Bielefeld: Aisthesis.

Langer, Lawrence L. (1975): *The Holocaust and the Literary Imagination*. New Haven: Yale University Press.

—— (1991): *Holocaust Testimonies: The Ruins of Memory*. New Haven: Yale University Press.

—— (1998): *Preempting the Holocaust*. New Haven: Yale University Press.

Lethen, Helmut (1994): *Verhaltenslehren der Kälte. Lebensversuche zwischen den Kriegen*. Frankfurt/Main: Suhrkamp.

—— (2002): *Cool Conduct. The Culture of Distance in Weimar Germany*. Trans. Don Reneau. Berkeley: University of California Press.

Lewis, Richard W. B. (1960): *The Picaresque Saint. Representative Figures in Contemporary Fiction*. London: Gollancz.

Lindberg, Gary H. (1982): *The Confidence Man in American Literature*. Oxford University Press.

Lorenz, Dagmar C. G. (1992): *Verfolgung bis zum Massenmord. Holocaust-Diskurse in deutscher Sprache aus der Sicht der Verfolgten*. New York: Lang.

Luhmann, Niklas (1977): 'Interpenetration. Zum Verhältnis personaler und sozialer Systeme'. In *Zeitschrift für Soziologie* 6, 62–76.

—— (1979): *Trust and Power. Two Works by Niklas Luhmann*. New York: John Wiley & Sons.

—— (1981): *Soziologische Aufklärung*, vol. 3: *Soziales System, Gesellschaft, Organisation*. Opladen: Westdeutscher Verlag.

—— (1984): *Soziale Systeme*. Frankfurt/Main: Suhrkamp.

—— (1986): 'The Individuality of the Individual: Historical Meanings and Contemporary Problems'. In Thomas C. Heller *et al.* (eds): *Reconstructing Individualism. Autonomy, Individuality, and the Self in Western Thought*. Stanford University Press, 313–25.

—— (1988): *Die Wirtschaft der Gesellschaft*. Frankfurt/Main: Suhrkamp.

—— (1993): 'Individuum, Individualität, Individualismus'. In *Gesellschaftsstruktur und Semantik. Studien zur Wissenssoziologie der modernen Gesellschaft*, vol. 3. Frankfurt/Main: Suhrkamp, 149–258.

—— (1997): *Die Gesellschaft der Gesellschaft*. 2 vols. Frankfurt/Main: Suhrkamp.

—— (1998): *Observations on Modernity*. Stanford University Press.

Lukács, Georg (1955): 'Das Spielerische und seine Hintergründe'. *Aufbau* 11/6, 501–24.

—— (1973): *The Theory of the Novel*. Trans. Anna Bostock. Cambridge/MA: MIT Press.

Lyotard, Jean-François (1993): *Political Writings*. Trans. Bill Readings and Kevin Paul Geiman. Minneapolis: University of Minnesota Press.

Mach, Ernst (1991): *Die Analyse der Empfindungen und das Verhältnis des Physischen zum Psychischen*. Darmstadt: Wissenschaftliche Buchgesellschaft. [1886]

Mahlendorf, Ursula R. (1986): 'Schelm und Verbrecher: Döblins *Berlin Alexanderplatz*'. In Gerhart Hoffmeister (ed.): *Der moderne deutsche Schelmenroman. Interpretationen*. Amsterdam: Rodopi, 77–108.

Malkmus, Bernhard (2007): 'The Picaresque Hero and Economies of Circulation'. In Christoph Ehland and Robert Fajen (eds): *The Paradigm of the Picaresque*. Heidelberg: Winter, 179–200.

—— (2009): 'The Birth of the Modern Pícaro out of the Spirit of Self-Reliance: Herman Melville's *Confidence-Man*'. *Amerikastudien* 54/4, 603–20.

—— (2010): 'Vom Hoch- und Tiefstapeln: Der Pícaro zwischen den Systemen der Moderne'. In Thomas Bedorf *et al.* (eds): *Triadische Sozialität. Der Dritte in interdisziplinärer Perspektive*. Munich: Fink, 289–315.

Marckwort, Ulf-Heiner (1984): *Der deutsche Schelmenroman der Gegenwart. Betrachtungen zur sozialistischen Rezeption pikaresker Topoi und Motive*. Köln: Pahl-Rugenstein.

Martinich, Aloysius P. (1992): *The Two Gods of Leviathan. Thomas Hobbes on Religion and Politics*. Cambridge University Press.

Mattenklott, Gert (1983): 'Der mythische Leib: Physiognomisches Denken bei Nietzsche, Simmel und Kassner'. In Karl Heinz Bohrer (ed.): *Mythos und*

Moderne. Begriff und Bild einer Rekonstruktion. Frankfurt/Main: Suhrkamp, 138–56.

Menninghaus, Winfried (1999): *Ekel. Theorie und Geschichte einer starken Empfindung.* Frankfurt/Main: Suhrkamp.

Meyer, Theo (1991): *Nietzsche. Kunstauffassung und Lebensbegriff.* Tübingen: Francke.

Midgley, David (2000): *Writing Weimar. Critical Realism in German Literature 1918–1933.* Oxford University Press.

Miles, David H. (1974): 'The Picaro's Journey to the Confessional: The Changing Image of the Hero in the German *Bildungsroman*'. *PMLA* 89, 980–92.

Minden, Michael (1997): *The German* Bildungsroman. Cambridge University Press.

Monteser, Frederick (1975): *The Picaresque Element in Western Literature.* University of Alabama Press.

Moretti, Franco (1987): *The Way of the World. The* Bildungsroman *in European Culture.* London: Verso.

—— (1999): *Atlas of the European Novel 1800–1900.* London: Verso.

—— (ed.) (2006): *The Novel.* 2 vols. Princeton University Press.

Nassehi, Armin (1992): 'Wie wirklich sind Systeme? Zum ontologischen und epistemologischen Status von Luhmanns Theorie selbstreferentieller Systeme'. In Werner Krawietz and Michael Welker (eds): *Kritik der Theorie sozialer Systeme. Auseinandersetzungen mit Luhmanns Hauptwerk.* Frankfurt/Main: Suhrkamp, 43–70.

Nehamas, Alexander (1985): *Nietzsche. Life as Literature.* Cambridge/MA. Harvard University Press.

Nerlich, Michael (1968): 'Plädoyer für Lázaro: Bemerkungen zu einer "Gattung"'. *Romanische Forschungen* 80/2–3, 354–94.

—— (1997): *Abenteuer oder das verlorene Selbstverständnis der Moderne.* Munich: Gerling Akademie Verlag.

Nietzsche, Friedrich (1988): *Sämtliche Werke: Kritische Studienausgabe in 15 Einzelbänden.* [*KSA*] Ed. Giorgio Colli and Mazzino Montinari. Berlin: de Gruyter. [1967–77]

—— *Geburt der Tragödie* (*KSA* 1).

—— *Die Fröhliche Wissenschaft* (*KSA* 3).

—— *Also sprach Zarathustra* (*KSA* 4).

—— *Jenseits von Gut und Böse. Genealogie der Moral* (*KSA* 5).

—— *Ecce Homo. Wie man wird, was man ist* (*KSA* 6, 255–374).

—— *Nachgelassene Fragmente 1882–1884* (*KSA* 10).

—— *Nachgelassene Fragmente 1884–1885* (*KSA* 11).

—— *Nachgelassene Fragmente 1885–1887* (*KSA* 12).

—— (1999): *The Birth of Tragedy and Other Writings.* Ed. Raymond Geuss and Ronald Speirs, trans. Ronald Speirs. Cambridge University Press.

—— (2001): *The Gay Science.* Ed. Bernard Williams, trans. Josefine Nauckhoff. Cambridge University Press.

—— (2002): *Beyond Good and Evil. Prelude to a Philosophy of the Future.* Ed. R.-P. Horstmann and Judith Norman, trans. Judith Norman. Cambridge University Press.

—— (2003): *Writings from the Late Notebooks.* Ed. Rüdiger Bittner, trans. Kate Sturge. Cambridge University Press.

—— (2003): *Thus Spoke Zarathustra.* Trans. R. J. Hollingdale. Harmondsworth: Penguin.

Olney, James (1972): *Metaphors of Self: The Meaning of Autobiography*. Princeton University Press.

Orlowsky, Ursula and Rebekka Orlowsky (1992): *Narziß und Narzißmus im Spiegel von Literatur, Bildender Kunst und Psychoanalyse. Vom Mythos zur leeren Selbstinszenierung*. Munich: Fink.

Ortega y Gasset, José (1941): *Toward a Philosophy of History*. New York: Norton.

—— (1961–83): *Obras completas*. Madrid: Revista de Occidente.

Ötsch, Walter (2000): 'Objekt, Subjekt und Wert'. In Jürgen G. Backhaus and Hans-Joachim Stadermann (eds): *Georg Simmels Philosophie des Geldes. Einhundert Jahre danach*. Marburg: Metropolis, 271–93.

Parsons, Talcott and Edward A. Shils (1951): *Towards a General Theory of Action*. Cambridge/MA: Harvard University Press.

Paul, Jean (1973): *Vorschule der Ästhetik. Levana oder Erziehlehre*. Munich: Hanser.

—— (1992): *A Reader*. Ed. Timothy J. Casey, trans. Erika Casey. Baltimore: Johns Hopkins University Press.

Pavel, Thomas (2001): 'The Novel in Search of Itself: A Historical Morphology'. In Franco Moretti (ed.): *The Novel*, vol. 2. Princeton University Press, 3–31.

Pellón, Gustavo and Julio Rodríguez-Luis (eds) (1986): *Upstarts, Wanderers or Swindlers. Anatomy of the Picaro. A Critical Anthology*. Amsterdam: Rodopi.

—— (1986): 'Introduction'. In *Upstarts, Wanderers or Swindlers. Anatomy of the Picaro. A Critical Anthology*. Amsterdam: Rodopi, 8–21.

Peuter, Jennifer de (1998): 'The Dialogics of Narrative Identity'. In Michael Mayerfeld Bell and Michael Gardiner (ed.): *Bakhtin and the Human Sciences. No Last Words*. London: Sage, 30–48.

Pietzker, Carl (1980): 'Das Groteske'. In Otto F. Best (ed.): *Das Groteske in der Dichtung*. Darmstadt: Wissenschaftliche Buchgesellschaft, 85–102.

Preisendanz, Wolfgang (1963): *Humor als dichterische Einbildungskraft. Studien zur Erzählkunst des poetischen Realismus*. Munich: Eidos.

—— (1976): 'Zum Vorrang des Komischen bei der Darstellung von Geschichtserfahrung in deutschen Romanen unserer Zeit'. In Wolfgang Preisendanz and Rainer Warning: *Das Komische*. Munich: Fink, 153–64.

—— (1976): 'Das Komische, das Satirische und das Ironische'. In Wolfgang Preisendanz and Rainer Warning: *Das Komische*. Munich: Fink, 411–13.

—— (1979): 'Humor als Rolle'. In Odo Marquard and Karlheinz Stierle: *Identität*. Munich: Fink, 423–34.

—— (1998): 'Komik als Komplement der Erfassung von Kontingenzen'. In Gerhart von Graevenitz and Odo Marquard: *Kontingenz*. Munich: Fink, 383–401.

Radin, Paul (1956): *The Trickster: A Study in American Indian Mythology*. London: Routledge & Kegan Paul.

Rank, Otto (1993): 'Narcissism and the Double'. In Emanuel Berman (ed.): *Essential Papers on Literature and Psychoanalysis*. New York University Press, 122–38.

Rasch, William (2000): *Niklas Luhmann's Modernity. The Paradoxes of Differentiation*. Stanford University Press.

—— (2007): 'From Sovereign Ban to Banning Sovereignty'. In Matthew Calarco and Steven DeCaroli (eds): *Giorgio Agamben. Sovereignty and Life*. Stanford University Press, 92–108.

Reed, Helen H. (1984): *The Reader in the Picaresque Novel*. London: Tamesis.

Reed, Walter R. (1981): *An Exemplary History of the Novel: The Quixotic versus the Picaresque*. University of Chicago Press.

Reginster, Bernard (2006): *The Affirmation of Life. Nietzsche on Overcoming Nihilism.* Cambridge/MA: Harvard University Press.

Riedel, Wolfgang (1999): 'Die Macht der Metapher. Zur Modernität von Jean Pauls Ästhetik'. *Jahrbuch der Jean-Paul-Gesellschaft* 34, 56–94.

Ritter, Joachim (1974): *Subjektivität. Sechs Aufsätze.* Frankfurt/Main: Suhrkamp.

Robertson, Alton Kim (1997): *The Grotesque Interface. Deformity, Debasement, Dissolution.* Frankfurt/Main: Lang.

Robertson, Ritchie (1999): *The 'Jewish Question' in German Literature 1749–1939. Emancipation and its Discontents.* Oxford University Press.

—— (2002): 'Modernism and the Self 1890–1924'. In Nicholas Saul (ed.): *Philosophy and German Literature 1700–1990.* Cambridge University Press, 150–96.

—— (ed.) (2002): *The Cambridge Companion to Thomas Mann.* Cambridge University Press.

Röcke, Werner (1987): 'Wahrheit und 'eigenes' Erleben. Zur Poetik von Schwankdichtung und Schelmenroman im 16./17. Jahrhundert'. In Gerhart Hoffmeister (ed.): *Der deutsche Schelmenroman im europäischen Kontext. Rezeption, Interpretation, Bibliographie.* Amsterdam: Rodopi, 13–28.

Rodríguez-Luis, Julio (1979): 'Pícaras: The Modal Approach to the Picaresque'. *Comparative Literature* 31/1, 32–46.

Roskothen, Johannes (1992): *Hermetische Pikareske. Beiträge zu einer Poetik des Schelmenromans.* Frankfurt/Main: Lang.

Rötzer, Hans Gerd (1972): *Picaro—Landstörtzer—Simplicius. Studien zum niederen Roman in Spanien und Deutschland.* Darmstadt: Wissenschaftliche Buchgesellschaft.

—— (1983): 'Der Schelmenroman und seine Nachfolge'. In Helmut Koopmann (ed.): *Handbuch des deutschen Romans.* Düsseldorf: Bagel, 131–50.

Ryan, Judith (1983): *The Uncompleted Past: Postwar German Novels and the Third Reich.* Detroit: Wayne State University Press.

—— (1991): *The Vanishing Subject. Early Psychology and Literary Modernism.* University of Chicago Press.

Schiller, Friedrich (1967): *On the Aesthetic Education of Man.* Ed. and trans. Elizabeth M. Wilkinson and L. A. Willoughby. Oxford: Clarendon Press.

—— (⁷1984): *Über die Ästhetische Erziehung des Menschen in einer Reihe von Briefen.* In *Sämtliche Werke*, vol. V. Ed. Gerhard Fricke and Herbert G. Göpfert. Munich: Hanser, 570–669.

Schinkel, Anders (2005): 'Imagination as a Category of History: An Essay Concerning Reinhart Koselleck's Concepts of *Erfahrungsraum* and *Erwartungshorizont*'. *History and Theory* 44, 42–54.

Schlenker, Barry R. and Beth A. Pontari (2000): 'The Strategic Control of Information: Impression Management and Self-Presentation in Daily Life'. In Abraham Tesser *et al.* (eds): *Psychological Perspectives on Self and Identity.* Washington/DC: American Psychological Association, 199–232.

Scholes, Robert, Robert Kellog and James Phelan (2006): *The Nature of Narrative.* Oxford University Press. [1966]

Schöll, Norbert (1971): 'Der pikarische Held: Wiederaufleben einer literarischen Tradition seit 1945'. In Th. Koebner (ed.): *Tendenzen der deutschen Literatur seit 1945.* Stuttgart: Kröner, 302–21.

Schopenhauer, Arthur (1987): *Die Welt als Wille und Vorstellung.* In *Sämtliche Werke* 2 vols. Ed. Wolfgang Frhr. von Löhneysen. Stuttgart: Cotta. [1819]

Schumann, Willy (1966): 'Wiederkehr der Schelme'. *PMLA* 81, 467–74.

Schutz, Alfred (1971): 'The Stranger. An Essay in Social Psychology'. In *Collected Papers II: Studies in Social Theory*. Ed. Arvid Brodersen. The Hague: Martinus Nijhoff, 91–105.

Schütz, Anton (2008): 'The Fading Memory of Homo non Sacer'. In Justin Clemens, Nicholas Heron and Alex Murray (eds): *The Work of Giorgio Agamben. Law, Literature, Life*. Edinburgh University Press, 114–31.

Schweitzer, Christoph E. (2003): 'Grimmelshausen and the Picaresque Novel'. In Karl F. Otto (ed.): *A Companion to the Works of Grimmelshausen*. Rochester/NY: Camden House, 147–64.

Seifert, Walter (1971): 'Die pikareske Tradition im deutschen Roman der Gegenwart'. In Manfred Durzak (ed.): *Die deutsche Literatur der Gegenwart. Aspekte und Tendenzen*. Stuttgart: Reclam, 192–210.

Serres, Michel (1997): *Le Parasite*. Paris: Hachette Littératures. [1980]

Sharpe, Lesley (1991): *Friedrich Schiller. Drama, Thought and Politics*. Cambridge University Press.

—— (1995): *Schiller's Aesthetic Essay: Two Centuries of Criticism*. Rochester/NY: Camden House.

Siguan Boehmer, Marisa (2007): 'Wenn es Calderón nicht gegeben hätte, die Deutschen hätten ihn erfunden: Deutsche Romantik und spanisches Barock'. *Jahrbuch der Jean-Paul-Gesellschaft* 42, 123–47.

Sillitoe, Alan (1993): *The Mentality of the Picaresque Hero*. London: Turret.

Simmel, Georg (1955): 'The Web of Group-Affiliations'. Trans. Reinhard Bendix. Glencoe/IL: The Free Press, 125–95.

—— (1971): *On Individuality and Social Forms. Selected Writings*. Ed. Donald N. Levine. University of Chicago Press.

—— (1989): 'Zur Psychologie des Geldes'. In *Gesamtausgabe* 2: *Aufsätze 1887 bis 1890*. Ed. H.-J. Dahme. Frankfurt/Main: Suhrkamp, 49–65.

—— (1989): *Über sociale Differenzierung*. In *Gesamtausgabe* 2: *Aufsätze 1887 bis 1890*. Ed. H.-J. Dahme. Frankfurt/Main: Suhrkamp, 109–295. [1890]

—— (1989): *Philosophie des Geldes*. In *Gesamtausgabe* 6. Ed. D. P. Frisby and K. C. Köhnke. Frankfurt/Main: Suhrkamp.

—— (1992): 'Zur Psychologie und Soziologie der Lüge'. In *Gesamtausgabe* 5: *Aufsätze und Abhandlungen 1894 bis 1900*. Ed. H.-J. Dahme and D. P. Frisby. Frankfurt/Main: Suhrkamp, 406–19.

—— (1992): 'Das Geld in der modernen Kultur'. In *Gesamtausgabe* 5: *Aufsätze und Abhandlungen 1894 bis 1900*. Ed. H.-J. Dahme and D. P. Frisby. Frankfurt/Main: Suhrkamp, 178-96.

—— (1992): 'Exkurs über den Fremden'. In *Gesamtausgabe* 11: *Soziologie. Untersuchungen über die Formen der Vergesellschaftung*. Ed. Otthein Rammstedt. Frankfurt/Main: Suhrkamp, 764–71.

—— (1995): 'Die Großstädte und das Geistesleben'. In *Gesamtausgabe* 7: *Aufsätze und Abhandlungen 1901–1908*, vol. 1. Ed. Rüdiger Kramme, Angela Rammstedt and Otthein Rammstedt. Frankfurt/Main: Suhrkamp, 116–31.

—— (1996): 'Das Abenteuer'. In *Gesamtausgabe* 14: *Hauptprobleme der Philosophie*. Ed. Rüdiger Kramme and Otthein Rammstedt. Frankfurt/Main: Suhrkamp, 168–86.

—— (1996): 'Der Begriff und die Tragödie der Kultur'. In *Gesamtausgabe* 14: *Hauptprobleme der Philosophie*. Ed. Rüdiger Kramme and Otthein Rammstedt. Frankfurt/Main: Suhrkamp, 385–416

—— (1996): 'The Stranger'. In Werner Sollors (ed.): *Theories of Ethnicity. A Classical Reader*. New York University Press, 37–42.

—— (1997): 'The Concept and Tragedy of Culture'. In *Simmel on Culture. Selected Writings*. Ed. David Frisby and Mike Featherstone. London: Sage, 55–101.

—— (1997): 'The Metropolis and Mental Life'. In *Simmel on Culture. Selected Writings*. Ed. David Frisby and Mike Featherstone. London: Sage, 174–85.

—— (1997): 'The Adventure'. In *Simmel on Culture. Selected Writings*. Ed. David Frisby and Mike Featherstone. London: Sage, 221–32.

—— (1997): 'On the Psychology of Money'. In *Simmel on Culture. Selected Writings*. Ed. David Frisby and Mike Featherstone. London: Sage, 233–43.

Slezkine, Yuri (2004): *The Jewish Century*. Princeton University Press.

Sloterdijk, Peter (1987): *Kritik der zynischen Vernunft*. Frankfurt/Main: Suhrkamp.

Smith, Gregory W. H. (2000): 'Snapshots "Sub Specie Aeternitatis": Simmel, Goffman and Formal Sociology'. In Gary A. Fine and Gregory W. H. Smith (eds) (2000): *Erving Goffman*. London: Sage, 370–99.

Sorell, Tom (1986): *Hobbes*. London: Routledge.

Stambaugh, Joan (1972): *Nietzsche's Thought of Eternal Return*. Baltimore: Johns Hopkins University Press.

Stanzel, Franz K. (1979): *Theorie des Erzählens*. Göttingen: Vandenhoeck & Ruprecht.

Steiner, George (1996): *No Passion Spent. Essays 1978–96*. London: Faber & Faber.

Stern, J. Peter. (1995): *The Dear Purchase. A Theme in German Modernism*. Cambridge University Press.

Strobel, Katja (1998): *Wandern, Mäandern, Erzählen. Die Pikara als Grenzgängerin des Subjekts*. Munich: Fink.

Suleiman Susan R. (1980): *The Reader in the Text. Essays on Audience and Interpretation*. Princeton University Press.

Taylor, Charles (2004): *Modern Social Imaginaries*. Durham: Duke University Press.

Tholen, Toni (2005): 'Leben und Form. Zu Schillers Briefen *Über die ästhetische Erziehung des Menschen*'. *Germanisch-Romanische Monatsschrift* 55/2, 175–90.

—— (2005): *Verlust der Nähe. Reflexion von Männlichkeit in der Literatur*. Heidelberg: Winter.

Tugendhat, Ernst (1979): *Selbstbewußtsein und Selbstbestimmung. Sprachanalytische Interpretationen*. Frankfurt/Main: Suhrkamp.

Tyrell, Albrecht (1975): *Vom 'Trommler' zum 'Führer'. Der Wandel von Hitlers Selbstverständnis zwischen 1919 und 1924 und die Entwicklung der NSDAP*. Munich: Fink.

Wellbery, David (1999): 'Die Ausblendung der Genese. Grenzen der systemtheoretischen Reform der Kulturwissenschaften'. In Albrecht Koschorke and Cornelia Vismann (eds): *Widerstände der Systemtheorie. Kulturtheoretische Analysen zum Werk von Niklas Luhmann*. Berlin: Akademie Verlag, 19–27.

Wicks, Ulrich (1974): 'The Nature of the Picaresque Narrative: A Modal Approach'. *PMLA* 89/2, 240–9.

—— (1986): 'Picaro, Picaresque: The Picaresque in Literary Scholarship'. In Gustavo Pellón and Julio Rodríguez-Luis (eds) (1986): *Upstarts, Wanderers or Swindlers. Anatomy of the Picaro. A Critical Anthology*, 23–51.

—— (1989): *Picaresque Narrative, Picaresque Fictions: A Theory and Research Guide*. New York: Greenwood.

Will, Wilfried van der (1967): *Pikaro heute*. Stuttgart: Kohlhammer.

Yerushalmi, Yosef Hayim (1992): *Assimilation and Racial Anti-Semitism: the Iberian and the German Models*. New York: Leo Baeck Institute.

Index